About Island Press

Since 1984, the nonprofit organization Island Press has been stimulating, shaping, and communicating ideas that are essential for solving environmental problems worldwide. With more than 1,000 titles in print and some 30 new releases each year, we are the nation's leading publisher on environmental issues. We identify innovative thinkers and emerging trends in the environmental field. We work with world-renowned experts and authors to develop cross-disciplinary solutions to environmental challenges.

Island Press designs and executes educational campaigns, in conjunction with our authors, to communicate their critical messages in print, in person, and online using the latest technologies, innovative programs, and the media. Our goal is to reach targeted audiences—scientists, policy makers, environmental advocates, urban planners, the media, and concerned citizens—with information that can be used to create the framework for long-term ecological health and human well-being.

Island Press gratefully acknowledges major support from The Bobolink Foundation, Caldera Foundation, The Curtis and Edith Munson Foundation, The Forrest C. and Frances H. Lattner Foundation, The JPB Foundation, The Kresge Foundation, The Summit Charitable Foundation, Inc., and many other generous organizations and individuals.

The opinions expressed in this book are those of the author(s) and do not necessarily reflect the views of our supporters.

Poisoning the Well

Poisoning the Well

HOW FOREVER CHEMICALS CONTAMINATED AMERICA

Sharon Udasin and Rachel Frazin

ISLANDPRESS | Washington | Covelo

Library of Congress Control Number: 2024947206

All Island Press books are printed on environmentally responsible materials.

Manufactured in the United States of America
10 9 8 7 6 5 4 3 2 1

Keywords: 3M; cancer cluster; Cape Fear River; carcinogens; chemical
exposure; chemical regulation; contaminated drinking water; contaminated military bases; Decatur, Alabama; DuPont; environmental health;
firefighting foam; GenX; per- and polyfluoroalkyl substances; Peterson
Space Force Base; PFAS; PFOA; PFOS; Rob Bilott; sludge fertilizer;
Teflon; toxic chemicals; water quality

Contents

Forever and Everywhere

Brenda Hampton thought she had finally gotten her blood pressure under control. She gratefully gulped down her new medication and kept a watchful eye on her vital signs, which had been volatile, to say the least.

Having faced years of renal failure with just one kidney, Brenda had been coping with "uncontrollable" highs and lows as the semi-functioning organ worked overtime. But with her blood pressure now stabilized, her doctors remained relatively unfazed about her laggard pulse of 40 beats per minute. Perhaps, they surmised, her body had just become accustomed to functioning at a heart rate that Brenda described as nearly "undetectable."[1]

But things changed when Brenda got home at the end of the day, in December 2021.

"My shoulders were bothering me, and so I administered a heating pad, went to sleep," she said. "I woke up nauseated, sweat popping off of me—I felt like an elephant was sitting on my chest."

Breathless after eventually falling, Brenda knocked on the floor to her downstairs neighbor, who ultimately called her sister and an ambulance, which shuttled her to the hospital.

"I would never become dizzy or anything until I fell here—at the time when I had a heart attack," she said. "It was an unusual heart attack. I had worked that Monday."

Her medical team was puzzled by the circumstances of the heart attack but told Brenda that the event was likely connected to her kidney issues. And while there was no blood clot and Brenda didn't require a stent, her bloodstream did contain the cardiac enzymes that marked a recent heart attack. The mysterious episode concluded with warnings from her doctors that she might be "leading up to a big one."

Sitting next to her monitor a couple weeks after the attack, Brenda observed that her heart rate wasn't even reaching 40 beats per minute— the lowest measure to register on her machine.

"I'm just sitting. I'm not doing anything stressful. I'm not worried about anything," Hampton said. "I know it's from getting in those chemicals."

⌒

Experiences like Brenda's—life-threatening illness following long-term exposure to toxic chemicals—have become disquietingly familiar in recent years. But what makes her story especially insidious is the nature of the chemicals that had infiltrated her drinking water. As it turns out, Brenda, and in fact, everyone in her small hometown of Courtland, Alabama, had been contaminated by compounds known as PFAS.

While just a brief acronym, PFAS stands for a much lengthier chemical name—the umbrella group called per- and polyfluoroalkyl substances, which include thousands of manmade chemicals. They have waterproof and stain-resistant properties and are used in all sorts of products—from Teflon pans to raincoats, mascara, and even certain types of firefighting foam. And unfortunately for the people of Courtland, PFAS also have a habit of leaching into nearby waterways.

Worse yet, these substances are known as "forever chemicals" for a reason: unlike many compounds, they don't break down over time. Instead, they build up in the environment, and many also accumulate in animals and people, growing evermore concentrated and dangerous. Along with kidney and testicular cancer, studies have linked PFAS to a variety of other ills, from low birth weights and high cholesterol to thyroid dysfunction and liver damage.

PFAS chemicals are not only toxic and long-lasting; they are, as environmental activist Erin Brockovich points out, omnipresent. "All this time it's been in the water. It's gotten into the food chain. We're eating it. It's in plastics. We're sleeping in it. It's in everything we touch."[2] Overall, the contamination is so widespread that the Centers for Disease Control and Prevention (CDC) estimated that PFAS are in the blood of at least 97 percent of Americans.[3]

Although most of us have PFAS coursing through our veins, these chemicals, like all pollutants, are not distributed evenly or equitably. Instead, communities like Brenda's, downstream from production facilities, are particularly hard hit. So, too, are those who live near military bases, where soldiers used PFAS-laden firefighting foam in training drills; and farm towns, where chemical sludge was used to fertilize crops.

Throughout the following pages, we will meet a wide range of individuals who have become painfully familiar with the awkward acronym PFAS. The toxic compounds that trickled through Brenda's tap have also infiltrated the infrastructure of Mark Favors's faithful military family in Colorado, Lawrence and Penny Higgins's agricultural oasis in Maine, Emily Donovan's riverside community in North Carolina, and every American household.

In a note of hope, we will explore how these communities are pushing back against the chemicals and companies that have imperiled their health and happiness. As in so many cases of pollution, opportunism and sleight of hand by industry are central to this story. So, too, is government neglect. On a federal level, it took decades for just six of what could be as many as 15,000 compounds to be regulated.

"We said ten years ago this is going to be the largest emerging contaminant in the history of this country, and it is," added Brockovich. "It's very scary, because it's not going to go away."

They're forever, they're everywhere, and they're wreaking havoc across the nation and in every corner of the planet.

CHAPTER 1

A Glorious Future

TALL GRASS BORDERS EACH SIDE of northern Alabama's County Road 150 as it passes by farm homes, groups of grain silos, and centuries-old plantations. The fields taper off toward a traffic intersection where the area's lone gas station looms large: a Chevron-signed gateway to the Jesse Jackson Parkway and the town of North Courtland. By the time the road reaches a once predominantly Black high school, shuttered by the school board in 2022 following years of neglect, green has turned to gaunt.

Passing by the empty school, Brenda Hampton gestured through the sealed car window toward an adjacent house, announcing that the father and son who lived there are now deceased.

"The next house, the mother died," she said, as the car crept down the quiet parkway on a humid day in March 2023. "The next house coming down the street, the husband and wife died. The next house was husband and wife. The next house was a female that died—a young girl died here, in this house, here."[1]

In two streets alone in this small section of North Courtland, the sixty-seven-year-old mother of three recounted, she has identified fifty-four cases of cancer and fourteen cases of kidney failure. This in a town of fewer than 500 residents. "We've had a lot of people in this area to die from renal failure, a lot of them from rare cancers, very rare cancers," Brenda said.

The death-rattled thoroughfare rolls right into adjacent Courtland, a stop sign serving as a de facto dividing line between the two towns. An abandoned Foodvalu supermarket sits vacant alongside the parkway: now the Dollar General is the sole place to buy groceries, and only canned goods and packaged food at that. Although more than 30 percent of the people in Courtland live below the poverty line, the town is dotted with relics of an affluent past—decaying but expansive plantation homes and a vacant, historic downtown—while its northern neighbor (one of the poorest communities in Alabama) hangs on by a vestigial limb.

"They don't care for me over in North Courtland," Brenda said. "They're like a little nervous of me over there when I come in."

Despite her neighbors' suspicions, Brenda has long "serviced" both areas, offering families bottled water, adult diapers, and rides to medical appointments, free of charge. For nearly a decade, she has been supporting residents in need through her primarily self-funded nonprofit organization.

"My phone is constantly ringing from people in the community that need things," she said.[2]

Like North Courtland, Courtland has experienced more than its fair share of death and disease. Across the town line, Brenda pointed out yet another home racked by illness. "I service this house—the husband died in there. He had renal failure," she said. "The wife is still alive in there."[3]

Within Brenda's own circle, many of her nuclear family members, distant relatives, and friends have passed from unexplained illnesses. Her grandparents both died of kidney failure, as did her mother in 2001, just four years after Brenda had given her a kidney. In one single week, her family experienced six deaths—related to causes including cancer, kidney failure, liver failure, and heart attacks.[4]

"We were at one funeral and then there was another. We buried my brother and my cousin on the same day," she said, recalling the "double funerals" of her thirty-nine-year-old brother and her thirty-seven-year-old cousin. "It's something to grieve one, but when you have double caskets, it just sort of messes with you."

Brenda knew that her family had suffered tremendous loss, but it wasn't until she experienced her own health scare that she started to suspect a link to her hometown. Brenda had grown up in Courtland before the single town split into central and northern townships. She attended the now-abandoned R. A. Hubbard High School, but a graduation gift from her aunt led her to Boston. For a while, she worked as a paralegal for her godmother and then started doing court-appointed investigative work for a variety of legal firms after she realized the importance of delving into the details of each defendant's story.[5] "That's where I come in at—I knock on the door to actually see," Brenda said.[6]

Working as a manager for McDonald's in 2015, Brenda transferred from Boston to Tennessee to help her ailing father—and underwent a routine physical examination as part of that shift. When her tests came back, the results were shocking. "My kidneys and everything were off the charts," she said. "They just said that I was going through renal failure then, that I had been exposed to something toxic, and I knew at the time that what I was working with, it was nothing toxic—hamburgers and fries."[7]

After moving back to Courtland following the alarming physical exam, Brenda started to notice just how many people in town were sick. Her informal door-to-door survey revealed dozens of cancer cases, along with many instances of renal failure.

While she had lived in Boston since 1973, she made frequent trips home to Alabama, eating the same food and drinking the same water as the residents of Courtland. "*Voilà*, I'm at death's door," she recalled. "And then they're telling me that I'm affected by industrial toxins, and I'm like, what? How am I affected by industrial toxins?"[8]

⌒

Brenda's story begins nearly a thousand miles away and almost ninety years ago, with an Ohio farm-boy-turned-chemist fresh out of graduate studies. The postdoctoral student, Roy Plunkett, had taken on his first job at a New Jersey laboratory of E. I. du Pont de Nemours and Company—which was also known as DuPont.[9]

In 1938, Roy was seeking out an alternative for the hazardous refrigerants that were used to keep food cold at the time. As part of this process, he stored a gas called tetrafluoroethylene (TFE) in cylinders at very low temperatures—assuming that he would still find a gas afterward. Yet when he sawed open the cylinder, he found a white powder instead.[10] Roy's initial reaction was one of disappointment; *Now we'll have to start all over again!* he thought.[11]

What had happened was that the substance had gone through a process called "polymerization," in which a double bond between two carbon atoms in one TFE compound came apart in such a way that it could "attack" other TFE compounds.

"One of them hooked up with another one, with another one, with another one, until there were hundreds, thousands, millions of tetrafluoroethylenes," said Kathy Davis, an associate professor of chemistry at Indiana's Manchester University, Roy's alma mater.[12]

Roy noticed that the powder was heat resistant, chemically inert, and so low in surface friction that most other materials would not stick to it.[13] Yet the young scientist hadn't yet realized what he had stumbled upon: an entirely new chemical that would eventually become a cash cow for DuPont—and one of the biggest environmental problems the world has ever seen.

The company ultimately trademarked Roy's white powder, called polytetrafluoroethylene (PTFE), as Teflon in 1944.[14] Teflon had unique properties that made it particularly appealing to the US military: it was persistent, nonstick, nonreactive with other chemicals, and resistant to both high temperatures and corrosion. In fact, one of its first uses was to contain highly reactive materials, like uranium, in the making of the atomic bomb. Collectively, PTFE and chemicals like it came to be known as PFAS.

Though these chemicals had early roots in World War II, their military application took off in the 1960s. At that time, the US Navy partnered with the Minnesota Mining and Manufacturing Company (3M) to develop a PFAS-based foam that could suppress jet-fuel-based fires by smothering the flammable liquids responsible for their ignition. The primary PFAS ingredient in the new "aqueous film-forming foam" (AFFF) was for many years perfluorooctanesulfonic acid (PFOS), one of the most notorious types of forever chemicals.

PFAS provided armor not only on the battlefield, but also in kitchenware and in other consumer products—with the surge in popularity of a Teflon-based nonstick coating. Before mass production of the material could occur, however, scientists had to overcome a tremendous hurdle: figuring out how to bond a nonstick powder to other solids. Techniques that ultimately proved effective included heating the PTFE to high temperatures, blending it with hydrocarbons, and mixing it with solvents that extracted some of the fluorine atoms. Early on, Teflon was used for insulating electrical equipment, coating industrial valve and pump components, and eventually, commercial food processing.[15]

Though Roy Plunkett may have been the brains behind the Teflon chemical, the scientist "had nothing to do with putting it on a frying pan," his daughter-in-law, Susan Plunkett, wrote in a February 2022 text message. She did recall, however, that "a man approached Roy at a social event and told him that his discovery had saved his life because he had received an artificial heart valve made of Teflon." And when Roy received a medal for his invention in 1951, each guest went home with a nonstick muffin tin.[16]

The first person to commercialize nonstick pans coated with the material was actually across the Atlantic, in France. Engineer Marc Grégoire's invention was the result of a friendly marital challenge. An avid fisherman eager to avoid tangles,[17] Grégoire decided to heat Teflon powder just below its melting point to coat his aluminum fishing gear.[18] When his wife, Colette, got wind of his new hobby, she challenged him to coat her cookware with the material as well. He patented the technology in 1954 and the couple launched a company, Tefal, in 1956.

Soon after, Tefal opened a factory in Rumilly, a small town in the French Alps near the Swiss border. It attracted employees by offering relatively high salaries, even if the working environment was far from ideal. Bernard Truffet, the second-ever employee at the Rumilly factory, recounted "difficult conditions" from his first days on the job, lamenting how they "were building things cheaply." He recalled one situation in which he was tasked with acquiring dozens of meters of bicycle chains for a conveyor belt and another in which a flood of Teflon erupted from a centrifuge. But the company's eventual transformation into an industrial titan brought significant change to the verdant Alps community, and many residents relished their boost in lifestyle. Henry Bouvier, an employee from 1967 to 2007, described the factory as "somewhat of an institution" in the region, noting that salaries were "obviously much higher" than those paid by small pharmacies or artisan shops in town.[19]

The forever-changed village still houses the Tefal global headquarters and continues to boast the coveted title of "the world frying pan capital." In 2016, officials erected a monument of a giant metal frying pan at the town's entrance for the company's sixtieth anniversary, while celebrating with festivities along "Tefal Street"—the original home of a product that unexpectedly became a post–World War II phenomenon.[20]

Nonstick pans became a major hit, both in Europe and across the pond. Tefal's products made it to the US market in December 1960, with stores ordering a million pans each month by mid-1961.[21] That year, a photo of First Lady Jackie Kennedy holding a Tefal pan caused a significant boost in company sales.[22] Historic promotions for the cookware introduced a so-called happy pan as an "amazing new concept in cooking" and the savior from getting "stuck in the kitchen."[23]

A 1968 ad from Mirro Aluminum Company, a former cookware giant, promises "Hard-Bond Super-Tough Teflon" pots and pans, as a woman with a sixties-style flip-do glances flirtatiously from the stove at a man. A tagline trumpets the products as "for ladies who want more than just slickness from their Teflon."[24]

Another ad, this time from DuPont, depicts a glowering woman, struggling to scrub off layers of grease from a steel pan.

"What a way to start married life," the ad declares in bold print. "There are better things in life than being married to a sink. Talking, walking, having a night out with your bread-winner. Anything, rather than scrubbing leftovers out of a pan."[25]

The ads worked, and soon, nonstick pans became a cookware staple in households across America. Yet with heavy demand also came heavy manufacturing.

In 1951, DuPont opened a major plant called Washington Works, in Washington, West Virginia, along the Ohio River. At the plant, the Teflon manufacturing process also made use of a chemical called perfluorooctanoic acid (PFOA), which DuPont bought from 3M. The mining and manufacturing giant, meanwhile, opened several plants of its own, including a facility in Cottage Grove, Minnesota, in 1948.[26]

Irene Dalbotten, who began her forty-year tenure at the plant shortly after it opened, told a local newspaper in 2008 that the factory started out small "but it grew fast."[27]

One of the products the company manufactured there was

Scotchgard, a fabric protector that repels water and prevents stains.[28] Like Teflon, Scotchgard was also synthesized by accident—when a lab assistant spilled a liquid rubber concoction, which then splashed onto chemist Patsy Sherman's shoes. As the scientists scrambled to clean her shoes with water and other substances, every attempt was repelled by the mixture. Sherman and fellow chemist Sam Smith transformed this inadvertent discovery into a product of its own, and sales of the Scotchgard stain repellent kicked off in 1956.[29] What they didn't know, however, is that in addition to generating a lot of sales, this product would also turn out to have deadly consequences.

Over time, 3M grew, eventually launching plants all around the world that made not only PFAS but a wide range of products—from office supplies to electrical equipment to masks used during the COVID-19 pandemic. And one lucky spot to gain a massive manufacturing branch was an industrial complex just outside of Decatur, Alabama, right in Brenda Hampton's neck of the woods.

Continuing her tour of Courtland, Brenda approached the silent downtown square, proclaiming there's "nothing happening"—and not just because it was a Sunday. Dusty windows betrayed dark, vacant spaces, shadows of the lives no longer there.[30]

"The lady that lived in here—she's dead," Brenda said, gesturing to a historic old house. "This used to be Hughes Drug Store. It is gone. This was the movie theater."

An ice cream parlor next door hinted at some signs of life, but blank windows quickly revealed that there was no one working and certainly no ice cream inside. Brenda was quick to confirm that "nothing happens in there" and that "they just decorate it." This was, however, the space where she had launched her community service effort.

"I gave out water, food, clothing, and everything from this ice cream shop," Brenda said. An adjacent antique store—which now sells JAX

Wholesale, Amazon, and Target returns—became a regular gathering site for her meetings with other volunteers.

Red brick building facades—deemed historic by the National Parks Service[31]—stood largely intact, but no guests frequented the long-shuttered Old Sherrod Hotel, a 1930s hub for the construction crews who built the nearby Wheeler Dam. Nor were there any patrons in the locked and dark Ms. Jane's Antiques, whose wares lined the windows of the historic A. F. Rebman and Company's 1890 building.

Courtland on occasion gets families from "up north" seeking out an idyllic Southern spot to settle down. "A lot of them have been requesting, like, a little Mayberry town, laid back, cost of living pretty cheap," Brenda said. "I've had several families that have come in this town, and then, they'd be asking me, 'Well, where's downtown Courtland?' And I go, 'You're *in* downtown Courtland.'"

"This used to be a thriving town. There used to be a clothing shop right there," she recalled. "My mother had a restaurant over here where they got the City Hall at. That's where all the Black businesses were at."

A wrought-iron street clock, two stories high, stands in front of the A. F. Rebman building, ticking toward a future that has left Courtland behind. Still stuck in place beneath the clock is a mounting block (also called a horse block or carriage block), its three stone steps used for a far more sinister purpose than simply climbing onto a saddle.

"These used to be where they sold a lot of slaves," Brenda said. "This would be for the expensive one, this is one that's not so good," she continued, pointing to the top and middle steps. Then gesturing toward the third, she added, "That's the bottom of the totem pole."

Courtland, like so many other former hubs of the Deep South, still bears emblems of its pre–Civil War history. While plantations tended to have fewer enslaved people in this region, which was far less fertile than many other parts of the South, the town remained largely segregated for more than a century after emancipation, and the legacy of slavery is still woven into the town fabric.

"People did grow cotton around here, but it was mostly smaller farms," said John Allison, archivist for Morgan County, home to the city of Decatur and adjacent to Lawrence County, where Courtland is located.[32]

Brenda described a slow-paced rural culture that defines Alabama, which she views as less developed than other Southern states. "That's why they are still taking advantage of Alabama," she said. "Nobody goes by any rules, nobody questions anything."[33]

Brenda holds that attitude—and the region's limited agricultural potential—responsible for the twentieth-century drive that lured industrial giants like 3M to erect their plants along the banks of the Tennessee River.

About twenty miles upstream from Courtland, Decatur was once a sparkling Southern city replete with dress shops, cab service, and culture, as Brenda recalled from her grandparents' lore. They, and their parents before them, worked as sharecroppers in the surrounding farm fields and came into Decatur to enjoy the vibrancy of urban life.

"They would hang their head in shame—they couldn't believe it," she said, of the current landscape.[34]

In its early days in the 1800s, Decatur's location along the Tennessee River at the intersection of two railway lines made it a hub of trade and transport, while the creation of the Tennessee Valley Authority in 1933 and subsequent construction of the Wheeler Dam brought further development to the region. In 1953, the *Alabama Municipal Journal* deemed Decatur "Alabama's fastest growing industrial empire," and a Chamber of Commerce pamphlet from 1961 proclaimed, "Nowhere in America can be found a better balance between agriculture and industry," noting that the city's seven-mile waterfront included thirty-three industries representing a total investment of over 100 million dollars."[35]

The City of Decatur and the larger Morgan County made things easy for companies and manufacturers, offering an industry-friendly environment to those interested in entertaining a move to this corner of the Deep South, particularly in unincorporated rural areas.

"That's how these plants come in here—they sit on the outskirts of the city," Brenda said.[36]

It was during this period that residents of Decatur first became acquainted with 3M. Phil Raths, who would end up managing the Decatur plant until his retirement in 1984, began eyeing the spot in 1959, and the company opened its factory within two years. Among the lures of the city was the presence of manufacturing giants—legacy chemical company Chemstrand, as well as Wolverine, Goodyear, and a flour mill—employers that had made the region ripe for industrial expansion while promoting river development and job growth.

"Those were all significant workplaces for Decatur," Raths told *The Decatur Daily*. "Before that, people had to leave Decatur to make a living."

The local news story attributed much of the plant's early successes to Raths, surmising that "perhaps his years as a plant manager at 3M made him a problem-solver, or maybe it was growing up on a ranch in Roundup, Montana, or rearing ten children." After his retirement from the company, Raths also "put his business and family skills to work to improve Decatur in many ways: as a city councilman."[37]

Historical literature commissioned by the mayor and city council of Decatur in 1968 and published in 1970 hailed 3M as "a great and nationally famous corporation." Noting that 3M specialized in a broad range of industrial chemicals, the literature explained that the plant hosted a division, managed at the time by Raths, that produced materials like plastics and textile-treating compounds. Another part of the company with a major Decatur presence was a separate division responsible for manufacturing film.[38]

The number of workers at the Decatur 3M plant continued to grow over time. Beginning with 100 employees in 1961, the factory rapidly expanded its workforce—employing more than 1,000 people for a collective $11.3 million in wages and salaries in 1975.[39]

But back in 1961, when this tenfold rise in employment was just a dream, the Alabama Chamber of Commerce declared in its pamphlet that this "Fresh Water Fishing Capital of the South" had "every reason to look forward to a glorious future," thanks to the combination of an "enlightened citizenry" and "devoted community leaders."

"Decatur's future growth and success can most certainly be assured," the pamphlet boasted.[40]

For a while, during Brenda's childhood, those golden promises seemed to materialize. "People were able to afford better homes and better transportation," Brenda said. "And in the area where 3M is, once that comes in, CEOs always talk to another plant to find out how the area is, so it brought in other plants."

The lure of jobs kept 3M popular in the community. Yet as the chemical giant grew and grew, decades-old mom-and-pop businesses, along with legacy industries, eventually began to shut their doors. When, for example, the International Paper mill closed down in 2014, it was Lawrence County's largest employer, taking with it 1,096 jobs and $771,000 annual tax revenue from Courtland.[41]

As of mid-2022, manufacturing still made up a significant share of both Courtland and North Courtland's economies, responsible for about 35 percent and 39 percent of jobs, respectively, while Decatur clocked in at 20 percent.[42] Yet the dream of middle-class livelihoods appears to have gone up in smoke alongside the plumes from the manufacturing plants. Courtland's median household income was almost $40,000, while North Courtland's was nearly $31,000 in a 2022 federal survey.[43] Decatur, less reliant on manufacturing jobs, was higher at more than $55,000—but still a good $20,000 below the national average.[44]

The economic push and pull of the chemical industry was already a significant burden for Brenda and her neighbors to shoulder. But whether 3M and its compatriots were creating jobs or hurting the community's other financial prospects, they were certainly producing vast amounts of waste—byproducts that ended up in landfills that were unequipped to handle them and in waterways that carried the pollution to nearby towns. And although that waste was there to stay, the same could not be said for all the companies and the jobs they provided. That eventual emptiness and contamination, Brenda said, caught up with the area and "everything just died out."[45]

"It changed the landscape here," she recalled. "Then the stores and things closed—no grocery store, things like that. That's what happened in this area. . . . It was devastated." And in the case of PFAS, the threat wasn't just to neighborhood stores and historic town centers but to the residents themselves.

CHAPTER 2

A Very Toxic Compound

As the Decatur 3m plant was ramping up production of PFAS and the popularity of products like Teflon surged in the middle of the twentieth century, evidence was emerging that the substances also had a dark side.

In the 1950s, researchers inside and outside DuPont started to see an odd phenomenon: people exposed to heated Teflon developed flu-like symptoms, feeling chest discomfort, followed by a dry cough, increased heart and breathing rates, fever, shivering, and sweats. A 1951 paper in *The Lancet* documented four such cases—including two that involved DuPont employees.[1] The accounts continued to trickle in, with an internal memo from 1959 discussing the experience of employee John Kropenski, who came down with a case of the "shakes." Earlier in the day that he developed these symptoms, Kropenski had cut a Teflon pipe while he had an open pack of cigarettes in his pocket. The tremors began after he smoked the cigarettes later that evening.[2]

About a year later, a New York–based doctor documented a similar phenomenon in one of his patients, a middle-aged man who worked with Teflon. The doctor, Henry Wharton, said in a letter to the FDA that the man was experiencing "angina-like" chest pain as well as dizziness and shortness of breath. The patient noticed that his co-workers had similar symptoms, and his foreman told him that these symptoms were "caused by Teflon and that they all know about it," the doctor wrote. Wharton took a chest X-ray of the patient, observing abnormalities and questioning whether "Teflon might be carcinogenic or whether it might produce" a lung disease. In response, an FDA official said the agency had "relatively little occasion to consider" Teflon's health effects—a response that foreshadowed years of regulatory neglect to come.

By the early 1960s, stories about what came to be called "polymer fume fever," along with other ill-effects of inhaling Teflon, were circulating beyond company walls. One account, published in a letter to the *Canadian Medical Association Journal*, alleged that a person who smoked a Teflon-contaminated cigarette had died—though the writer later retracted the story.[3]

Nevertheless, in response to these stories, DuPont published a pamphlet called "The Anatomy of a Rumor," decrying the accusations. The pamphlet's author, DuPont toxicologist John A. Zapp Jr., acknowledged the existence of polymer fume fever—likening it to influenza—but stressed that there are "no lasting physiological effects" and linked the symptoms to soot pollution, as opposed to gases related to Teflon. In addition to redirecting blame for polymer fume fever, Zapp also emphasized the safety of Teflon pans.[4]

A manager at a company that used Teflon wrote to the *Journal of Teflon* in June 1962 to praise the missive as "extremely informative"— and he requested thirty copies to distribute to his employees, who had regular contact with the material. "We have all been exposed to these rumors in various forms, and possibly unknowingly some of our people have assisted in passing some of them as impressions along to our customers," he wrote.

Despite these assurances, even prior to the 1960s scientists were beginning to demonstrate that the impacts of PFAS exposure might extend beyond a temporary "flu." In a 1956 paper, researchers with Stanford University found that PFOA could bind to human blood.*[5] It was also during this era that evidence began to emerge about the potential of these substances to harm animal organs. For example, a 1955 study published in the journal *Cancer Research* found that embedding Teflon under rats' skin could trigger the growth of cancerous tumors.[6]

As alarming findings began to accumulate, DuPont's own personnel also started to discover adverse health effects in animals. Toxicologist Dorothy Hood wrote in a 1961 company memo that several PFAS, including PFOA, were toxic and could cause the enlargement of rat livers in low doses. She described another PFAS, known by the initialism AHT as "a very toxic compound." "It is recommended that all three materials . . . be handled with extreme care," Hood wrote. "Contact with the skin should be strictly avoided."[7]

By the following February, and at the same time in 1962 that Dupont was downplaying health hazards associated with inhaling Teflon, company scientists documented additional health issues stemming from PFOA. DuPont pathologist G.W.H. Schepers wrote that month in an internal company memo that rats fed PFOA had moderately enlarged livers, shrunken pancreases, and slightly enlarged kidneys, adrenal glands, and testes.[8] A few days later, Schepers followed up to explain that in three experiments, rats fed PFOA were killed by damage to their stomachs, intestines, brains, lungs, and pancreases. Meanwhile, another company document suggested that the problem might apply to an entire group of PFAS compounds known as surfactants—substances such as soaps, detergents, and lubricants that decrease a liquid's surface tension and, in the case of PFAS, enable water and oil to mix into a foaming agent.[9]

---

* References to PFOA in this book also include variations of the substance known as APFO, an ammonium salt of PFOA.

Following these initial findings, DuPont researchers extended their experiments to also include dogs, noting that the canine research "might be useful in detecting liver injury in personnel."[10] Sure enough, the studies showed liver enlargement.[11] By 1966, DuPont was trying to figure out how to get rid of waste from its Teflon plant. While acknowledging that some of the solid wastes contained "toxic" PFAS, the company claimed to have found a suitable method of disposal—as long as the toxic parts were "reduced to an acceptable level." All one needed to do was bake the waste for five hours. Without taking this action, it warned, some of the toxic PFAS "would be leached into the groundwater."

DuPont may have been grappling with its PFAS waste problem in the mid-1960s, but federal regulators had already begun to take notice of the potential issues posed by the substances in 1959. In February of that year, a man named Henry McNulty wrote to the Food and Drug Administration (FDA) asking for its views on the use of "Teflon-Tefal" in cooking utensils, as he had hoped to import them to the United States from France. However, his business aspirations would hit a speed bump after he received negative responses from the FDA's A. J. Lehman.[12] Replying that he could not "comment favorably" on the use of the product in cooking utensils, Lehman explained that the material "appears to be unstable under cooking temperatures" and that "some of its decomposition products are quite toxic."[13]

McNulty tried again, following up with additional information, but Lehman's opinion remained unchanged. "I have reviewed the data and have again discussed the problems with others of the staff," the FDA official stated. "I am sorry to say that I cannot offer any other opinion than that expressed in my letter of Feb. 10."[14]

But later that same year, in September of 1959, Lehman appeared to change his tune. He, alongside other FDA officials, met with DuPont representatives to discuss the company's own foray into PFAS-coated cookware. At the meeting, the employees discussed two problems—"the inhalation hazard and the ingestion hazard"—hazards that Zapp, the DuPont toxicologist who also wrote the "Anatomy of a Rumor" pamphlet, roundly refuted. Some back-and-forth followed, according to a DuPont memo, but ultimately an FDA toxicologist agreed that no hazard existed. DuPont employees, meanwhile, presented data showing that "only minute bits" of the coating transferred to food when the Teflon pans were used.

"It's like bits of glass or porcelain coming off," Lehman understood.

The agency ultimately did require some further clarification from DuPont, but the company received "no major objections" from the FDA officials, who foresaw "no major obstacles" in getting federal approval.[15] A few months earlier, the FDA also authorized Teflon's use in handling milk. Similar issues later cropped up for another DuPont product: Zonyl, which used PFAS to make food wrappers resistant to grease. The FDA raised objections in 1966 about the substance leaching into food and causing liver problems. However, DuPont was able to stave off the regulators once again, even though, after the product got FDA approval, it would again find that dogs who ate it experienced liver issues.[16]

While the FDA gave PFAS the green light, pesky questions about the health effects of the chemicals would continue to plague 3M and Dupont in the years that followed. After university researchers found organic fluorine—a possible indicator for PFAS—in 104 out of 106 blood samples from five different US cities in the 1970s, they alerted 3M that they were suspicious of its own Scotchgard and DuPont's Teflon.[17] In 1975, 3M sought to tamp down any qualms, telling University of Florida scientist Warren Guy—who had expressed concerns about the role of Teflon or Scotchgard in fluorine's pervasiveness—that "this was no time for speculation." In an internal memo, 3M employee G. H. Crawford described these concerns as "far-fetched" and "unlikely," but said that of the products Guy had flagged as possibly responsible, Teflon was "least unlikely." However, Crawford downplayed the matter, writing, "This was not (I hasten to say) suggested to Dr. Guy."[18]

Despite brushing off the researchers, 3M started to look for the substance in the blood of its employees—and found it. In fact, in 1978, the company described fluorine concentrations in their blood to be "proportional to the length of time" that they worked there, persisting in people who had previously been exposed to PFAS but hadn't been around the compounds for fifteen to twenty years.[19] There was also some early evidence that the substances' reach was global. A 1979 DuPont memo cited 3M's detections of organic fluorine in the blood of peasants in a Chinese village, though at levels "significantly lower . . . than values found in developed countries."[20] DuPont also found fluorine in the blood of its workers, but the company decided against informing the EPA.

Worse yet, there were signs that these chemicals were taking a significant health toll—not just in animal studies but in people. A 1978 internal review of the medical records of those workers who had long-term exposure to PFOA revealed "borderline elevation of liver function tests," wrote Sidney Pell, a manager of DuPont's epidemiology section.[21]

The finding may have presented a legal quandary for DuPont—not only putting their own employees at risk, but also causing potential harm to contractors who worked at the plant. In fact, there was some internal debate at DuPont over whether to inform West Virginia janitorial company Winans about the risks to their staff. Ultimately, Dupont decided—in the interest of preempting any legal or media scrutiny—to come clean and recommend taking employee blood samples.

"This sampling is required to place DuPont in the best legal and ethical position should something happen with C-8 [i.e., PFOA] in the future or if we're investigated by either the media and/or government," Dupont's A. R. Behnke wrote in a memo.[22]

He then laid out a playbook as to how such investigations have occurred at other plants, which involved a beneficial opportunity for DuPont: an offer to conduct the tests for Winans, for a price. "The contractor pays DuPont to test his people w/ the testing cost added to the price of the contract," Behnke explained in the handwritten note. "This is the route I'd advise taking."[23]

As the 1980s rolled around, 3M identified something it considered so problematic about PFOA that it took the rare step of informing the EPA: evidence of a link to birth defects. In a study from 1981, 3M researchers found that the fetuses of pregnant rats that had consumed the substance developed eye deformities, confirming two previous studies. Yet in its alert to the EPA, 3M stressed that "no human health problems have been observed" that were related to PFAS exposure.[24]

In addition to notifying the EPA about the issue, 3M also alerted its customer, DuPont, in March 1981. Within days of hearing from 3M, DuPont acted—moving women out of jobs that could potentially expose them to the substance.[25] Bruce Karrh, DuPont's medical director, wrote that there had been one employee with "heavy" PFOA exposure who had experienced a miscarriage.[26] 3M took similar action, moving twenty-five Decatur women "of childbearing potential" out of jobs to prevent their exposure.[27] By mid-May, DuPont had compiled a list of employee pregnancies and recent births. Three were listed as having had a "normal child" (though PFOA was found in one of these women's umbilical cord blood), while two other women gave birth to babies with eye abnormalities. One also had a nose abnormality. Yet within a few months, DuPont appeared to reverse course. A November 1981 staff meeting memo from DuPont said that it seems "very unlikely" that PFAS exposure causes birth defects.[28]

Yet other, even deadlier illnesses were also cropping up, with DuPont finding an excess of certain cancers in its employees. In April 1989, the company said that its scientists had identified more cases of leukemia than expected, while that December, they detected high levels of mouth, throat, and kidney or other urinary cancers among male employees. The company ultimately determined that there was no statistically significant excess in cancers overall.[29]

Nevertheless, 3M was beginning to worry not only about its employees' unusual illnesses, but also about what they could mean for its bottom line. An internal memo noted that since 1984, blood levels had started increasing. The document listed two primary concerns: "employee health" and "corporate liability."[30]

In 2000, the health effects—and their potential liability—had become so stark that, after pressure from the EPA, the company agreed to begin phasing out PFOS and PFOA, though it would continue to produce many of their chemical cousins.

When asked about this long and sordid history, 3M did not respond directly to any particular findings, but the company commented on the toxicity studies broadly. Carolyn LaViolette, a spokesperson for 3M, said in a May 2024 statement that such studies "are typically designed to produce adverse effects and identify the doses at which toxicity occurs." These doses are "generally many orders of magnitude higher" than what humans are exposed to through the environment, she added.

"Subsequent animal studies performed by 3M at lower exposure levels did not show adverse effects at exposure concentrations still well above environmental exposure levels in humans," LaViolette said.

Referring to the studies in general, she added that 3M has "shared significant information about PFAS over the decades," while also publishing many of its related findings "in publicly available scientific journals dating back to the early 1980s."[31]

As for DuPont, the company spun off its PFAS business in 2015—and then later underwent a merger and a separation. A spokesperson for the corporation argued that as a result, DuPont is no longer the same company that carried out these studies, and therefore did not provide a response. The company to which it spun off its PFAS business also declined to comment, declaring that it did not exist until 2015.

⌒

As executives at DuPont and 3M were discovering the lethal effects of PFAS, the consequences were becoming painfully obvious at the plant outside Decatur. Even in the glory days, when 3M seemed like an economic savior for communities along the Tennessee River, red flags were popping up along its banks. Fifteen years after it opened the Decatur plant, 3M found PFOS in a Decatur plant worker's blood sample—a finding that repeated itself in several employees in 1979 and became even more striking in the decades that followed.[32]

3M was finding not only a wide presence of the chemicals in Decatur workers' blood, but also that the exposures were making people sick. One study based on data collected in the 1990s found high risk levels for prostate and colorectal cancers, while another noted that workers had an increased risk of death from bladder cancer. The first study revealed that around the time that 3M was downplaying any potential health harms of PFOS to the EPA,[33] the company was internally identifying conditions to watch among its own personnel. 3M scientists listed liver and bladder cancers, as well as endocrine and reproductive disorders, as being of interest based on "a substantial body of literature," including PFOA and PFOS research.[34]

There was also evidence that the exposures were not limited to within the walls of the facility; in 1979, PFAS compounds were discovered in fish caught in the Tennessee River around Wheeler Dam, about twenty-six nautical miles from the company's Decatur plant.[35]

While 3M's facilities have long been landmarks on the Tennessee River shores, they are by no means the only such plants in the region— or the only ones polluting local waterways. Steps away from 3M Decatur sits another industrial giant: Daikin, an appliance manufacturer head-quartered in Osaka, Japan. Driving along the highway adjacent to the area, passersby can see the company's cream-colored buildings flanked by intersecting gray structures. On a warm June 2023 day, as Brenda's car careened past the compound, at least one chimney was emitting a white substance into the atmosphere.

In addition to making air-conditioning equipment, Daikin also deals in PFAS. The company began making fluoropolymers—coatings that resist heat, oil, stains, grease, and water and can be made from PFAS—at the Decatur site in 1994. But the chemicals Daikin used didn't stay on Daikin's property—they went into the nearby air, water, and of course, the Tennessee River. A 2004 presentation stated as much; while stressing that soil monitoring showed "no clear pattern," it lists the application of sludge to the land and residue from air emissions as "potential sources of contamination."[36]

While for years—and indeed decades—troubling findings were being discussed behind closed doors in corporate offices and government agencies, by the 1990s the local media was starting to take notice. A November 1999 article in *The Decatur Daily* sounded the alarm, citing the area industry's own descriptions of "their ultimate potential disaster."

"At the Daikin America Inc. and 3M chemical plants, the worst-case scenario for a chemical accident would be the total release of a railcar filled with up to 180,000 pounds of hydrogen fluoride,[37] a dangerous toxic chemical," the article stated. Any potential accidents involving the substance—which is required in the synthesis of PFAS, among other compounds—"could also span 25 miles and affect an estimated population of more than 75,000 people," the article added. However, to mollify readers, it noted that "the worst-case scenario is extremely unlikely to happen."[38]

Likely or not, the threats posed by PFAS were becoming more widely recognized, with tangible consequences for its manufacturers and their factories. It was around this time that 3M agreed to stop producing PFOS and PFOA, a move that affected the products churned out on the banks of the Tennessee River, and by extension, about a hundred of 3M's 975 Decatur employees.

"It has already been a year of change for 3M," a December 2000 *Decatur Daily* article stated, citing the May 2000 corporate decision to phase out certain product lines that contained "persistent chemicals that do not easily break down in the environment."[39]

Among the items they shelved were certain Scotchgard products and firefighting foams, as well as grease-proof paper, pet food packaging, and some surfactants that were used in paint to smooth its spread. While Jim King, 3M's Decatur plant manager, stressed that the chemicals had not been proven dangerous, he acknowledged that their persistence was unsettling nonetheless.

"It's not a good public image if you're dealing with something that lingers in the environment, even if there's nothing wrong with it," he said.

The plant at that point started refocusing its efforts on a light adhesive used on the back of 3M Post-it notes and an adhesive for reflective strips on firefighter's outer clothing. Despite the news, King said at the time that "Scotchgard is alive and well," noting that affected products would be reformulated.[40] King went on to retire just a year later, in 2001, and he died in 2019.

But things at 3M were perhaps not as "alive and well" as they seemed. A series of tests from the early 2000s detected PFAS in the Tennessee River,[41] showing that the pollution was flowing downstream: the water and fish collected there had higher concentrations than those upstream.[42, 43] The levels identified in these fish were "very high," according to Rutgers environmental and occupational health professor Robert Laumbach.[44] PFOS was also found in the wastewater leaching out of Decatur's landfill, in local sediment, and in sludge coming out of the city's wastewater treatment plant.[45]

Unsurprisingly, given the prevalence of PFAS in the Tennessee River—where many communities downstream of the factories source their water—the substances were also detected in local public water networks,[46] including that of West Morgan–East Lawrence (WMEL) Water and Sewer Authority, which serves Brenda's community in Courtland and most unincorporated areas of Morgan and Lawrence Counties.[47]

Either PFOA or PFOS was also contaminating water systems serving other nearby communities, like those located in the towns of Muscle Shoals and Florence, each more than forty miles from the 3M Decatur plant.[48]

More recently—from 2007 to 2010—after an unnamed manufacturer notified the EPA that it had "unknowingly discharged large amounts" of PFAS just upstream and into the Decatur Utilities' Dry Creek Wastewater Treatment Plant, federal agencies stepped in. The EPA tested and identified biosolids from the plant that had been distributed to farms as sludge from 1996 to 2008. EPA samples showed elevated PFAS levels in the area's soil, as well as in groundwater and drinking water. After enacting its first health advisories in 2009 for PFOA and PFOS, the agency then found elevated concentrations of PFOA in two private wells in the area.[49]

That same year, the EPA asked the Centers for Disease Control's Agency for Toxic Substances and Disease Registry (ATSDR) to enter the fray as well. ATSDR tested blood levels of several varieties of PFAS in a community cohort and observed in a report published in 2013 that concentrations of PFOA and PFOS "were two to four times higher than average levels in the United States."[50]

To this day, numerous chemical plants and manufacturing hubs still dot the banks of the Tennessee River, their tall smokestacks puncturing the sky with puffy white plumes. Amid other structures both wiry and rotund, these back-to-back buildings pump out the products that bring Americans comfort and convenience. Around 100 are still allowed to dump pollutants into the river, though the EPA's website lists the stretch of water they sit along as "impaired" with contaminants including PFOS as well as agricultural nutrients.[51]

While these "discharges" are lawful, the companies have not infrequently overstepped their legal bounds, with PFAS becoming the focal point in a series of local scandals. In November 2017, it came to light that 3M had alerted the Alabama Department of Environmental Management (ADEM) that it had been underreporting its discharge of PFAS into the Tennessee River—for three years and by a factor of a thousand.

In response, 3M's legal counsel pinned the mistakes on the fact that the government's new electronic filing metrics were different from the old manual submission process. But a 3M engineer's letter said that the errors had been occurring even before the switch to that system.[52]

Carl Cole, an attorney who would soon become a key partner to Brenda in her pursuit of justice,[53] slammed regulators for failing to revoke the company's discharge permit as a punishment.[54] Looking back at this incident, Cole recalled his certainty that the company was going to "get away with it" and would receive no more than a "slap on the wrist."

"The reason for that is that the Alabama Department of Environmental Management is toothless," he said. "They don't have the resources to battle somebody like 3M."

ADEM did not respond to multiple requests for comment.

3M once again faced scrutiny in late September 2019, when a self-investigation revealed that the Decatur facility released another type of PFAS into the Tennessee River, and in doing so, violated a 2009 legal agreement the company had entered with the EPA. That contract allowed 3M to manufacture two replacement PFAS by forbidding their discharge into federally protected waters like the Tennessee River.[55]

That same month, another news report exposed further inaccuracies in 3M's reporting data from the past few years. This time, the company found that contamination levels of 289 of the PFAS discharges it had reported in 2015 and 2016 were wrong—and that it had delayed reporting this matter to both the EPA and ADEM.[56]

The pace at which 3M was appearing in local headlines with connection to PFAS was picking up, and the residents whose faucets were overflowing with that discharge downstream were getting frustrated and alarmed.

CHAPTER 3

So Many Ailments

ONCE BRENDA HAMPTON REALIZED that forever chemicals were wreaking havoc on her community, she dove into action. She not only opened a center in downtown Courtland to hand out supplies to her neighbors—she also paid the rent out of her own pocket.

At this makeshift location, in 2017 or 2018, she met Lamont Dupree, associate director of the Huntsville-based North Alabama Area Health Education Center. Dupree recalled his awe upon learning how Brenda was single-handedly investigating the breadth of Courtland's PFAS plague. It was Brenda, he later said, who discovered "what was going on with the health of the people."[1]

"Every time we have a conversation," he added, "it seems like she's telling me something else, where there's some other family that has been impacted. It's unreal to think about how many people have passed from some of the same kind of things, and then there are just those strange cancers."

Dupree couldn't precisely recall the date when Brenda officially came on board as an employee, because far before receiving a salary, she was volunteering for his organization. He marveled that rather than spending that money on herself, Brenda allocates most of it toward buying more water, food, and adult diapers. "She's just using what we're giving her to still continue to pour into the community," he explained.

"I keep telling her to try to find someone that can help her, because she's picking up people, dropping them to appointments up here in Huntsville," he continued, noting that Brenda is simply incapable of disconnecting. "Her heart is just so tuned in and locked into people's needs."

☞

Whether Brenda is delivering supplies or ferrying a reporter around town, she always runs into one or two or a dozen people she knows. At the local Dollar General, she was greeted by yet another friendly face—Katronica Jones, a forty-three-year-old mom of two who works at the store.

Like so many others in her community, Katronica attributed the tragedy she endured—the stillbirth of a daughter eighteen years ago— to contamination. Recalling how her daughter was healthy all nine months and born at 7 pounds, 12 ounces, Katronica was still engulfed by her grief.

"I went the night before, she was doing fine," she said. "The next morning I went, she was dead."[2]

While she couldn't prove that PFAS was responsible for her daughter's death, Katronica was firm in her belief that this was the cause. "There won't be no justice because I ain't got my baby. I couldn't celebrate her eighteenth birthday—this year," said Katronica, who has two other children in their mid-twenties and one grandchild.

"Every day it hurts to even think about it," Katronica continued. "We had all them clothes at a baby shower. I had to take all those clothes back. . . . Really, my folks had to do it because I couldn't do it."

It's a story that's almost too painful to bear, but one that is repeated over and over, in various forms, throughout the area. After talking with Katronica, Brenda took the half-hour drive to Decatur to visit one of her regulars, in the Wesley Acres senior housing complex. (The building made headlines in 2008, after flyover footage revealed its eerie swastika shape.)[3]

Stepping out of the car, Brenda greeted a beaming man sporting a bushy off-white beard, mustache, and a set of silver rings.

Howard "Buster" Branham led the way toward his modest apartment through a common room, which he said still contains a copy of Adolf Hitler's *Mein Kampf.* The book was anathema to Buster, seventy-three, a long-time proponent of equal rights and a self-described "outlaw" from his motorcycling days.[4]

"I rode with a club for a lot of years in California, and I learned how to respect people. And this lady needs a lot more respect than what she gets," Buster said.

Brenda's friendship with Buster, a cancer patient whom she helped regularly, happened by chance, while she was shopping with her grandson at another Dollar Tree, this one in Decatur.

"Are you Brenda Hampton?" Buster asked her at the store that day.

It turns out that Buster had long been following Brenda's "Concerned Citizens of WMEL Water Authority (GRASSROOTS)" group on Facebook. The recently widowed veteran had become fascinated by her drive due to his own 1960s and '70s advocacy work, which included an internship for social justice activist Rev. Cecil Williams in California.

"It didn't matter what kind of people—she was there to help," Buster said. "I got to thinking, man, this kid's got a lot of heart, and heart is what gets it done."

After Buster's wife died in February 2020, he recalled having trouble "keeping things together" and maintaining focus. But once he started reading Brenda's Facebook posts, he felt new enthusiasm and appreciation for the way "she'd go after the system."

"She put the fight back in me is what it was," Buster said of Brenda. "She goes right at them—she don't hide behind no bush, and she don't talk about nobody, she just goes right at it."

"You're not going to find a better person," he continued. "If there's an angel, she's one, a good one, too."

Buster was between chemotherapy treatments for bone cancer at the time of the visit, explaining that he went twice a week for the IV drip and took a chemo pill every night—not to mention his diabetes and high blood pressure. Through it all, he kept a wry sense of humor, quipping, "Mainly, they say, I've got brain damage."

Eventually, the illness took even that. By April 2024, Buster had succumbed to his bone cancer.

"I saw him right up until the death," Brenda said. "He still recognized me at some point, and then later that afternoon, he got to the point where he didn't recognize no one."[5]

It's experiences like Katronica's and Buster's that drove Brenda to take on the adjacent industrial giants, to go head-to-head with local public officials, and to make sure that the health of her community wasn't entirely forsaken. She recruited a small contingent of fellow activists—as well as scientists from across the state and around the nation—to her side. They've pushed forward lawsuits, helped secure settlements, and have regularly exposed injustices in the media. In doing so, however, Brenda has made herself an enemy of local leadership and of some neighbors—who have, at best, downplayed or ignored her efforts, and at worst, made her worry about her personal safety.

Her fight to bring transparency to local industrial operations has even cost her threats to her life. She said she was shot at and had two of her cars destroyed when her efforts started making headlines. After exiting a meeting at the time, she discovered that someone had broken into her truck and left behind the cut-up head of a Chucky doll.[6]

"I point out a lot of things to them that they're doing wrong," she said. "Any type of injustice that is done wrong, whether it's environmental, mentally, or physically, housing, whatever. It's an injustice."[7]

Her ultimate goal is to get the state of Alabama to revoke the polluters' permits. "I want this governor now, Kay Ivey, to rescind those permits that Governor [Robert] Bentley put out because they're dumping a million pounds of this stuff into the river and it's still going to kill us," she said.[8]

Given the losses that both Brenda and members of her community have endured, she also believes the perpetrators should be prosecuted—a rare remedy under the United States' legal system.

"If I knowingly poison you, I'm going to jail," she said. "So how can these people poison thousands of people and just pay a fine? I don't understand that." Money simply can't make up for the multitude of illnesses she's witnessed.

Brenda's sense of justice developed early. Growing up as the eldest of five sisters and four brothers, she was always willing to act against the grain, to do what she believed to be right, regardless of the consequences.

"She was very verbal, I'll put it that way," said one of her brothers, Larry Hampton, seven years her junior.[9] Laughing with Larry on his Courtland front porch, Brenda backed up his assessment and recalled how she was "pulled out of school in seventh grade."

Her teacher had assigned the students to do independent projects on the Civil War—using information from any documented source, as long as it was accurate—so Brenda turned to a set of encyclopedias that her mother had purchased.

"We were about the only Black family in our immediate community that had encyclopedias," she said. "Along with our encyclopedias came three Black books on Black history."

Brenda ended up writing about the "Buffalo Soldiers," an African American regiment that fought against Indigenous people during the country's westward expansion after the Civil War. The class was interested in her findings, but apparently the teacher was not.

"He kicked me out and it was right in semester exams, so I had to go to summer school because they said that I was inciting a riot," she said.

⌒

Between visits to ailing community members, Brenda occasionally takes a break at a sprawling riverside property just next to Courtland, where she said she sometimes likes to just sit and watch the quiet ripples of the water lapping the shore. The land is home to retired couple Tom and Rose Adams, whom Brenda recruited several years ago to her food- and water-distribution campaign.

Tom recalled how, at first, he just accompanied Brenda to purchase pallets of water. "Next thing you know, I'm walking around handing water to everybody on the streets for weeks at a time," Tom said.[10]

But these deliveries weren't always welcomed by Courtland-area residents. Occupants of many households resented Brenda's advocacy efforts, as they depended on 3M and other industrial giants for their livelihoods.

"We didn't even get a thank-you," Tom said. "They'd be sitting in a chair. They wouldn't even get up and come and get the water."

"They would send down kids," Brenda interjected, explaining that the adults seemed not to want to face her.

Describing in a separate conversation just how difficult it was for her to carry a thirty-two-bottle pack of water, Brenda said she wasn't going to let children lug such a massive load.

"I knocked on the door and I counted five adults, and I said, 'Come get your water,'" she recalled from one delivery, reiterating that she had bought and paid for the water. "I went as far as Birmingham; we bought out all the Office Depots one day."

She wasn't exaggerating. Brenda was quick to open a binder of files and pull out a list tabulating all the purchases she had made during one supply run.

"I must have spent about $3,000 or $4,000 in water, in every Dollar

Tree in Decatur, Hartselle, Athens, Huntsville—we hit all the immediate area," she said.

But Brenda and her helpers have persevered, and ultimately recruited Tom's wife Rose to join their battalion as well.

"Tom comes home and he says, 'Brenda'—like I know who Brenda is," Rose laughed. "'Brenda needs help to do this and that and the other,' and I sat there and I said, 'Okay.'"

The Adamses are relative newcomers to the region—arriving from Florida later in life due to a job opportunity for Tom, a carpenter by trade. After their son began working for NASA in nearby Huntsville, Tom joined him for a six-month stint designing model spaceships that astronauts would use in training, and ended up staying. Rose followed five years later.

But they soon discovered that the picturesque waterside plot they had purchased was not quite as beautiful beneath the vibrant green grass and fertile farmland.

"If you purposely do something and you know it's going to contaminate the fish, it's going to make people ill, it's going to kill people—why are you doing it?" Rose asked.

Not far from Tom and Rose's house, a country road ambles toward the Tennessee River, tall grasses sandwiching the asphalt on either side of the quiet corridor. But anything growing there does so in the midst of industrial pollution—coated with toxic sludge billed as free fertilizer all over area farmland, according to Brenda. And while it is distributed from landfills, that sludge has origins in the area's manufacturing sites.

"What happened is that the landfills give them their sludge," Brenda explained, referring to public utilities in the region.[11] "When you've got acreage like this and you have to put fertilizer on it, and you're growing corn, it would cut deeply into profit. So if someone tells you that we can give you free fertilizer that'll make your product grow faster, yield more product, what are you going to do? You're going to go and get it."[12]

Across the country, wastewater treatment plants have a long history of asking area farmers to take the residual sludge—marketed as "biosolids," byproducts of the purification process—and spread it on their lands in lieu of expensive fertilizers. While this sludge does tend to include nutrients that boost crop yields, it also often contains toxic chemicals. Some states are considering banning sludge-spread entirely, but Alabama is not one of them.

Meanwhile, the runoff from these fields goes downstream, compounding the existing pollution and raw sewage releases that already plague the Tennessee River. Conditions are even worse for households in the immediate vicinity of the waterway—about five miles north of downtown Courtland—as they are "getting a double whammy" of PFAS pollution, Brenda noted.

Already in 2009, EPA scientists were investigating "very high levels" of PFAS in agricultural soils near Decatur. Gail Mitchell, then deputy director of water management for EPA Region 4, confirmed that the source of the contamination was municipal sewage sludge applied to about 5,000 acres of farmland. Nonetheless, researchers concluded that the Tennessee River was "unlikely to be affected by sludge because the river's volume is so large." Yet at the same time, the EPA was also in the process of sampling private drinking water wells closer to the fields, which served fewer than 100 people.[13]

Regardless of the sludge that may have seeped into their land, area residents haven't abandoned their fields and homes entirely, and some are even attempting to remediate the area by planting sunflowers, Brenda pointed out. She glanced at the expanse of green and its winsome beauty, observing that it's "like you just want to run out and play in it."

As bountiful as the surface might seem, the contamination it contains is even more problematic due to its precise positioning upstream from the Wheeler Dam.

This 1933 hydroelectric fortress, located about twelve miles northwest of downtown Courtland, is operated by the Tennessee Valley Authority (TVA) and stretches roughly a mile across the river. The TVA promotes the dam as "a major recreation and tourist center" for fishing, boating, and camping, with the Wheeler National Wildlife Refuge, home to Alabama's only wintering Canadian geese population, just next door.[14]

"This is owned by the bad TVA—this is who I want to get," Brenda said. "I want to get them because they were supposed to have an adequate water flow out here on the Tennessee River."

Brenda explained that after the dam closes at midnight, operations don't restart until around 7:00 a.m.—meaning that there is no water gushing through the dam to dilute pollutants. She recalled that prior to the installation of a new filtration system, local tap water was not only "a brown tea" color, but was also "stinking to high heaven."

A spokesperson for TVA claimed that the dam's flows "are monitored around the clock to ensure that all minimum flow conditions are met at all times," while stressing that "TVA is not responsible for enforcing the specific state laws regarding municipal, industrial, or individual discharges to the river," as that duty is in the hands of state agencies. Asked whether it is true that the TVA shuts down the dam at midnight, the spokesperson didn't respond directly, but admitted that it regularly turns off or releases less water from its hydroelectric generators when power demand declines.[15]

The handful of people fishing in the waters next to the dam one March 2023 morning were neither deterred by the less-than-appetizing conditions nor by local government warnings about eating the fish.

"A lot of them in this area will say, 'I've been eating those fish for 100 years, I'm going to continue, I'm all right,'" Brenda said. "The next thing you know, you may hear that they had cancer or something like that."

A 2023 Alabama state advisory recommended that people "do not eat any" fish caught at certain points in the reservoir and limit their consumption of certain species caught in other areas, due to the presence of both mercury and PFOS. But the pamphlet also noted that "PFOS is not considered to be a carcinogen in humans," asserting that "more research is needed" to determine whether the chemicals can harm human health.[16] While the EPA has not labeled PFOS as a definite carcinogen, the agency describes the compound as *likely* to be one.

Bimang So, a recent immigrant from Cambodia who was fishing at the dam with his father, said that he and his family do eat some of the fish and that they were unaware of the contamination.

Several local fishermen, gathered a few steps away, were quick to flee as soon as they were in danger of being similarly questioned. Another three anglers a bit farther along the riverbank declined to be interviewed, with one saying that he was just trying to run a business and didn't want to talk about it. Brenda, meanwhile, kept her distance from the fishermen entirely.

"A lot of them have been in this area all their life," she said. "They're just determined to stay and continue what they did, their father did and so on, you know? But these plants are coming in here because we've got a government that's pushing industry."

From the banks of the Tennessee River, Brenda gestured across the channel to the opposite shores, noting that the people on that side are also dying from cancer.

Ronald Mixon, a stocky man with white hair and a handlebar mustache, spent more time in the river than the average resident. In the 1990s, he was a diver and collected mussels in an area downstream from Wheeler Dam known as "the Muscle Shoals."

Where Brenda advocates for the people of Courtland, Ronald has also stood up for his neighbors, having led a group called Warriors for

Clean Water that commissioned tests on the Tennessee River and found dangerous levels of PFOA and PFOS.[17]

While he still seeks to draw attention to the issue, Ronald eventually decided to take down his group's webpage because he was receiving threats. But, so far, those threats have been nothing compared to what he described as "horrible" health problems, including type 2 diabetes and a leg amputation following an infection.[18]

After doctors at first inserted pins in his leg when he was having trouble feeling the extremity, Ronald said that they eventually had to remove part of the limb—replacing it with titanium. His mother, Geraldine Knox Mixon, had kidney cancer, something he attributed to the river.

"She told everybody that this water was killing her," he said.

Given the substantial contamination coming from all sorts of factories—from industries such as chemical, agricultural, textile, food, lumber, metal fabrication, and transportation[19]—Ronald said that past tests showed many kinds of pollution in his blood: mercury, lead, cadmium, and, of course, PFAS. In his most recent blood test, he said that all the metals had finally cleared from his blood, but not the forever chemicals.

"I got PFAS in there like crazy because it don't come out," he said. And despite the toll it has taken on him, Ronald is also extraordinarily lucky. He dove with eleven other men, but he's the last survivor.

"I won the lottery. I'm still around and the rest of them died, most of them from cancer," he added.

☞

Neither Ronald nor his neighbors ever really won the lottery, but area residents did eventually score some victories.[20] In October of 2015, attorney Carl Cole and colleagues filed a lawsuit against 3M on behalf of the West Morgan–East Lawrence Water (WMEL) Authority, which serves Brenda's community, accusing the company of "negligent, willful, and wanton conduct" in releasing PFAS downstream.[21] Three and a half years later, 3M settled for $35 million. In addition to doling out small checks to affected residents (before he died, Buster expressed gratitude for his $400 piece of the pie), the settlement enabled WMEL to pay for the construction of a reverse osmosis water treatment plant. While this expensive filtration technology cannot destroy PFAS—which must be discarded elsewhere—it is able to eliminate the compounds from community drinking water supplies.

Yet in the lead-up to the April 2019 settlement, 3M was not only arguing against such a plant, but it was also continuing to contaminate the water that needed treatment—and violating EPA orders in doing so. When WMEL general manager Don Sims demanded the reverse osmosis system, a 3M spokesperson countered that the plant had already installed carbon filtration technology to remove PFOS and PFOA from water. Sims, however, wanted a system that could also remove "the hundreds of lightly researched replacement chemicals" that were under manufacture at the time.[22] Ultimately, settlement negotiations went in Sims's favor, and WMEL's reverse osmosis system was up and running by May 2021.[23]

"That settlement worked out great. And quite honestly, it was the framework and the template that so many other of these cases has followed,"[24] Cole said in April 2024, referring to similar lawsuits that have since unfolded nationwide.

The water system upgrade worked out better for some than for others: while Courtland installed a new pipeline network to connect to WMEL's state-of-the-art facility, North Courtland had yet to do so. Residents of that town were therefore still getting water via galvanized pipes contaminated with sediment and other pollutants.

Whether the PFAS issue would have been addressed to the degree it has been without Brenda's return to Courtland is "a very good question," said Lamont Dupree, with the health education center.[25]

Although Brenda has become notorious across the region for her fierce crusade against 3M and other chemical powerhouses, the allure of industry has even touched her own family. Her brother Larry, now a truck driver, previously worked at the former Champion factory in Decatur, as well as at other area factories along the river. He recalled his summer contracting jobs as a teenager, performing duties like cleaning tanks and pressure washing.

"At the time, I didn't realize what was going on," Larry recalled. "But they were dumping it directly into the river."[26]

"We used to drink a whole lot of the water from the water fountains and the faucet and stuff," he continued. "There were just so many ailments going around—you know, young people dying and you know, for no reason at all. And that was scary."

As far as Larry's own health is concerned, he said that he has endured "diabetes, kidney problems, a little of everything—all kinds of ailments that [he] didn't have before." And although the water in his faucet is now considered safe, he doesn't trust it and only drinks bottled beverages.

Larry, who looked back at the jobs from his youth with alarm, is far from Brenda's only close family member who has worked for the region's industrial giants, including 3M.

"Our daughter . . . hates that I'm doing this, and she denies that she's my daughter, she works there," Brenda said.[27]

CHAPTER 4

All Settled?

Pᴀᴛ Uɴᴅᴇʀᴡᴏᴏᴅ ᴄᴏᴜɴᴛꜱ ʜɪꜱ ᴛɪᴍᴇ ꜱᴘᴇɴᴛ at Brookhaven Middle School in Decatur among his most formative years, filled not only with turn-of-the-century Y2K parties but also with students who would become his lifelong friends.[1]

"Middle school was a time when you're trying to find yourself, you're trying to find your tribe to fit in to, and I just have very fond memories of the friends that I made there," said Pat, a thirty-seven-year-old martial arts expert and environmental activist known locally as the "Trash Ninja."[2]

Pat reminisced about the "raw, institutional" design of the building, constructed with cinder blocks and featuring windowless pod-style classrooms. During his years there, from 1996 to 1999, he only saw daylight during gym class, when the boys went out to the basketball courts while the girls usually played volleyball inside the gymnasium.

It wasn't the only strange thing about Brookhaven. "We all knew that the school was built on a landfill—like it wasn't a hidden thing, we all were in on it," said Pat, who previously volunteered as cleanup director for the Decatur-based Tennessee Riverkeeper, while working as a lead field technician for the Osprey Initiative environmental contracting service. "And the joke that we all just subscribed to is that the school was sinking, three inches or something a year. And that eventually when we were old . . . that the school was just going to sink into the ground."

That wasn't a far cry from the site's appearance on a sunny March 2023 morning, when plumes of dust hovered over a crumbling demolition site and a discolored stream gushed into an adjacent drainage ditch. The property was indeed home to a landfill from the 1940s through the 1960s, during which time 3M has admitted to dumping waste there for about a year. After the site's closure, the spot was transformed into a stomping ground for generations of kids and teachers—from 1971 until 2018.

"The land was free," Ward Webster, the first principal of Brookhaven, told local news in 2019. "Of course everybody had concerns in the community," he added. "You built a school on a garbage dump."[3] (Webster died of cancer at age eighty-five on August 15, 2023.)[4]

Ultimately, it wasn't concern about pollution that closed the school, but structural issues, along with major heating and cooling problems. After Brookhaven shut its doors in 2018, a local nonprofit started using the building to host activities for kids from lower-income households. But that didn't last long.

While federal and state regulators had been monitoring the property for contamination since the 1980s and '90s, with the latter scrapping the need for testing in the early 2000s, around 2018 gossip started swirling that Brookhaven was riddled with PFAS.[5]

"It was known that it was a dump—it was not known that it was a dump for anything hazardous," said Carl Cole, the attorney who represented the West Morgan–East Lawrence Water (WMEL) Authority in its $35-million settlement.[6]

With the rumors in the back of his mind, Cole attended his son's practice at the Brookhaven-adjacent "Aquadome baseball field." On the sidelines, Cole asked the other parents if they knew anything about a site known colloquially as the "Aquadome dump." They didn't—but fortunately, an older grandparent showed up for pickup that day. "You're standing on it," the grandfather stated.

The baseball field and former landfill picked up their nicknames from the adjacent Aquadome Recreation Center, a hemispheric swimming pool that—along with neighboring Brookhaven—would end up at the core of Decatur's contamination controversy.

With that information, Cole soon after approached the superintendent, whom he said had already been given a heads-up about the possible contamination while handling other building issues. Municipal and school district officials received official news of Brookhaven's contamination in 2019, after the City of Decatur asked 3M to investigate the site, as well as two shuttered landfills that summer.

Cole was determined that 3M should answer for polluting a site where children had attended school for nearly fifty years, and he began discussing a potential lawsuit against the company with school board members. They "wanted to get rid of the liability" that Brookhaven had become, Cole explained. And because they "did not trust the city administration and certainly did not trust the legal representation for the city," according to Cole, the school board members retained him instead.

As for the City of Decatur—and Morgan County as a whole—Cole described its leaders and industry as "exactly on the same page."

"3M, I believed then, and would believe now, knew they had most of the leaders of the county in their pocket, on their side," Cole said.

Decatur City Schools and 3M reached an agreement in May 2020.[7] While 3M claimed to have only used the former landfill for about a year, a corporate statement said that from the mid-1940s to 1964, local manufacturers unaffiliated with the company had released waste there.[8] Regardless of who dumped what, where, or when, the company agreed to purchase the fifteen-acre site for $1.25 million—despite its assessed property value of only $487,500.[9]

Marveling at the threefold discrepancy between the purchase price and the site's actual value, Pat watched as his former school was "being torn down piece by piece by multinational corporations, with a big 3M sign." In November 2023—about eight months after the visit to the grounds with Pat—3M announced that it had completed the first phase of its revitalization plans, having recycled nearly 80 percent of the former building and declared that "the green space is suitable for public use."[10]

Nevertheless, work plans filed by 3M ahead of the demolition showed significant PFOS levels at test sites across Brookhaven.[11] Were any samples taken afterwards? Officials from the Alabama Department of Environmental Management (ADEM) simply referred back to the original plans, with a spokesperson noting that PFOS levels in the soil "were below the applicable screening levels to support the community green space as interim use."[12]

Brookhaven might now appear green on its surface, but Pat repeatedly described the surrounding neighborhood as a "sacrifice zone," where residents who voice complaints are told to just "move away."

"Then you've got another camp of people that are like, 'Well, 3M didn't know any better back then,'" Pat said, imitating a thick Southern drawl. "'Now they're doing right by us.'"

As it turns out, Brookhaven Middle School is far from the only PFAS-polluted property that appears to have been purchased either by 3M or by a mysterious company that shares its address.[13] In early 2019, Tennessee Riverkeeper volunteers identified contamination in a stream adjacent to what appeared to be an illegal dump on the outskirts of Decatur. The site was situated behind the pastoral San Souci Cave Road—hidden in a tree-covered area upstream from a wealthy McMansion neighborhood called Woodtrail Estates.[14] Ultimately, results released in February 2020 revealed excessive levels of both PFOS and PFOA.[15] Pat, who took part in the effort, recalled finding sinkholes filled with garbage and other debris in the surrounding woods.

Immediately downstream from the contamination zone was an expansive site designated for new development—a subdivision in a larger, spacious neighborhood. Pat remembered that, at one point, the remainder of that subdivision was about to be put up for sale via Jeff Parker, a local real estate broker, and H. M. Nowlin, an attorney. While the partners had already started advertising the new properties, things swiftly changed when Tennessee Riverkeeper revealed its findings.

About six months after news of the contamination surfaced, Pat combed through the tax records of the still-undeveloped residential properties. Sure enough, he found that Jeff Parker and H. M. Nowlin were no longer listed on these records. Instead, the lots were owned by a "Woodtrail Estates, LLC," whose taxpayer address was listed as 3M Center in St. Paul, Minnesota,[16] with records showing an incorporation date of June 22, 2020, in Delaware.[17] Describing the lots as "dead on arrival," Pat noted that there have only been about five houses built in this phase of the subdivision—either already completed or under construction before the contamination became apparent. Many plots therefore sat empty during the March 2023 visit.

The entire Woodtrail Estates area transaction was a multi-property sale that occurred on June 29, 2020, for a total of $3,864,740—just a few months after Tennessee Riverkeeper's discovery of the contamination.[18] The sale included eighteen different neighborhood properties that had been marketed as prime real estate.

In a cold call to Parker to ask him if he did, in fact, sell these lots to 3M, Pat recalled the real estate broker responding, "Well, if the tax records say that, that's what the tax records say."[19] Later, in an April 2024 email, Parker said that he could not speak about the Woodtrail Estates transaction because "there are confidentiality agreements in place."[20] 3M did not respond to questions about Woodtrail Estates or the properties.

Thinking about the land buyouts, Pat was cynical about the neighborhood's future—perhaps in years to come when memories have faded, the LLC could resell the properties to other buyers. Meanwhile, Pat remains uncomfortable drinking local tap water despite Decatur City reassurances that the municipal system is clean, and he therefore regularly refills a five-gallon jug at a Publix purified water station.

While Pat has not endured health problems that he would attribute to PFAS exposure, he said he suspects that others might be far less fortunate. He thought specifically about his favorite middle school music teacher, who "beat cancer three times and is still with us."[21]

Watching the building of his adolescent years crumbling before his eyes, Pat described the Brookhaven demolition as "bittersweet."[22]

"It's a step forward in trying to either do something different, or it's a step forward in repeating the same mistake," Pat said. "3M owns that property now, and they can do what they want with it."

Since his days at Brookhaven, Pat has traveled outside the area, making a name for himself in martial arts—but he always finds himself back where he started. "It's a risk to continue to stay here in Decatur and raise a family," Pat said, noting that the city will remain his "home base" nonetheless.

"I'm not giving up on Decatur," he insisted.

Like Pat, Paige Bibbee still deems Decatur her forever home, but the former city council president bemoans the ways both chemicals and corruption have contaminated her community. Bibbee has lived nearly all her life in Decatur, aside from the time she spent in college and law school—although both were also in Alabama. After coming home and serving as a youth minister for about six years, she decided to take care of her young kids full-time—until she dipped her toes in the local, city, and then state parent–teacher association (PTA). Inspired by her fire-fighter father's longtime devotion to Decatur, she ran for city council in 2015.[23]

Both Bibbee and her colleague, former city councilman Charles Kirby, view themselves as political independents. At a meeting at the local library in 2023, Bibbee said she is a registered Republican simply because a courthouse clerk advised her "to put something that can get elected," but she describes herself as "financially conservative" and "very liberal on many other issues."

Kirby, on the other hand, said he has never registered any party affiliation. After serving her first year on the city council as president pro tempore, Bibbee was appointed president—a one-year, annually elected position—in 2017. It was only when she assumed the presidency that she understood the gravity and the extent of her community's PFAS problem.

Bibbee learned about the situation mainly from Rickey Terry,[24] who performed various municipal roles over the years, including management of the Decatur/Morgan County Landfill—a regional dump site that is not related to the former Brookhaven facility.

"This was new and emerging information," Kirby added, noting that council members had been given little background.[25]

Terry, who retired in 2021, recalled a situation in which "nobody knew how tough it's going to be, what difficulties we're going to have dealing with it."[26]

"We were receiving waste from all of those facilities immediately because there was nowhere else for it to go," the sixty-seven-year-old said, noting that the facility had opened in 1982.

His first introduction with the landfill's PFAS problem came around 2001 or 2002, when the facility's operators informed him of the presence of the chemicals—and advised that they should no longer keep the wastewater sitting in the ponds. Instead, the operators built a loop system that pumped it back into and out of the dump in a "continuous flow" back and forth."

While he and his colleagues tried to make improvements over the years, Terry said he's certain that they weren't able to contain all the PFAS—noting that the facility is only about a mile from the Tennessee River.

"For all practical purposes, you can't contain every drop . . . and keep it within the landfill—it's impossible," he said, adding that rain can cause the substances to leach out.

During his lengthy tenure overseeing the landfill, Terry harbored more "animosity" toward 3M than to the political leadership of the city, as his facility needed to invest more and more funds in handling the company's PFAS-polluted waste. He surmised that the various mayors were "tiptoeing" around 3M due to its role as a major employer.

☞

Even as the nearby WMEL and in-town school district settlements started to roll in, one of the biggest watershed moments in Decatur's PFAS saga was yet to come—in the form of a 3M internal earnings call in January 2020. It was on this call with investors that 3M CEO Mike Roman revealed that "3M discovered and voluntarily informed the EPA and appropriate state authorities that discharges from our Decatur, Alabama, facility may not have complied with permit requirements."[27]

Prior to that announcement, Bibbee, the former city council president, heard rumors in the summer of 2019 that 3M was "having mediations with ADEM and EPA, trying to decide on what they're going to do."[28] When she approached City Attorney Herman Marks to ask if he should represent Decatur in the negotiations, she said he responded that the city was planning to leave those deliberations in state and federal hands. But Bibbee stressed that the city council would have to approve any potential settlement and that she would not vote on anything without doing sufficient research.

Bibbee said she was finally invited to an informational meeting in summer 2019 with Marks, Chuck Ard, then–president pro tempore, and Barney Lovelace, an external legal counsel retained by the city. At the next meeting, which didn't occur until December, Bibbee learned that the others had met three times without her. When she walked into that December meeting, everyone else was already there.

Bibbee recalled Lovelace handing her a nondisclosure agreement (NDA) and demanding her signature before they began discussions.

"I'm going to step out and call my attorney because I'm just really having a problem with this one," Bibbee remembered telling the group. And when Lovelace became angry, she said, "You can get mad. I'm not going to sign it."[29]

After calling her attorney, from whom she received instructions not to sign the agreement, she stepped back into the room.

"I said, 'I'm sorry, gentlemen, I'm going to have to leave because I'm not going to sign this,'" Bibbee recounted. Nevertheless, she neither left the meeting nor signed the NDA, as the men launched into a multi-hour discussion of a pending settlement among the City of Decatur, Morgan County, and the PFAS polluters—including 3M, Daikin, and a few others. Bibbee also recalled some talk about how one of the riverside plants was discharging a newer type of PFAS into the waterway—and that the general consensus was that they shouldn't say anything about that compound because they "really don't know much right now."

"It was like, you think we're idiots," she said.

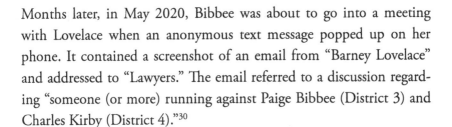

Months later, in May 2020, Bibbee was about to go into a meeting with Lovelace when an anonymous text message popped up on her phone. It contained a screenshot of an email from "Barney Lovelace" and addressed to "Lawyers." The email referred to a discussion regarding "someone (or more) running against Paige Bibbee (District 3) and Charles Kirby (District 4)."[30]

"If you can think of someone who should be approached about running, please let me know. It does not necessarily have to be someone you have heard is interested in running, it could just be someone who you think would be a good Council or School Board member," the email read.

In the email sent to Bibbee, Lovelace went on to describe the election as "critical for the future of Decatur," adding that he told Willie LaFavor and John Seymour, then chairman and president, respectively, of the Decatur–Morgan County Chamber of Commerce, that he "could not be publicly involved in this effort," but would assist as needed "very deeply behind the scenes."[31]

Bibbee and Kirby were convinced that this involvement led to their subsequent ouster. "The reason we're not in office today is because we asked about having meetings open to the public and being honest with the people about what's going on—that meant we had to go," Kirby said. "We were elected by the public to protect the public. Our feeling was, if we're withholding information, that makes us guilty."

Bibbee pointed to the mystery email screenshot as the event "that kind of blew the lid off." Because the chamber of commerce was immediately adjacent to her office, Bibbee stepped out and went next door to approach Seymour, who retired about a year later.

"I laid my phone down and I said, 'I just got that. What do you have to say about it?' And he looked physically sick at the time when he was reading it," Bibbee said, noting that he denied the chamber's involvement in any interactions mentioned in the email.

Asked about the incident in April 2024, Seymour responded that he could "barely remember" the details but was certain that nothing had alarmed him at the time.[32]

"A lot of folks were trying to get people to run for various offices," Seymour wrote. "There was an obvious lack of leadership at city hall, which resulted in Paige failing to be reelected."

After her visit with Seymour, Bibbee went back to her scheduled meeting with Lovelace, which she said she recorded.

"The first forty minutes, I just got screamed at and threatened with things that are not illegal or anything—it was just, I think he thought he could scare me," Bibbee said.

Those tactics included telling her that she was being followed and letting her know that he had pictures of her car and a variety of locations at different times.

"That was a really eye-opening conversation," she said.

In July 2020, she shared the eighty-two-minute recording with a local journalist, who quoted Lovelace as threatening, "I will burn you down," in response to Bibbee's suggestion that she might publicize the email.[33] While Bibbee played the recording for the reporter one time, she declined to play it again.

At the time, Lovelace said that he took offense at any accusations of inappropriate behavior, noting that he has "represented the city well" and that he has had his "legs cut out from under [him] at every turn without any communications or discussion."[34]

Following their conversation, Bibbee became more vigilant about her safety, assuming that she might be under physical threat. She soon found her tires slashed in the parking lot and her radiator punched with a flathead screwdriver.

"I've always had a carry license [for a firearm], but I never really felt any need to carry. From that point on I carried," she said during the March 2023 visit. "And I didn't like doing that. But I felt it was necessary at the time."

On an April 2024 phone call, Lovelace declined to comment on the 3M case itself because of "potentially ongoing litigation." But he expressed general satisfaction with the terms of the eventual settlement. And he vehemently denied threatening Bibbee, saying: "I've never threatened her in any shape, form, or fashion, or anyone else. That's just absurd."[35]

Regarding her alleged exclusion from meetings, Lovelace said he had no influence on scheduling, which was overseen by the mayor and the city attorney.

"It didn't really matter because she got beat. And she wasn't around when the settlement was reached," Lovelace added.

The attorney did admit to sending the contentious email, responding when asked about efforts to recruit opposing candidates that this "is not at all what that email says."

"I said in that email that some people in a meeting had discussed that," Lovelace said. "I did not ever recruit anybody to run against Paige Bibbee. And if I did, it didn't really matter because she only got 21 percent of the vote when she ran."

During the race for the city council seat, Mayor Tab Bowling and three council candidates—including Carlton McMasters, Bibbee's opponent—received campaign donations from the same political action committee. In addition, both Bowling and McMasters received donations from individuals linked to the Decatur–Morgan County Chamber of Commerce.[36]

In October 2019, Bowling received a $2,000 donation from the head of a political action committee (PAC) called Alabama Leadership Now, and about a year later, he also got $1,000 from Contractor Service & Fabrication, Inc.[37]—the company led by Willie LaFavor, who was then the chairman of the chamber of commerce and featured in Lovelace's email.

In August 2020, meanwhile, McMasters received $500 from Alabama Leadership Now and $1,000 from Gary LaFavor, whose donation shared the same address as Contractor Service & Fabrication Inc., of which Willie LaFavor is president.[38] The latter donations occurred despite a chamber of commerce declaration that its political action committee, ProsperityPAC, had decided not to support candidates in the municipal election. Individual chamber members, however, were encouraged to back whomever they personally favored for the city council positions.[39] Willie LaFavor never responded to multiple requests for comment.

From Kirby's perspective, the mystery email and other campaign issues were no less than a crusade to get him and Bibbee out of office. He lost to eighteen-year-old Hunter Pepper by thirty-three votes, in a district where only 9 percent of the residents voted.

Kirby noted that Mayor Tab Bowling "actually showed up on Election Day and campaigned for the kid, asking people to vote for the kid."

"That little kid came in in like four weeks of a campaign and won," Bibbee said. But that "little kid" attributed his motivation for running—as a high school senior—to his "big-citizen, small-government" instincts, and he denied any suggestion of outside influences.

"I did a lot of research and I said, 'Holy crap, this is something I want to do,'" Pepper added. "It's ridiculous that we don't have individuals that want to help civilians, and in my opinion, they just want to do what makes them look better."

The 2020 high school graduate unseated Kirby, a nine-year, two-term incumbent. The last candidate Kirby had defeated—in 2016—was Pepper's uncle, Eugene McNutt,[40] who worked for the company owned by the Chamber of Commerce chairman Willie LaFavor.[41]

☞

In October 2021, less than a year after Bibbee and Kirby had relinquished their council seats, the City of Decatur, along with Morgan County and Decatur Utilities, settled with 3M for nearly $100 million.

That sum was divided among multiple recipients: $35 million to Decatur to pay for a new recreation center—to replace the massive Aquadome; $25 million split among the city, Morgan County, and Decatur Utilities for community projects;[42] $7 million to Lovelace's firm;[43] $22.25 million to cap portions of the Decatur/Morgan County Landfill; $9.27 million to the city and Decatur Utilities for past PFOS-related expenses; and $7 million for future sludge removal at the utility company's treatment plant. The settlement also stressed that the agreement is "no admission of wrongdoing or liability."[44]

Just prior to the vote on whether to adopt the settlement, Billy Jackson—the only council member who opposed it—stressed at a public meeting that over his twenty-five years on the council, he had begun to find it "increasingly difficult to just . . . accept what Mr. Lovelace says on face value."

"I have great concern about the amount of the settlement," Jackson said. "I have concern about the settlement as to the amount that goes to our attorney—we all know that the company was paid on an hourly rate, and now, they're getting a contingency, so I have concerns about that."[45]

Kirby's perspective on the settlement was that "the city's legal staff hung the city out to dry." Similarly, Bibbee cited a March 2020 city council session where Marks, the city attorney, suggested that in "less than ten days," he would propose an external environmental law expert to represent the city.[46]

"He never came back to us—ever," Bibbee said.

Echoing these sentiments, Carl Cole—the attorney who represented both WMEL and Decatur City Schools in their lawsuits—said that the agreement's main problem lies not in the amount of money but in its allocation. In terms of the total dollar figure, Decatur has fared relatively well, compared to other communities. Among the many other PFAS settlements materializing in the same era was a 2021 agreement for $50 million between the State of Delaware and DuPont, Corteva, and Chemours over Delaware River pollution, following a lawsuit from the town of Blades, Delaware.[47] Meanwhile, a class-action suit in Kent County, Michigan, was settled with 3M and the Wolverine Worldwide footwear company in September 2022 for $54 million.[48]

"Everyone associated with the lawsuits from an environmental side thought that the lion's share of the money would go to prevent further contamination and clean up existing contamination in the water," Cole said, noting that Decatur Utilities could have fought for a reverse osmosis facility similar to that of WMEL, but the city maintained that its PFAS levels were low enough.

At the October 2021 meeting to adopt the settlement, Lovelace told members of the public that recent PFAS levels in their water were about 2.158 parts per trillion (ppt) for PFOA and 3.308 ppt for PFOS[49]—values that are below the 2024 federal limits of 4 ppt but exceed the EPA's health goals of zero for each of these substances. For reference, one part per trillion is equivalent to a few drops of water in twenty Olympic-sized swimming pools.

"Our drinking water is safe—no questions about it," Lovelace said. "There is PFAS in drinking water everywhere."[50]

But Cole criticized city leadership for giving up "an opportunity to have the cleanest water in North Alabama" and instead negotiating "something that politicians can put their name on in the form of a new recreation center."

If Bibbee and Kirby were still on the council, the vote likely would have failed—being 3–2 against rather than the actual outcome of 4–1 in favor.[51]

For his part, Lovelace described the settlement as "historic" and stressed that Decatur isn't prohibited from all legal action against 3M. He added that "3M is addressing the PFAS issue in this area, as required by that settlement."

The mayor and city attorney's office were asked multiple times to comment about the settlement, the political melee, and other accusations against them, but only Bowling replied. His message was succinct: "We received your previous inquiries. We are not interested in participating in an interview."[52] The mayor did not respond to specific follow-up questions, which included topics such as alleged support of Pepper's campaign.

A Decatur city clerk, meanwhile, said that she couldn't fulfill a request to view internal emails from 2009 to 2016 under Alabama's public records law, characterizing such correspondence as "so old." The clerk also admitted that emails are kept "up to two years and then removed" in the interest of preserving storage space.[53]

According to Alabama state code, government agencies must request preapproval from the Alabama Department of Archives and History for the destruction of permanent records—including correspondence with public officials.[54] Decatur's destruction permits, obtained from the relevant state agency, do not include approvals to destroy emails.[55]

Asked whether this omission might violate the law, Cole said that, although "there's nothing you can do about it," his "instinct would be yes, it's illegal."[56]

While some city officials were not eager to share emails or thoughts about the settlement, Kirby's replacement, Hunter Pepper, had plenty to say. He argued that because there was no PFAS regulation in Alabama at the time, 3M "didn't have to give us a dime."[57]

"The City of Decatur settlement was just fine and dandy," he said. "We may not be able to take legal action against them, but 3M has done a tremendous deal for the City of Decatur."

Leaving aside the recent legal settlements, 3M has long cultivated the image of a public benefactor in Decatur, sponsoring countless community events and parties, Bibbee explained.

"Look at Decatur's history, anything and everything we have. If it's to the hospital benefit or anybody—you look on the program, who is the platinum giver? 3M," she said.[58]

Yet when it comes to tax dollars, Decatur reaps few financial benefits from 3M operating near its shores. Since the company is technically located in an unincorporated "State Docks" section of Morgan County,[59] rather than in Decatur proper, it pays no municipal property taxes. It does, however, rely on Decatur's first-responder services; the city even had to invest in a truck equipped with foam to be used for fighting chemical fires—a truck housed at the station closest to the industrial zone, Bibbee added while musing about whether that foam might contain PFAS.

Meanwhile, Kirby noted that most of Decatur's working adults drive across the Tennessee River every morning to travel to jobs outside the area. It's hardly the "glorious future" the Alabama Chamber of Commerce envisioned when 3M first set up shop in 1961. Instead, Kirby described a Decatur ridden with poverty and devoid of youth, noting that if young adults "get a chance to do anything in life, they move off somewhere."

Those remarks hit close to home for Bibbee, as neither of her two adult daughters had stayed in Decatur. "I don't blame them one bit now for not coming back, which breaks my heart," she said. "That's all I wanted to raise them to do, is to love it like I do."

Despite her frustrations and her 2020 election loss, Bibbee isn't quite ready to give up on Decatur, noting that she would consider an eventual run for mayor. Ever since high school she was determined to stay put, while most kids wanted to leave.

"Even after knowing all I know about the local politics and all of the stuff, I still love Decatur," she said. "It's just part of who I am."

Reversing the town's decline will require electing officials who are not intimidated by industry, the two former council members agreed. Reminiscing about days gone by, Kirby recalled how those driving on the causeway into Decatur used to be greeted with a sign that read "City of Opportunity."

"That sign hasn't been there in half a century now," Kirby added.

CHAPTER 5

Miracle Foam

FOLLOWING THE EVENTS OF JULY 29, 1967, John McCain (yes, that John McCain, the longtime US senator from Arizona often branded a "maverick") was lucky to be alive. The thirty-one-year-old navy pilot was stationed on the USS *Forrestal*, an aircraft carrier deployed in the South China Sea during the Vietnam War.

Just after McCain finished his preflight routine that morning, a missile onboard the *Forrestal* accidentally discharged and struck an airplane's fuel tank, setting 200 gallons of jet fuel on fire and spilling them onto the ship's flight deck, as McCain recalled in his 1999 memoir.[1]

"I looked out at a rolling fireball as the burning fuel spread across the deck," he wrote. The future presidential candidate described an officer running ahead of him with a portable fire extinguisher, pointing it at a bomb that had been dislodged from his plane. That officer was killed when the bomb went off—and as additional explosives detonated, the ship was engulfed by burning planes, pieces of the vessel, and body parts.

Servicemen finally put out the blaze later that afternoon, though it took another day to extinguish fires raging beneath it. McCain described

men of just eighteen or nineteen who "fought the inferno with a tenac-
ity usually reserved for hand-to-hand combat."[2]

Though the *Forrestal* survived the fire, 134 men perished in the
flames. After this tragic lesson, the military would expedite its search for
equipment capable of staving off such catastrophes.

As fate would have it, about a year prior, the navy had received a
patent for just the thing: foam that could extinguish jet fuel fires. The
patent for "aqueous film-forming foam" (AFFF) described the material
as displaying "remarkable" potential to prevent resurgent fire—exhib-
iting a "self-sealing ability," unlike other foams that would break down
and allow fires to reignite.[3] Soon, the US Navy would require its vessels
to carry AFFF on board.[4]

The adoption of AFFF was quick. A 1972 navy report said that the
new material had "widely replaced" the navy's previous firefighting foam
by the time it was issued.[5] By 1979, acceptance of the foam extended
beyond the military to more than ninety US airports and a number of
civilian fire departments.[6] But nowhere was AFFF more popular than
on the nation's military bases. Hundreds of bases began using the foam
not only in emergencies but also in training drills, in which fires were
intentionally set and then doused with AFFF to prepare soldiers for
experiences like John McCain's.

For the military, the foam seemed like a virtual silver bullet,
while for the makers of AFFF, it was a guaranteed cash cow. Eventually, several major corporations got in on the action, including specialty manufacturers such as Tyco Fire Products. But the
Navy's original partner in developing AFFF? None other than 3M,
the same company that set had set up shop on the banks of Decatur. And the primary ingredient in the new miracle foam? Perfluorooctanesulfonic acid (PFOS), one of the most notorious types of
forever chemicals.

More than 1,200 miles northwest of Alabama, Colorado Springs doesn't share much in common with Decatur—except for the specter of 3M. The Colorado city and its suburbs in El Paso County are surrounded not only by natural wonders like the Garden of the Gods, a massive park filled with red rock formations, but also several military installations, including Peterson Space Force Base, the US Air Force Academy, and the US Army's Fort Carson.

Mark Favors grew up in the shadow of these bases, part of a tightly knit Black family within the largely White Colorado Springs. As Mark tells it, Cold War–era patriotism molded the city into a libertarian stronghold in which the small-government ideology reigned and "politics was highly, highly, highly discouraged."[7] Military service, on the other hand, was the bread and butter of the community, a major source of jobs in a rural region. The area is home to about 45,000 military personnel and 15,000 federal employees, as well as approximately 90,000 veterans.[8]

Mark's family is no different. Today an ICU nurse in New York City, Mark is himself a veteran, as is his uncle and multiple other relatives. His large squadron of cousins, multiple-times-removed—some blood relations, and others not—have served in most branches of the military, leaving an intercontinental web of bootprints in their wake. Likewise, his mom, Lillian Clark Favors, is a retired Air Force security manager, and his grandmother, Arletha, spent thirty-six years working as a civil servant at Fort Carson. It is a staunchly patriot family—but one that has, in recent years, begun to question why this long history of military service seems to dovetail with an extensive pattern of disease.

Sitting at his mother's dining room table in Colorado Springs, Mark attempted to tabulate exactly how many people in his extended family had suffered from various iterations of cancer and other sometimes-fatal illnesses. That headcount, he estimated, includes more than two dozen cousins, siblings, and in-laws—but does not even begin to touch upon the friends and neighbors who have similar stories.

"Another one of my cousins, he's getting a port now," Mark said, referring to the under-skin catheters used in kidney dialysis. At least five of his sick family members suffered from kidney-related diseases.

Mark has also noticed how tightly the illness tracks with proximity to certain bases. As far back as 1987, when his mother's department was transferred from the older Ent Air Force Base, near downtown Colorado Springs, to a new building at Peterson Space Base, on the outskirts of the city, colleagues started falling ill. A colonel in her group, Lillian remembered, decided to retire so that he would be able to take his grandson to kindergarten every day. "And then he got sick, and it was like, in two months, he was dead," she said.[9]

Most striking for Mark's family, however, is the number of relatives who developed diseases after moving to Widefield, about five miles southwest of Peterson. On retirement from the base, Mark's grandmother decided to turn her hobby of making porcelain dolls into a second career and relocated to the suburb with her husband and son (Mark's father) in the late 1970s.[10]

Mark's cousin Vikki recalled the moment when her grandmother pulled the family together one Thanksgiving in the late 1980s—with the news that her doctors had discovered a lump and that she was going to need surgery. Following the diagnosis and the surgery, Arletha went through a course of chemotherapy.

"And then she started having issues breathing," Vikki continued.[11]

Her cancer had returned. She succumbed to her illness on November 19, 1991, after about a week in the hospital.[12]

"She just never was able to recover," Vikki said.

Members of the immediate family who never moved from Colorado Springs to Widefield enjoyed long lives, several living into their nineties. Meanwhile, Arletha's husband also died of cancer, and her son, who had no kidney issues prior to living in Widefield, developed renal failure and had a subsequent kidney transplant. But after the new kidney became cancerous, he too passed away, at the age of sixty-nine, in 2017.

Less than a year later, Mark was visiting his mother when a CBS *This Morning* special came on TV.[13] As they watched an episode about perfluorochemicals—PFCs, the common abbreviation for PFAS at the time—Mark had an unsettling epiphany.

"I just started doing more research into it," Mark remembered, detailing how he began exploring PFAS mapping data on the Colorado Department of Public Health and Environment's website.

Among his first moves was to talk to local politicians, as well as try to get his family's water tested. Ultimately, Mark discovered that the Widefield property[14] was contaminated with PFAS at levels that far surpassed the EPA's drinking water health advisories at the time. Several sets of groundwater samples taken just a half mile west of the property between 2016 and 2018 indicated that the area's contamination was up to four times those safety thresholds.[15]

Rising from his seat at the dining table, Mark milled around the room and picked up a framed certificate that honored his mother for her four decades of service at Peterson. Similar certificates are likely sitting in houses all over Colorado Springs, documenting not only years of service but years of exposure to toxic chemicals.

Members of the Favors family had no idea that the firefighting foam being used on nearby bases contained PFAS, or that those chemicals were dangerous, or that they were leaching into the local water supply. But the military, like industry, already had some indication of AFFF's toxic effects decades before such information became public knowledge. In 1971, the Air Force Research Laboratory flagged the foam in use at the time—3M's "Light Water"—as both a possible threat to certain fish and a "serious pollutant," due to its inability to easily break down in water.[16] A few years later, Air Force researchers tested another iteration of Light Water and deemed it "less toxic" than previous PFAS-based foams, but still said it should not be released in substantial quantities if animals would be exposed for several days after the release.[17]

In the same era, a 1975 report prepared by a contractor for the Defense Department affirmed that AFFF foams contain PFAS "which are largely resistant to biodegradation."[18] Five years later, a navy review suggested that AFFF shouldn't be used in training at all, noting that it "may present serious environmental pollution problems" and that existing treatment facilities cannot process the substance.[19] Other problematic aspects of PFAS that are more widely known today, such as their toxic byproducts when PFAS are heated, were also noted in the 1970s and 1980s.[20]

There did appear to be some knowledge gaps, however, including, as one naval commander put it in correspondence accompanying a 1978 report, 3M's failure to disclose "any useful information" about the foam's ingredients.[21]

Nevertheless, a 1979 navy guide had also already listed "firefighting agents (e.g., AFFF)" as "hazardous."[22] Meanwhile, a 1981 document went as far as raising legal concerns, flagging AFFF sludge for evaluation as potentially hazardous waste "to assess the Navy's responsibility" under a waste cleanup law.[23]

The knowledge soon trickled down to the installation level, with a 1985 report conducted at Peterson likewise describing AFFF as a "hazardous material," though the report said that it did not produce hazardous waste.[24] In 1991, assessments from the Army Corps of Engineers conducted at Fort Campbell in Kentucky, Fort Ord in California, and Fort Carson in Colorado all recommended a transition to "nonhazardous substitutes."[25]

These warnings did have some effect—at least at select military installations. The Colorado Army base started using water rather than foam for training exercises in 1993, according to a Fort Carson spokesperson.

Subsequent policy allowed AFFF to be used only in emergencies, until the base replaced it entirely in 2018.

Meanwhile, neighboring Peterson took much longer to act—despite a 1989 internal analysis that demanded better management of AFFF waste.[26] But a central issue was that the air force simply has more planes on their installations than does the army on theirs, and jet fuel is particularly flammable when vaporized at high temperatures. In fact, the Federal Aviation Administration for years required all airport firefighters to test their AFFF supplies—and until 2019, the foam was discharged into the environment.[27]

Regardless of exactly why the military continued to use AFFF long after the hazards were known, the results were hard-hitting: in communities like Widefield, the firefighting foam flowed into the local water supply—and ultimately tainted residential taps. To Mark Favors, that fact embodies the region's symbiotic yet subservient relationship with the Defense Department, which he said has left a "trail of human devastation" in its path.

Given the extent of the contamination and the onslaught of illnesses that have rattled families across El Paso County, both Mark and his mother, Lillian, now look back at past years with newfound suspicion.

"It just kind of makes you wonder, as I say, did they know there was a problem from the beginning, when they started buying the foam or whatever?" Lillian asked. "Did they know?"

For years, Peterson, and many other installations around the country, continued to use AFFF despite all the red flags. Eventually, though, the military took systemic action to reduce the substance's presence—with a Department of Defense (DOD) decision in January 2016 to prevent "uncontrolled" AFFF releases during training and testing.[28] Ultimately, under direction from the 2020 National Defense Authorization Act passed by Congress, DOD committed to phase out AFFF altogether, declaring that it intended to stop purchasing PFAS-based foam in 2023 and stop using the material entirely in 2024.[29]

While the military was beginning to phase out AFFF for training, an important move by the EPA focused new scrutiny on contamination at bases. In 2016, the agency revised its health advisories—levels at which a substance is considered unsafe to consume—from 400 ppt for PFOA and 200 ppt for PFOS to 70 ppt for PFOA and PFOS, individually or combined.[30] This revision sent utilities nationwide scrambling to meet the new guidelines and also to determine the sources of contamination.

By November 2016, the US Army Corps of Engineers had detected PFAS at Peterson—noting that the chemicals "may present potential, non-carcinogenic risks to human health and the environment."[31] Subsequent inspections, published the following year, found significant levels of PFAS in the groundwater at the base's fire training area. Although no drinking water wells were immediately adjacent to that area, the "migration of PFAS-impacted groundwater offsite is possible and downgradient drinking water wells could be impacted," the authors concluded.[32]

Even down the I-25 highway at Fort Carson, the US Army base where AFFF hadn't been used in more than three decades, the environment has remained contaminated both on and off the base itself. At multiple spots cited in a January 2022 report, levels of several types of PFAS exceeded risk thresholds set by military leadership—who use those levels to determine the need for further investigation of a given site.[33] In response to the findings, a spokesperson said that the army would evaluate "the nature and extent of PFAS releases and conduct risk assessments using the latest EPA toxicity data."[34]

Such contamination is by no means limited to Colorado, but it has reached military families via vastly different pathways. Peterson's PFAS pollution has largely flowed into the faucets of off-installation communities downstream, while households on-base have benefited from clean drinking water supplied by Colorado Springs Utilities. This was not necessarily the case on other Defense Department establishments: an internal memorandum showed that as of December 2019, the military served as the direct drinking water provider for about 175,000 people in twenty-four on-site neighborhoods in which levels of PFOA, PFOS, or both were considered unsafe.[35] After the EPA updated the levels that were considered safe in 2022, an advocacy organization called the Environmental Working Group estimated that 600,000 service members were imbibing contaminated water.[36] Meanwhile, blood tests issued to military firefighters over the past few years—as mandated by Congress—have revealed PFAS in virtually all samples.[37]

At least one scathing assessment of the military's behavior has come from within—from the inspector general (IG), an independent internal watchdog for the Defense Department. In 2021, the watchdog dinged the military for declining to "proactively mitigate" risks related to AFFF, contrary to its own policies. While officials had issued a "risk alert" for the foam in 2011, that warning was never elevated, and administrators therefore did not have to respond—and they didn't until 2016. The watchdog also found "no evidence" that officials on bases, including firefighters, were made aware of the alert.

"As a result, people and the environment may have been exposed to preventable risks from PFAS-containing AFFF," the report said.[38]

Richard Kidd, a high-ranking military official overseeing environmental issues, justified the behavior on the grounds that the military "learned about the health hazards posed by PFAS basically at the same pace as the rest of America." Only when the EPA issued a final health advisory in 2016 could the Defense Department "take objective, measurable actions," he added.[39]

Yet to many, the military's actions are too little, too late. Former congressman Dan Kildee, a Democrat from Michigan and vocal advocate for PFAS action, lamented in a March 2024 interview what he described as "the lack of urgency at the very top of the Defense Department" across presidential administrations.[40]

A spokesperson for the Pentagon's leadership declined to answer a list of questions about the military's use of AFFF, its early knowledge about the substance's pollution potential, or suggestions that it should have been more proactive.

☞

Snow-capped mountains peek out over the asphalt stretch of runways that straddle the expansive grounds of Peterson Space Force Base and the adjacent Colorado Springs Airport.

While technically part and parcel of Colorado Springs, the base is itself a small town, with 550 houses and 2,000 people living on-site. But the working population—which includes those who commute to the base—is even bigger, totaling somewhere between 10,000 and 15,000, explained Sean Houseworth, chief of installation support at the Air Force Civil Engineer Center, while conducting a tour of the base in May 2023.

The installation is not only a hub for all things space control, but it also houses the 302nd Airlift Wing flying mission, which operates over-sized cargo transport aircraft, according to public affairs officer Stephen Brady, who led the tour together with Houseworth.

"Peterson's a good stopping point for folks that are going cross-country,"[41] said Houseworth.

Because the base is situated on property leased from Colorado Springs Airport, the air force also provides its landlord with first-responder services. For decades, that meant the presence of AFFF, which Brady described as "one of the tools in their toolbox." And in the past, the material was used not only in aircraft response but also in training, he acknowledged.

"Invariably, some of that foam escaped into the environment," he said.

While AFFF was once a mainstay for Peterson, neither Brady nor Houseworth could recall any operational use of the foam since the 2016 emergency-only orders took effect.

"We've had a couple accidental releases, where the firefighters are using water out on the fire training area, and they accidentally press the wrong button and some foam comes out for a minute," Houseworth acknowledged. "We respond to that just like it's a hazardous waste spill."

Brady confirmed in May 2024 that Peterson was in the process of replacing AFFF for *all* purposes, per rules laid out in the 2020 national defense bill. The base, he said, had received fluorine-free foam and was "awaiting arrival of disposal containers," after which the site would "transition one vehicle at a time, in order to maintain emergency response readiness."[42]

At Peterson's main fire station, giant bay doors give way to the flight line, where an asphalt stretch of runways borders the expansive grounds. Adjacent to the doors is a volleyball court, which Houseworth said used to be "a spot where they may have spray-tested" AFFF. But such tests, he stressed, only occurred "before we knew what the foam may be doing to the environment."[43]

The Air Force Civil Engineer Center in 2021 launched several pilot studies to remove PFAS from groundwater in highly polluted areas—such as the former fire training and fire station—with results expected later in 2024, according to Mark Kinkade, a spokesperson for the branch's Installation and Mission Support Center. Through 2023, the air force had spent a total of $103,245,840 on PFAS investigations, responses, and mitigation efforts at Peterson, Kinkade added.[44]

Separately, the military as a whole is evaluating hundreds of potentially polluted bases to see which might require PFAS cleanup.[45] By the end of 2023, the Defense Department had assessed more than 700 bases and found that 574 of them needed remediation. But such widespread restoration could take years—well into the 2030s for some bases and through 2048 for one particularly problematic site.[46] Nonetheless, the military was taking some intermediate cleanup steps at a small fraction of these polluted installations—just forty as of 2024—while the larger process played out. Amid the lucky locations were Peterson and Fort Carson.[47]

Efforts to rid the environment of PFAS may have begun, but forever chemicals have earned their name for a reason and past pollution remains problematic. This predicament was clear at another spot at Peterson, where a dried-out lawn stretches toward the foothills of the Rockies. The crackled fields are now vacant, aside from a couple of defunct aircraft collecting dust—and rust. But the old planes sit atop what Houseworth said might be the most PFAS-polluted point on the entire installation.

Prior to the 2016 ban on training with AFFF, exercises to prepare for aircraft blazes were regularly performed here—with PFAS-laden foam. Even though the military installed a lined pit and recirculating water system, the chemicals still find their way out due to factors such as "wind pushing the foam."

PFAS is in the base's soil, but even higher concentrations are found in the local aquifer. When conducting quarterly samples to monitor PFAS levels, Houseworth said, he and his team have seen higher levels in the groundwater "because this stuff is very mobile," particularly when it rains.

While the adjacent Sand Creek—which regularly overflowed onto Lillian Favors's childhood farm—is typically a dry bed, it has a shallow water table, Houseworth noted. This means that when contamination flows through the creek, it doesn't take very long for the pollutants to reach the aquifer, and ultimately residents' taps.

The most recently updated PFAS test results (from 2022) included samples from 86 locations in the communities of Colorado Springs, Security, Widefield, and Fountain in El Paso County. Out of 106 total samples, 41 contained PFAS levels that exceeded the guidelines set in 2016.[48] But through the lens of a new standard set in 2024, nearly 80 percent of the results would be considered unsafe.

Thus far, the air force has only identified off-base contamination near Peterson and not at the Air Force Academy, noted Houseworth, whose office also oversees PFAS-related action there. The team has tested residential wells in the adjacent Woodman Valley neighborhood and has not detected any PFAS, Houseworth confirmed.

"Peterson was just very unique—all the science and the hydrology and the geography sort of all came together in one package where we had to respond off the installation," he said.

Those responsible for delivering water to the neighborhoods downstream from Peterson have no trouble recalling the date and time when their world turned upside down.

"It was January 14, 2016, at approximately 12:30 p.m.," Roy Heald, general manager of the Security Water & Sanitation Districts, said.[49]

It was at that moment, he explained, that a reporter from the now defunct *Fountain Valley News* called to ask about PFAS after reading a story in the *Colorado Springs Business Journal* that cited findings about the compounds nationwide, including in Colorado.[50]

When Heald got that call, he said that he "didn't even know what she was talking about." But once he did, he and his team pored over recent well-water tests that had been mandated by the EPA—prompting them to shut down the worst offenders within a matter of days.

Regulators at the Colorado Department of Public Health and Environment (CDPHE) recounted a similar early 2016 scramble, in which they were tasked with protecting a drinking water source for 65,000 people. For Tracie White, director of CDPHE's Hazardous Materials and Waste Management Division, getting a phone call from the State Emergency Operations Center was a complete surprise, as she was accustomed to handling hazardous waste cleanups rather than drinking water issues. But she grabbed a map and considered the area's groundwater flow.

"My first call was to the air force," White said.

She then visited Washington, DC, to meet with officials at the Pentagon, noting that within two weeks of first identifying the issue, the military "had contractors on the ground at Peterson looking for potential sources."[51]

But water utility officials in the Security–Widefield census-designated area were still contending with the daunting news that much of their water supply was no longer drinkable. Heald identified in particular a "really hard hit" area just downstream of Peterson that tested as high as about 1,100–1,300 ppt for PFOS: about six times greater than the 200 ppt health advisory at the time.[52] But the contamination source was still a mystery at that point, he remembered, recalling "all kinds of speculation internally."

As the district rushed to accelerate a new water project that had already been in the works, Heald felt that the "EPA really blindsided" utilities by tightening its safety guidelines for PFOA and PFOS to 70 ppt.

"We didn't have any wells that would comply with that, not a single one," he added. "It was literally the week before Memorial Day, before summer starts. They couldn't have done it at a worse time for us."

Amid sizzling summer temperatures, Heald said that the district sometimes had to use contaminated wells to ensure adequate supply.[53] Only when the new project came online in September 2016 could water managers take a breather, while also preparing for the following summer—by signing a costly water purchase agreement with Colorado Springs Utilities. That utility gets its water from untouched snowmelt, according to a spokesperson. Tests done by the company in 2023 found only one type of PFAS, called perfluorobutanoic acid, for which the EPA had not issued safety guidelines.[54]

Alongside local water managers, the military is playing a role in mitigating the fallout from its contamination. In addition to long-term efforts to clean up contaminated soil and groundwater, in 2016 the Air Force Civil Engineer Center began working with public utilities and private well owners to supply clean drinking water to residents through bottled water and installed treatment systems. About two years after the crisis hit in Colorado Springs, the air force agreed to start building a shiny new ion exchange treatment facility, from which Heald, along with operations manager Brandon Bernard, were speaking in May 2023.[55]

The citadel of sparkling siphons and cisterns was up and running—greeting the visitor with a "raw water" tank that was shuttling in supplies via a five-mile pipeline. After flowing through a set of pre-filters that eliminate larger particles like sand, the water then enters a large green tube and is forced up into vessels stocked with resin, a porous material on which positively charged beads attract negatively charged ions. The PFAS, which naturally bonds with sodium that's already in the water, swaps places with the chloride on the resin beads.

"You've created sodium chloride—you're making salt," Bernard said.

The first drop of water ran through the plant in December 2020, while full operations began in August 2021. While Bernard touted the system as the best solution available for this region, he acknowledged its limitations, noting that it targets just a few PFAS compounds.

After years of push and pull, and ultimately, collaboration, Heald said that he and his colleagues "are very appreciative of what the air force has done, because this would have bankrupted us." That appreciation, however, is not without qualifications.

"Of the eight or nine hours I work today, probably five or six of them will involve PFAS. And prior to 2016, it would have been zero hours," Heald mused.

"PFAS is all-encompassing," Bernard added. "If you don't have to deal with it, you really have no understanding or clue about it. But the reality of the situation is, at some point you're going to."

CHAPTER 6

Boots on the Ground

Regardless of the military's early efforts to clean up its massive PFAS mess, Mark Favors and his relatives still have unresolved questions about whether the very entity that they have served could have contributed to the inconceivable losses within their community.

One of those family members, Mark's cousin Steve Patterson, served in the military until 1976 and recalled seeing AFFF at various points throughout his career.[1] Yet his run-ins with the substance began years earlier. Steve, his sister Princess, and their other siblings spent their entire childhood living in one of the most contaminated areas of Colorado Springs—a sprawling neighborhood at the southern edge of the city known as Stratmoor Valley.

When Princess was only about sixteen years old, she already started showing signs of being sick, according to Steve, who had gathered at his Colorado Springs taekwondo studio with Mark and several other relatives on a May 2023 morning.

"She used to come home tired all the time and all that stuff," Steve recalled, adding that "nobody really knew" why she was feeling this way.[2]

Around that time, she started to notice a butterfly patch—a red facial rash that is often associated with the autoimmune condition lupus. She received her official diagnosis at about age eighteen. By that time, the air force had already been contaminating the area for approximately a decade, Mark noted.

Princess was able to finish high school and college, going on to teach at Colorado Springs schools for more than three decades. She also earned master's degrees in education and in marriage and family therapy[3]—and she had a son, Yazeed Saajid (born Kenneth Callum).

But she was never able to shake her illness entirely. Princess ended up on dialysis as lupus ravaged her kidneys, and then she developed bladder cancer. "It got really bad when around the time I was born, it was the first time that she almost didn't make it," said Yazeed, who himself was born with one kidney and has irritable bowel syndrome.[4]

During Yazeed's early childhood, he and his mother lived in the area of Colorado Springs that has remained relatively unscathed by water contamination. Yet every time Princess got sick, she would recover at her childhood home in Stratmoor, where PFAS levels were off the charts. "I've never drank out of the fountain," Yazeed declared. "The water didn't even taste clean."

"That was the nastiest," Steve recalled, clutching his abdomen.

"I would get out of the shower, and your skin would be white because the water was so hard," Yazeed added.

Steve remembered that they continued to drink the water during adulthood when they made their regular visits to his mother, noting that "the ice was made out of it, too."

The trips to Stratmoor became more and more common as Princess spent an ever-greater portion of her time at the hospital. Steve recalled a grueling, multistep process in which doctors tried to restore his sister's health. Once they had beaten back her initial bout of cancer, they had to construct a new bladder—which meant that she needed to stay on dialysis about five or six more years until she became eligible for a kidney transplant. Luckily, Steve was a perfect match, and he was able to give his sister a kidney in 2002.

Even in hopeful moments, Princess's illness weighed heavily on Yazeed. He coped by playing basketball and nearly earned an athletic scholarship—that is, until poor behavior and plummeting grades landed him in junior college, where he played basketball but also developed a habit of skipping classes. Things started to look up for Yazeed in 2005, when he converted to Islam—a decision that stemmed from his family's spirituality, his distaste for "the whole White Jesus thing," and his appreciation of the discipline involved in five-times-daily prayer. About two years later, he became a father.

Through his former junior college coach, who was then at Dickinson State in North Dakota, Yazeed was able to make a triumphant debut as a point guard for the university in early 2008.[5] Yet by the next year—his senior year—he left the university and returned to Colorado Springs, where his mother's health continued to deteriorate.[6]

The cancer had returned and eventually invaded her liver, kidneys, spine, anus, and brain. Yazeed and Steve watched as Princess lost organs and took more and more medicines, while continuing to unknowingly drink contaminated water.

To this day, Steve can't help but wonder about the kidney he donated to her, as he, too, would end up developing multiple types of cancer. "I gave my sister a kidney," he pondered. "Did I give her the one with cancer?"

For Yazeed, the only bright light at the time was the birth of his second son, Kareem, about two months before his mother passed, at age fifty-three. And in the years following Princess's death, drug-related activities would land Yazeed with on-and-off stays in the county jail.

"There's an old omen there that when somebody's come somebody has to go," he said.[7]

Yet for the Favors and Patterson clan, it has hardly been an equal balance. Steve's oldest brother, P.K., had just died of prostate cancer about six months before the May 2023 roundtable, while his younger brother, Mike, was undergoing treatment for his third round of the illness. Then in November of the same year, Steve's cousin Jerry died of cancer at seventy years old.

Just a couple months after Jerry's death, an unexpected phone call from Steve came with a personal health update: he had been diagnosed with rectal cancer in October 2023. While the doctors managed to remove the tumor, Steve said he would need to do a partial colonoscopy every three months for the next two years and then every six months for the three years after that. While he still owned his taekwondo studio, he said he was taking a break from teaching.

"I've got to get my strength, and mentally I'm just all screwed up," he said.[8]

So much remains uncertain for the Favors-Pattersons, yet they recognize that they are just one among many families that have endured similar tragedies. Steve noted that "this isn't the worst" that the military has done, citing a history of systemic racism that was already apparent during World War I: "When they captured the enemies, we still had to sit at the back of the bus. So they've always gotten away with this, and they'll probably get away with *this*, too."

As someone who served his country for years, Steve said he has been trying to receive the maximum support from the Department of Veterans Affairs, which allows those exposed to AFFF to apply for a higher disability rating.[9] While he did succeed in increasing that rating, he still is at only 90 percent, rather than the full 100 percent. This means that he is eligible for only $2,172–$2,643 in monthly disability payments, as opposed to $3,621–$4,148.[10]

Nonetheless, Steve took solace in the fact that his close, inclusive family has been able to remain resilient through decades of illness. His twenty-year-old grandson, Deonte Spratley, underwent a kidney transplant in the summer of 2017—weathering years of treatments and facing a lifetime of medications, but alive nonetheless.

"We're happy, we hang together, we laugh, we have fun—even though we just lost a brother, and just lost a cousin—but life goes on," Steve said. "We cry at the funeral. But sometimes we don't even cry because I don't think we have any more tears left."

Steve's son Najee, who was also at the taekwondo studio that May 2023 morning, was himself about to enlist. Steve thinks the choice is "good for him," a way to "get out there and see the world."[11]

Najee said he was heading into the navy with the feeling that "whatever happens is going to happen." Embracing a future of possibility alongside an imperfect past, the thirty-one-year-old looked around the circle of men surrounding him.

"Every time I get around the family together, I get history lessons," he said.[12]

But to Najee, that's just part of being home.

"My family built this city in my mind, they built Fort Carson," he said. "There's generations that have touched this town."

Yazeed agreed, explaining that while he's been to other places, Colorado Springs is "just home" and that "it's been like that for generations and generations."

"Environmentally, I think we're just like orcas," Mark added. "We're like a pod of orcas."[13]

☞

Orcas live in cohesive groups, traveling together through vast sea depths in multigenerational, matrilineal families.[14] But these massive marine mammals are also killer whales—fierce protectors of their offspring, whose deadly pods cooperatively hunt their prey.[15]

Within the Favors-Patterson pod, Mark's maternal family was deeply wounded by the passing of his grandmother, and subsequent deaths left the remaining members isolated and hurt. When a killer whale community breaks apart, confusion and anxiety reign. But for Mark, that distress has only driven him harder to pursue the people he holds responsible for his loss.

"Can you imagine somebody who says, 'Oh, I'm sorry, I poisoned your whole family for the last thirty years?'" he asked.[16]

The injustice of it gnaws at him, and given his background, his mind runs toward legal retribution. After leaving the military, Mark did a short volunteer stint with the Colorado Department of Corrections, where he often heard the refrain, "All these guys are here because they broke the law."

"So why would we hold the air force to any different standard when they said they've done it?" he asked.

If life had taken a slightly different turn, Mark might have been a prosecutor. In fact, he moved to New York to attend Seton Hall Law School, and working in a hospital was originally just a way to fund his degree. But the prospect of massive law school debt, paired with a low salary, made him decide to stick with nursing. Still, he volunteered during his free time—advocating for voting rights and teaching civics to middle school kids. Reminiscing about his Cold War–era childhood, he noted that he was raised with the idea that citizens need "to keep the federal government in check." From there, he said, it was "a natural evolution" to speak up for those affected by PFAS.

While Mark was pushing politicians to test the water around his family's home in Colorado and linking up with local advocates, he also started attending lectures on PFAS hosted by the Environmental Protection Agency on the East Coast. As he dabbled in the water-quality space, Mark eventually made the leap from New York activism to Capitol Hill, connecting with others who were fighting for a federal response to PFAS contamination. In addition to community members directly harmed by PFAS, epidemiologists and nonprofit organizations from the Silent Spring Institute to the Environmental Working Group and Toxic-Free

Future had begun to rally around the issue. Indeed, long before Mark (or Brenda or many of the other individuals described in these pages) had ever heard of PFAS, pods of advocates had been circling the makers of forever chemicals.

⌒

If one story is the posterchild for PFAS, it is that of a West Virginia farmer named Wilbur Tennant, who had the misfortune of living near a DuPont manufacturing hub.

Tennant noticed that strange health problems had begun to plague his cattle.

"You can see she's hemorrhaged out the nose," he said in a video of one of his cows—proclaiming that many others had suffered a similar fate. Dissecting the dead cow, he noted black teeth, red spots on her tongue, and something that looked "like milk" on her tissues.[17]

Tennant, with the help of Cincinnati-based lawyer Rob Bilott, sued DuPont in June 1999, alleging that "contaminants" had been released into the environment. But Tennant and Bilott were missing a major piece of the puzzle—a key contaminant that they hadn't heard of . . . yet.

Critical to the evolution of the case was the legal discovery process, which enabled Bilott to demand documents from DuPont as part of an effort to find evidence. And when he got that evidence, he got a lot of it. The company eventually gave the opposing lawyer tens of thousands of documents to sift through until, eventually, he stumbled upon something: a letter from DuPont telling the EPA about its use of a chemical called APFO—which he later learned was another form of a substance he was also not yet familiar with, PFOA.[18]

Wilbur's connection to the contamination, Bilott ultimately learned, could be traced back to the early 1980s, when his brother, Jim, agreed to sell land near Wilbur's farm to DuPont for what he was told would be a "non-hazardous, basically office trash type of landfill," Bilott said.

He has since "pieced together" that this was around the same time that DuPont began to realize that PFOA was seeping into drinking water near the plant. The problem may then have been out of sight, but it certainly wasn't out of mind: by 1990, DuPont had started sampling water that passed through the landfill and into the creek, where Bilott said the company "found high levels of PFOA."[19]

"At that point, though, they didn't say a peep to Mr. Tennant or his family," he added.

Bilott's digging led him to two key pieces information:

The EPA had recently said that a similar chemical called PFOS "could potentially pose a risk to human health and the environment."

PFOA was used to make a top-selling product for DuPont—Teflon.[20]

Eventually, the case led to a settlement, as well as a realization on Bilott's part that this problem stretched way past the farmer and his cattle. What he found most disturbing of all was that the companies knew since the 1970s that the chemicals were in the blood of the entire US population and that they didn't tell anyone. Bilott eventually took on another lawsuit: a class action that represented 70,000 area individuals who had been drinking contaminated water. In 2004, DuPont agreed to settle—paying out an initial $107 million and agreeing to an additional $235 million for long-term medical screenings if a team of scientists identified a link between PFOA and any health condition.[21]

Seven years after the initial class action settlement, the scientists began to release their findings. This "C8 Science Panel" ultimately linked PFOA to six conditions: high cholesterol, kidney cancer, ulcerative colitis, thyroid disease, testicular cancer, and pregnancy-induced hypertension.[22] These determinations not only secured health monitoring for the community, but they also opened the door for future cases around the nation. Without Tennant and Bilott, there may have been no settlements for the residents of Decatur and the Courtlands, and far less national attention on the PFAS scourge.

In the spring of 2019, the environment subpanel of the congressional House Oversight and Reform Committee began holding a series of hearings on PFAS. The first three sessions established scientific facts about the substances and featured witness testimony about the pervasiveness of the compounds. They also included corporate voices who downplayed the public health risk, as Harley Rouda—a California Democrat and subcommittee chairman at the time—told his colleagues. The goal of the fourth meeting, in November 2019, he explained, was to encourage "immediate federal action to regulate and cleanup these dangerous chemicals."

Mark Favors was there to testify, revisiting his family's painful experiences of cancer and death.[23] He spoke alongside actor Mark Ruffalo, who portrayed Bilott in *Dark Waters*—a film that dramatized the lawyer's fight against DuPont. Both Bilott and resident Bucky Bailey, born missing one nostril after his mother was exposed to PFOA from working at DuPont while pregnant, were sitting in the gallery during the testimonies.

At first, Mark Favors was confused as to why he, out of all PFAS activists, was chosen to speak alongside Ruffalo that day. But then he remembered the sheer number of cancer-related deaths that had stricken his family members, many of whom were veterans.

"Most of them survived either Korea, Vietnam, or Iraq, and they're now in a military cemetery—not for combat wounds but for being poisoned by the military," Mark said.

In addition to sharing his family's experiences, Mark's goal in testifying was to push for a congressional investigation into wrongdoing related to PFAS. At the helm of any such investigation, he believes, should be an impartial entity, independent of the Defense Department.

Mark noted that courts have held the air force accountable for other wrongs, like failing to notify the FBI about an assault conviction of a former serviceman. After that man went on to carry out a 2017 mass shooting, the air force had to pay $230 million to affected families.[24] But when it comes to contamination, the law dictates that the Department of Defense (DOD) leads all investigations of pollution that begins on its property, rather than the EPA. And at this point, Mark's confidence in the DOD has been badly shaken, to put it mildly.

During the November 2019 hearing, Republicans and Democrats alike professed a commitment to ensuring that American communities have access to clean, uncontaminated drinking water—although they had very different thoughts about how to get there.

Congressman James Comer, a Republican from Kentucky, cautioned against "taking any sweeping actions" that could harm the economy, while stressing that he does "wholeheartedly support if any families have been poisoned intentionally by corporate America that they get compensated for that."[25]

On the other side of the aisle, Congresswoman Alexandria Ocasio-Cortez, a Democrat from New York, used most of her time to revisit Mark's main points, reflecting on the notion that "the army has said this is dangerous."[26]

"That is why we need subpoenas issued for this and we need a comprehensive investigation from Congress," Mark said in his testimony.

"I concur. I concur with you, Mr. Favors," the congresswoman agreed.[27]

In Mark's recollection, following the hearing, Ocasio-Cortez asked him for a list of possible individuals to subpoena if an investigation did materialize. But soon after that conversation, the coronavirus pandemic emerged, disrupting any further action. (A spokesperson for Ocasio-Cortez was unable to confirm whether the exchange took place and did not answer directly when asked whether there were plans to pursue the issue.)[28]

A congressional investigation may be a pipe dream for Mark Favors, but his commitment to the cause has become a motivating force for other activists. Liz Rosenbaum, a friend and fellow advocate who was fighting PFAS around Colorado Springs before Mark entered the fray, summed up her admiration this way: "Who gets invited to the congressional Oversight Committee, and sits next to Mark Ruffalo? And gets a personal discussion with AOC? Mark Favors. Sold. After that, dude, whatever you need, I'm in, done."[29]

It was thanks to Mark's first cousin twice removed, the late Fannie Mae (Bragg) Duncan,[30] that the two activists first crossed paths. In 2018–2019, the city of Colorado Springs was nearing completion of a monument to Fannie Mae,[31] who in the 1950s had opened a local jazz club that hosted luminaries including Duke Ellington, Billie Holiday, and B. B. King. The Cotton Club also served customers of all races—a sign reading "Everybody Welcome" hung in the window—and became a symbol for desegregation and civil rights.

From the get-go, Mark was skeptical about the statue. Why would the city bother to build a monument to Fannie Mae while, in his view, failing to stand up to those who had contaminated her community's water? Nevertheless, the city's commemoration provided Mark's introduction to Liz, who at the time owned a restaurant called Her Story Cafe and had been commissioned to design a cookie in Fannie Mae's honor.[32] Soon after meeting at a local celebration, he dropped by a gathering of her PFAS activism group, the Fountain Valley Clean Water Coalition.

"He's like, 'Hey, I'm from New York. My family lives here.' And my first thought was, Okay, this is the one time I'll meet you," Liz recalled. She assumed that while he was concerned about his relatives, he was just passing through. Still, she would take any help she could get. But when Mark flew to Colorado to attend a small meeting that Liz had organized at a local Applebee's, she knew he was serious. "I'm like, son of a bitch, I think he's sticking around."[33]

That kind of commitment and determination to be heard speaks to Liz. With a fuchsia biker jacket, sparkly eye shadow, and seven binders full of color-coded documents related to PFAS, she is not what you would call shy in either her fashion or her advocacy. "It's a lot—you hear me and you see me," Liz said.

Liz first heard about PFAS in the summer of 2016—about thirteen years after she and her husband moved to the town of Widefield, where Mark's grandmother had also relocated. That fateful summer, she found out about the PFAS pollutants contaminating Fountain Creek—which flows into the aquifer that fed their drinking water utility. After reading about the compounds in a local newspaper and growing frustrated with local political inaction, she took on the fight herself and launched her coalition.[34] In the years since, she has scrapped extracurricular activities and family vacations in favor of PFAS-related meetings and legislative volunteer work—in addition to her day job as a health insurance broker, which followed stints as a restaurant owner and history teacher.

"I wasn't even crocheting for a while, which I like to do when I watch TV, because I'm doing PFAS shit," she said.

Her limited travels during the pandemic were likewise dominated by PFAS—including a June 2022 conference in North Carolina that she was able to attend with grant funding. But she arrived home on a Friday with what she thought were allergies but ended up being COVID.

"And then Sunday I almost died," she said, explaining that her condition quickly deteriorated and required emergency surgery.

Two and a half feet of her large intestine and most of her appendix were removed, but Liz and her doctors still have "no freaking clue" what was actually wrong.

"Imagine the worst contraction that you had for four hours straight," she said, noting that such trauma does not usually strike a forty-six-year-old.

With her diagnosis still unclear today, the only clear justification she received for removing parts of her abdominal organs was that her "insides were dying."

Liz points a finger at PFAS for much of her bodily chaos, explaining that these compounds can interfere with the activity of cellular proteins. When the body tries to process what it thinks is a protein, she explained, the interloping compound "makes everything screw up in your body."

Scientists have, in fact, determined the underlying molecular mechanism through which PFAS can bioaccumulate in the human body. Evidence has shown that the compounds have "high binding affinity"—an ability to cling—to blood albumin as well as to certain types of proteins in liver and kidney tissues.[35] Their subsequent buildup and refusal to leave then disrupts metabolism processes, enzyme activity, fatty acids transport, and other mechanisms.[36]

Liz's husband, Dan, who has an autoimmune disorder called primary hypophysitis, had almost exactly the same surgery about twelve or thirteen years earlier. As part of the disorder, immune cells penetrate the pituitary gland and collect into a mass that mimics a tumor—disrupting hormone function.[37] Dan gets two weekly hormone injections at a personal cost of more than $100 per month, as the jabs are not covered by health insurance.

Between the two of them, Liz said, "It's a constant health battle that we're fighting."

⌒

For Liz and many others, the health battle is a lonely one, with few knowledgeable doctors to offer care.

"There's no one here [in Widefield]. There's not an expert here to help me through this situation," she lamented. "My husband has to literally go to a men's clinic for hormone therapy, like erectile dysfunction stuff. And that wasn't his problem. That's the only place he can go to get the hormone shots that he needs."

The doctors that do work in her southern El Paso County region "are affiliated with, like, six other clinics," Liz added, noting that "they're never there."

Addressing Liz's concerns, John Adgate, a professor of environmental and occupational health at the Colorado School of Public Health, said that he and his colleagues have "tried really hard to engage the medical community there."[38] But he noted that physicians tend to have a multitude of demands on their plate and also do not generally have specialized training in toxicology.

"That's not part of the medical school curriculum, by and large, unless they've done occupational medicine," Adgate said.

He also expressed uncertainty as to how clinicians could draw population-level associations between exposure and illness, particularly because "they see people one at a time."

Adgate is a principal investigator for the Colorado portion of a federal PFAS research project—the Agency for Toxic Substances and Disease Registry's (ATSDR's) PFAS Multi-site Study[39]—called the Colorado Study on Community Outcomes from PFAS Exposure (CO SCOPE).[40]

A previous ATSDR exposure assessment,[41] which began in 2020 in eight hotspots across the country,[42] including El Paso County,[43] revealed that regional levels of both PFOA and perfluorohexane sulfonic acid (PFHxS), a type of PFAS used in AFFF, were up to 1.2 and 6.8 times the national average levels, respectively.[44]

The CO SCOPE study, which began in 2021 and was still in analysis stages in early 2024, is aimed at piecing together how PFAS has affected the health of residents in El Paso County. The investigators ended up recruiting 925 adults and 141 children to examine possible damage to the kidneys, liver, thyroid, metabolism, blood sugar, insulin, and immune function, as well as neurobehavioral outcomes in children.

Liz, who participated in CO SCOPE, got her initial blood test results in April 2024: alarming PFHxS levels of 13.1 micrograms per liter (μg/l)—more than ten times the national average.[45]

CHAPTER 7

Unqualified Immunity

Lɪᴢ Rᴏsᴇɴʙᴀᴜᴍ's ᴘᴇʀsᴏɴᴀʟ ʜᴇᴀʟᴛʜ ʙᴀᴛᴛʟᴇ has only strengthened her determination to rid her community of the contamination on which it unknowingly erected a house of cards.

When El Paso County water districts were slapped in 2016 with the unwelcome news that their systems were contaminated, politicians in the region "still didn't know what had happened to us," Liz recalled.[1]

But she said that lawmakers started picking up the pace on the issue, and that by 2018, they were finalizing the details of their first PFAS-related legislation.[2] Liz credited that initial success to local Democratic legislator Tony Exum—then a state representative, and by 2023, a state senator.

The first bill, a bipartisan and bicameral effort, was signed into law in June 2019—co-sponsored by Exum and his Republican colleague Lois Landgraf, as well as a state senator from each party. The legislation restricted the use of PFAS-based firefighting foams, on the grounds that these materials have polluted the drinking water of almost 100,000 Coloradans and five water systems located downstream from Peterson Space Force Base.[3]

Recognizing that "the full extent of contamination in Colorado has not yet been determined," the bill stressed that the removal of PFAS could take decades. The legislation also emphasized the needlessness of the chemicals for fighting fires, arguing that London's Heathrow Airport has "successfully used fluorine-free firefighting foams for years." Finally, the bill included a ban on both the foam's discharge and use in training exercises by August 2019, and a prohibition on its sale by August 2021.[4] (These efforts were in tandem with the military's own restrictions on use of the foam.)

Additional restrictions followed, and in July 2020 the Colorado Water Quality Control Commission approved the state's first surface and groundwater standards for PFAS, which were fairly similar to the EPA's nonbinding health advisories at the time but also included limits for additional types of PFAS.[5]

The state has also been cracking down on consumer products laced with the chemicals, prohibiting the sale of items that contain intentionally added PFAS, such as rugs, cosmetics, children's items, and food packaging.[6] By January 2028, the list of banned products will also include textiles, cleaning products, food equipment used in businesses, and outdoor apparel.[7]

Colorado is by no means the only state to move forward with such bans. Maine, Minnesota, and Washington have advanced legislation to ban PFAS in an expansive range of products, according to Safer States, a national alliance of environmental health groups.

California, Colorado, Connecticut, Maine, New York, and Vermont have enacted complete phase-outs of PFAS in apparel, while the same states—as well as Maryland, Minnesota, Rhode Island, and Washington—have adopted restrictions related to carpets and rugs. Bans on the sale of AFFF and PFAS-laden food packaging exist in at least a dozen states. Other PFAS phase-outs in multiple states apply to products like cookware, dental floss, menstrual items, and children's toys and textiles.[8]

When it comes to Colorado, Liz is proud of the state's progress, though she argues that the current laws do not go far enough—a shortcoming she attributes to Republican lawmakers watering down the bills.

☞

Just as Liz was scrambling to help get PFAS-related legislation off the ground, she also found herself in a new quandary at home. In 2018, she and her husband decided to move from Widefield to Wigwam, about ten miles to the southeast. Little did she know, however, that this community would end up plagued by the same problem.

She and her neighbors faced a rude awakening when Wigwam Mutual Water Company received word in January 2020 of PFAS contamination in its drinking water supply: 14 ppt for PFOA and 24 ppt for PFOS—below the EPA's 2016 health advisories, but well above the legal limits (4 ppt) finalized by the agency in April 2024.[9]

Alongside the PFOA and PFOS limits, the EPA at the time decided to consider certain types of PFAS in a mix—an approach long promoted by scientists. John Adgate, the professor at the Colorado School of Public Health, stressed that different types of PFAS tend to "travel together,"[10] meaning that disentangling one from another can be a formidable task. Kristy Richardson, Colorado's state toxicologist, likewise supported considering "the cumulative effects" of more emergent PFAS.[11]

Multiple types of PFAS have certainly been identified in Liz's new neighborhood, with Colorado's statewide PFAS map confirming elevated concentrations of the compounds in Wigwam—not only PFOA and PFOS, but also of perfluorobutane sulfonate (PFBS).[12]

The most recent samples from an El Paso County military base on the map were taken at Fort Carson—about fifteen miles upstream from Wigwam and twenty miles south of Peterson—where 2019 and 2020 test results were off the charts: up to 151,000 ppt for PFOA, 55,000 ppt for PFOS, and 9,800 ppt for PFBS. Concentrations were similarly high at Peterson, as well as at the adjacent municipal airport and at the Air Force Academy, just north of Colorado Springs.

Peterson personnel rejected the possibility that their installation could be the source of the Wigwam pollution, purely due to geographical reasons: the community is situated at a higher elevation than that of Peterson.

"We're not the only ones, though, who have historically used AFFF foam, either," said Sean Houseworth, chief of Peterson's Installation Support Section at the Air Force Civil Engineer Center.[13]

Asked whether some contamination could be coming from Fort Carson, Houseworth was uncertain. A US Army Corps of Engineers report from January 2022, meanwhile, included PFAS sample results from two off-base wells in the Fort Carson vicinity[14]—near the downstream portion of a creek that flows through the Wigwam area.[15] In both of these wells, the assessment detected PFOA and PFOS in excess of the military's risk-screening levels.[16]

While military and state officials are working to widen their areas of focus for remediation, such action can take years to materialize—time that, Liz felt, her community just couldn't wait. She therefore became involved in a Wigwam Mutual Water Company effort to obtain emergency grant funds that would provide residents with pitchers capable of filtering out PFAS.

"Did they ever play Oregon Trail and die of dysentery?" Liz asked, stressing that, unlike a case of dysentery, filtering out PFAS in Wigwam was something they could beat.[17]

In July 2023, Liz received welcome news via email that Wigwam had been awarded the necessary funding. A CDPHE official wrote that the grant was "intended to bridge the gap and provide temporary assistance until permanent treatment can be installed."

Despite the many years Liz has been involved in PFAS activism, the sense of loss she links to the contaminants was still raw on the sunny

Saturday morning in May 2023. As she looked both back at the past and toward the future, Pikes Peak—the highest summit in the region—poked out of the clouds due west, while a school-side mural in memory of Mark's late cousin, Princess Patterson, stood perhaps just as tall due north.

Like Princess, Liz's close friend Molly Miller—whom she described as her "number two person" in all things PFAS—spent years battling cancer. The two friends had met about fifteen years ago, when Molly's son was a student in Liz's history class.

Molly's husband, Greg Miller, recounted a journey that began with surprise results of a summer 2011 mammogram—a "stage zero" cancerous lump, but cancer nonetheless. When doctors identified another lump four years later, in 2015, Molly, then fifty-eight, requested a double mastectomy as a proactive measure.

After a couple years of respite, things again took a turn for the worse in 2017. An unrelated cardio-fitness test revealed that Molly's heart was in great shape, but also showed three lymph nodes that "lit up in her chest area," Greg recalled.[18]

"It was breast cancer," he said.

By the end of 2020, the tumors had become more aggressive and populous. Molly was able to join a clinical trial that initially shrank the masses, but only temporarily. As good news turned to bad, the doctors in early 2022 switched her medicine, which caused "terrible side effects."

"We'd maybe go out to eat somewhere, and she just would have to go to the bathroom and get sick," Greg recalled.

A switch to a standard chemotherapy drug proved insufficient, and she endured two episodes of severe swelling in her legs, landing her in the emergency room.

"I was really blessed and fortunate to be able to retire—like right at the end of August 2022," Greg said. Around that time, hospital personnel informed Molly that she had "about six months left."

During Molly's remaining months, Greg said they tried to "do some fun things," such as shopping at secondhand stores or driving to Cripple Creek—a former gold mining mountain town—in October, when "the aspens are just in full color."

"She took me out for coffee," Liz recounted, "and she just says, 'All the treatments and radiations aren't working anymore. And so we're just going to let everything naturally happen.' And I said, 'So what does that mean?' She said, 'Well, I've got a little bit of time left. But tell me about you, Liz—what's happening?'"[19]

Liz remembered exclaiming, "Molly, don't do this to me!"—to which her friend replied, "I'm going to do this to you."

By December, Molly was in full home hospice. She couldn't leave her living room hospital bed on Christmas Eve, but she was able to scroll through nostalgic photos with her family members. The next day, Greg recalled, Molly "was just able to say Merry Christmas, and that was all."

"We opened our presents, but she really wasn't alert enough," he said. "And then two days later, she passed away."

While Greg said he wished he could prove that PFAS had caused Molly's cancer, he knew this would be impossible—but credited his late wife for her willingness to "fight the fight."

"Justice was her work. She wanted justice," he added.

Pulling out one of her many PFAS-filled three-ring binders, Liz explained that Molly was the one who put these files together—an act that served as "one of her last gifts to us."

On that Saturday morning in May 2023, the adrenaline powering Liz's activism was still jogging, if no longer sprinting, through her veins, as she contended with the exhaustion brought on by both grief and the aftermath of a global pandemic.

"Now I'm mostly working within Wigwam Water District, like gentle nudges," she said.

But Liz's hard-earned breather was short-lived. By early 2024, she decided to launch a campaign for the Colorado General Assembly ahead of the November elections.[20] Liz, a Democrat, ultimately lost the race against a Republican incumbent in a historically red district.[21]

Whether she's on the campaign trail or affecting change, Liz wears her heart on her sleeve—boasting a multicolored tapestry of tattoos that tell both a political and personal story.

"And then after every election, the day after elections, I add to it," she said.

On one side, she bears a spiral stack of books topped with a steaming mug of coffee, whose vapors are woven into a heart. On the other, a skull is surrounded by a branched arrangement of colorful blossoms.[22] The skull, Liz said, is an indicator that "we're all the same" and is rooted in her love of history and anthropology. She motioned from the skull to a little flower, which she said is part of her signature.

Pointing to the image of a caterpillar, she said that the creature "doesn't know what it's like to be a butterfly, but a butterfly understands both," she said, pointing to additional tattoos. "And then flame because you're going to burn the shit down, a spoon because I like to stir shit up. It's got an F at the top because I fucking mean it."

Liz's long-time partner in the perpetual PFAS fight, Mark Favors, has pressed on in hopes that one distant Hail Mary might rattle the scoreboard that has thus far indicated repeated defeat. After all, he explained, the mission of "taking on the Pentagon is not for the weak."

He went so far as to chase down then senator Kamala Harris after a PFAS-related hearing, upon remembering that Harris's stepson had graduated from Colorado College in Colorado Springs in 2017.[23]

"You remember when you went to your stepson's graduation?" Mark asked her. "You know the creek behind Colorado College? . . . That's all contaminated with PFAS."[24]

Following that revelation, he recalled, Harris's "mouth literally hit the floor."

What Mark would want from a congressional investigation, in theory, is quite simple. He would aim to "to find out what really happened, how pervasive is it, what can be done to prevent it." Another critical component would involve holding "people accountable if there was something nefarious, as the documents imply."

A key reason behind the need for such an investigation, from Mark's perspective, is the lack of legal recourse. Mark has faced repeated stumbling blocks in his quest "to get justice and accountability," as he said in his 2019 congressional testimony.[25]

"Per Colorado's strict two-year statute of limitations," he added, "a lot of my grandparents and family members that fought in World War II and in Vietnam—because they died before 2014, they are not able to sue anyway."

The statute of limitations to which Mark was referring is a state-level law that defines just how much time victims of contamination and their family members have to bring a lawsuit.[26]

But Colorado's strict two-year statute is generous in comparison to that of Alabama, where Brenda Hampton lives. In Alabama, plaintiffs can sue only within two years of becoming ill, rather than within two years of becoming aware of the illness's cause, because the state lacks robust legal discovery rules for toxic exposures. While Colorado has a fast-ticking clock, victims there can at least postpone suing until they can identify a clear causal link for their conditions. Alabama law, on the other hand, renders such a pursuit nearly impossible.

Yet Mark noted that even if legal recourse were readily available to him, there isn't a sum of money that could make up for the losses his family has endured. Stressing that he was "raised in a matriarchy" and blaming the military for giving about a third of his family members kidney cancer, Mark said that "there's really no financial compensation."

"That's why I said there's not enough money in the US Treasury for my grandmother," he added.

Nevertheless, just before Mark's father died, he signed up for an expansive, nationwide legal procedure—called multidistrict litigation (MDL)—which has grouped thousands of claims against the manufacturers of PFAS-laden AFFF before a federal judge in South Carolina, Richard Gergel.[27] Liz did not file suit, in part because the illnesses she has experienced did not appear on a list used by attorneys litigating such cases.

During the initial MDL signups, the lawyers said that they were adhering to the results of the C8 Science Panel—the assessment that came from Rob Bilott's famous case against DuPont.[28] Paul Napoli, co-lead counsel for the MDL, said in 2021 that he was abiding by this strategy to ensure that he was using the strongest cases and avoiding giving "false hope" to potential clients.[29]

But Napoli's opinions have since changed. Given the ongoing advancements in epidemiology, he said in January 2024 that he might now be comfortable including several additional conditions, such as pancreatic cancer and prostate cancer, as well as possibly low birth weight and certain blood cancers.

"There's more and more connection between different injuries and exposure," Napoli said. "We're going to be able to look at communities and make some retrospective analysis."[30]

As for an illness like prostate cancer, which is common in men of a certain age and difficult to pin to a specific source, Napoli said that he supports conducting "a differential diagnosis"—determining whether the disease is in the family and whether the patient is, say, thirty years old or ninety years old.

"The doctors check the boxes," he said, stressing that "it'll be up to a jury to decide."

Mark Cuker, another lawyer involved in PFAS-related lawsuits, said that he personally would represent people with kidney, testicular, pancreatic, or bladder cancer. Although he acknowledged that some lawyers wouldn't represent claims involving the last two, Cuker said he is able to do so due to the significant incidence of these cancers among his clientele in New York, New Jersey, and Pennsylvania.

Regarding the idea of including more illnesses in personal injury cases, Adgate, the Colorado School of Public Health professor, said that determining "causality is hard."[31]

"In a courtroom, it's 51–49. For scientists, it's a little different," Adgate said, referring to the need for precise attribution in research. "It's a slowly moving target—it takes years to nail these things down."

Colorado State Toxicologist Kristy Richardson echoed Adgate's sentiments, stressing that scientists almost never get to the point where they have sufficient information to definitively link a single person's health to an exposure.

"Maybe most of us drink coffee, but what you put in your coffee is different than what I put in my coffee—we went to different gas stations, we breathed different air," Richardson said. "There's all these subtle differences between individuals."[32]

As Napoli moves forward with the MDL, he is doing so with extensive experience handling risky public health litigation. Among his most well-known battles was a quest for financial settlements for injured workers and first responders from 9/11.

"It's gotten easier over time, but thirty years ago, you couldn't find an expert that would testify because most of them were funded by these chemical companies," he said. "People didn't believe, if you couldn't see, smell, or taste it, that there was contamination."

Napoli attributed his own case of leukemia in 2014 due to the time he spent at the World Trade Center site as part of his 9/11 case work, which he said bolstered his understanding as to how pollution impacts people's lives.

His introduction to PFAS came from a place close to home. After a Long Island water district official called for legal counsel about high levels of the compounds, Napoli ended up testing for—and finding—PFAS in his own drinking water on the island's North Shore. From there, he got involved in places like Colorado Springs.

"The more I saw, I was really surprised by what the chemical was, how ubiquitous it was, that it was causing injury," he said, noting that his own daughter has "severe immune issues."

Within the MDL umbrella, the plaintiffs were sorted into several categories, including water providers, municipal property owners, personal injuries, medical monitoring cases for those exposed but not yet ill, state-based lawsuits, and challenges to the federal government.

With so many cases to sift through, the judge chose to start with water providers—from which he initially chose ten bellwether cases that would best represent others within that group. February and April 2024 brought about the finalization of the MDL's first settlements in that category.[33] DuPont—the successor company—and spinoff corporations, Chemours and Corteva, settled with the nation's water providers for $1.18 billion,[34] while 3M settled for between $10.5 billion and $12.5 billion.[35]

While these settlements won't directly influence future deals in other MDL categories, Napoli said they could provide some help: residents whose water was contaminated will have access to evidence proving their exposure through their water utility's data. It is Napoli's goal to get these individuals monetary compensation. But the number of personal injury cases, he noted, is poised to only grow over time. And this begs the question as to how even multibillion-dollar corporations would be able to afford to resolve such cases in the future.

The chemical manufacturers will likely be the first group of defendants to experience financial challenges, Napoli predicted. Then will come those who purchased PFAS for use in their own manufacturing processes. And after that are the other potentially responsible parties, including distributors and wastewater treatment facilities.

"There's going to be a series of lawsuits that go down this chain over time," Napoli said.

While several of Mark Favors's relatives have signed on to the MDL against the manufacturers, he still also holds the Department of Defense accountable for the damage.[36] Mark is well aware, however, of the hurdles associated with challenging the military in court.

One of the only ways that a plaintiff can sue the air force is through the Federal Tort Claims Act—a 1946 statute that deems government employees liable for negligent or wrongful acts and enables litigation on this basis.[37] But the military also has a unique shield, called "discretionary function immunity." This status exempts government employees from prosecution if an action "requires the exercise of judgment in carrying out official duties," unless evidence indicates that they should have known that the action was illegal or beyond their authority.[38]

In 2018, a US Court of Appeals judge ruled that at least one type of justice—healthcare screenings for people who have been exposed to PFAS—"is not barred by sovereign immunity." Yet the plaintiffs, Cuker's clients, were unable to get their government-subsidized exams because the court found that such payment would disrupt ongoing cleanup efforts.[39]

Napoli said that the MDL legal team had made some headway in circumventing immunity claims, through a new "track" of cases. At the forefront of this category is a November 2019 lawsuit against Cannon Air Force Base in New Mexico,[40] where a dairy farmer lost his milk license and had to euthanize thousands of cattle due to a mass discharge of AFFF.

As of January 2024, Napoli noted, the military was "refusing to remedy or pay [the farmer], citing immunity." The attorney described the case as "a state versus federal battle about who has control of the state waters" and who is therefore responsible for the pollution. The outcome,

Napoli explained, could prove "whether the US government has culpability and how much they have to pay."

Stressing that government entities "don't have a carte blanche to harm people," Napoli noted that the immunity function has "never relieved them of the obligations to be a good neighbor."

Napoli said it had recently come to light that the air force installation may have flouted multiple AFFF disposal protocols. He added that the base had even submitted notice of its infraction to the EPA while also admitting that the release trespassed onto neighboring property. Trespass, he explained, is not subject to immunity under Supreme Court case law.

Comparing Cannon to Peterson, Napoli said that the two bases are similar with respect to trespass. He had yet to determine, however, whether any site-specific rules were violated at Peterson, due to the government's slow rollout of such information.

"Until they're forced to by the court, they seem to be reluctant to provide it," Napoli said. "But I would find it odd if one base is making these types of updates without others also knowing about them and probably mirroring them."

Napoli said he could foresee a resolution of the entire MDL in the next few years, noting that the parties must work on not only identifying and quantifying the problem, but also on "digesting the ability to pay for it."

Reflecting on his initial immersion into what is now a global PFAS problem, Napoli recalled that one of the first such lawsuits, in 2016 or 2017, involved the El Paso County contamination in Colorado. At the time, there was hardly any national-level PFAS disclosure information available. But El Paso County was different.

"You had all three water providers contaminated—Security, Widefield, and Fountain, to varying degrees," Napoli said. "It was being studied, and it was so widespread."

CHAPTER 8

A Win–Win?

On a leafy tree-lined property in Fairfield, Maine, a red wooden structure with an A-frame roof shelters an artesian well. Both a relic of days gone by and a mainstay of modern Maine, this unassuming piece of engineering consists of a central pipe that delivers free-flowing water through an attached hose.

"It runs all the time, nonstop," said Lawrence Higgins, as he and his wife Penny ambled across their land on a sunny August 2023 morning.[1] Lawrence's solution to the soggy soil was to direct the water into a carve-out in the yard that was well-suited for a duck pond.

"She stopped laying eggs," he added, gesturing toward one of the ducks. "She was laying eggs before the PFAS—before we put them in here."

Little did the Higginses know, when they moved to this quaint corner of New England about three decades ago, that their sparkling well water would end up contaminating the entire property.

The lush landscape surrounds a modest ranch house and adjacent lean-to barn—a red fortress built with their bare hands as well as their retirement funds. Lawrence and Penny had sought to breathe new life into the property just a decade before, with no inkling that their efforts would be undermined by a plague of pollutants.

"Ten years ago, we decided that our old house was too old to invest any money, and so we buried it," Lawrence said earlier that morning, speaking from a dining table inside the renovated home.

Where the old house once stood there is now a shed with a "Products for Sale" sign, picturing a statuesque South American creature known for its quizzical looks and wild coiffures.

"We went and looked at an alpaca farm, and she fell in love with them," Lawrence said, referring to his wife in a thick New England accent.

"They're just different. They all have their little attitudes," Penny added.

The Higginses had been looking for "something to do" about six or seven years prior, after all their grandchildren grew old enough to attend elementary school. Lawrence was still working in machine shops at the time, while Penny was a certified nursing assistant, prior to her transition to full-time grandparent.

After an initial visit to an alpaca farm kindled love at first sight, the Higginses first adopted four of the animals. When they decided they wanted a few more, they built a barn—selling their camp site in northern Maine to fund the project. By that point, they had also gotten a pony, a miniature horse, a donkey, and a mule.

Inside the giant red barn, Penny pointed out the donkey and the horse, whom she scolded for his personal hygiene. "You're a mess, Tic Tac, look at your hair. Wow. I should put some color in it," Penny cooed.

When one of the barn residents gave out an assertive grunt, Lawrence was eager to present "Perry," an alpaca that clearly recognized him.

"You have to earn their respect," he said.

While visitors do come to see the alpacas, Penny said that it's more a labor of love than a gold mine. They send the excess alpaca fiber to a co-op in Massachusetts and then sell products in their store, but only enough to break even.

"We just started really growing our business," Lawrence said. "And our granddaughter loved it, and we thought she might want to take it over someday."

But "someday" now looks a lot foggier to the Higginses, after their retirement plans were torpedoed by toxic chemicals.

"And then, what, three years ago?" Lawrence asked his wife as they sat together at their dining table. "We found out that our water's contaminated with PFAS."

"My neighbor called me up and he says, 'Did the DEP come test your water?'" he recalled, using the acronym for Maine's Department of Environmental Protection. The neighbor's water was polluted with PFAS, and rumor had it that the contamination came from "sludge" that was spread across farm fields in the region.

This sludge is actually treated sewage—made up of the semisolid residuals from partially processed wastewater—that is applied to agricultural land, which has been common practice across the United States for decades. A 1979 EPA report noted that, at the time, more than 3,000 areas received municipal and industrial wastewater for "land treatment." The document traces the practice back to Greek and Roman times—when some of the "large piles of human excrement" were "used as fertilizers"—while more recognizable systems began to emerge in Britain in the mid-1800s.[2]

In Maine, much of the sludge is the result of paper production at the state's multitude of mills, some of which have a history of using PFAS in their pulping processes. Because paper mills generate so much debris, the facilities usually conduct wastewater treatment in on-site lagoons. But while that treatment method removes solid waste and biodegradable organic matter—creating a resultant sludge—it does nothing to address the presence of forever chemicals.

Local wastewater utilities were for decades peddling sludge to farmers as a win–win: the providers wouldn't have to pay the exorbitant fees associated with landfilling, while the recipients would get free fertilizer for their fields.[3] These transactions also benefited the state, which for years encouraged the practice. With a ban on new private waste-disposal sites since 1989—and housing just three large, state-owned landfills, one commercial facility, and a host of smaller municipal outfits—the state has long been contending with declining dump space.[4]

Little did the sludge suppliers know, however, that their nutrient-rich product also contained compounds capable of decimating the very farms they were purporting to empower. Applying sludge became so common that much of southern and central Maine is dotted with treated sewage; as of December 2022,[5] the DEP had flagged a total of 1,037 sites to be investigated for PFAS contamination.[6]

Nationwide, it's not clear how widespread the problem is, as the vast majority of states don't test sludge for PFAS.[7] However, the Environmental Working Group estimates that the substances may contaminate 20 million acres, or about 5 percent, of US croplands.[8] Consequently, farm towns around the country could soon be contending with the consequences of PFAS-laced crops and waterways.

Back in Fairfield, the Higginses recalled how their neighbor's surprise test results spurred them to action. Amid increasing chatter about the sludge, the Higginses asked the DEP to sample their water as well—and received unwelcome news in October 2020.[9]

"They called us up and said, 'Don't drink your water. Don't cook with it, don't give it to your animals, don't bathe in it. Don't do anything with it. It's contaminated,'" Lawrence remembered. "Well, we both kind of just lost it. You know, because we raised our kids here. This is our life investment. What do you do?"

The Higginses said that they initially purchased the property, including sixteen acres across the street, thirty years earlier for about $75,000.

They then eventually invested an additional $200,000 in the house and barn renovation. Without the contamination, they estimated that the property would now be worth about $500,000. Mulling over the numbers, Penny's face became sullen.

"I'm fine as long as I don't talk about it," Penny said.

Fine, that is, aside from high blood pressure, which Penny said runs in her family, and high cholesterol. Scientists have identified connections between PFAS exposure and these conditions, which can also both be hereditary. But given her healthy lifestyle, Penny said she suspects that PFAS may have played a role.

"I can't prove it," she acknowledged, then added a caveat: "Let them prove that it's not."

Regardless of whether decades of drinking polluted water had any meaningful impact on Penny and Lawrence's health, the fact of the matter is that the levels of PFAS in their blood are sky-high. Compared to samples taken in 2017 and 2018 as part of the CDC's National Health Survey,[10] Lawrence and Peggy's PFAS levels, collected in February 2021, were above the ninety-fifth percentile for almost every compound assessed. His were nearly six times the average for PFOS, forty-six times for PFOA, and five times for PFHxS,[11] while hers were four times the average for PFOS, sixty-nine times for PFOA, and nearly fifteen times for PFHxS.[12]

The Higginses also expressed concern about potential effects of PFAS exposure on the four-legged residents of their property, as well as chickens whose eggs have remained contaminated even though the animals reside on clean soil.

"We had a dog that lived here, and she was full of tumors. I had to have her put away. So we don't know if that was from the water or not," Penny said.

The alpacas have not exhibited any demonstrable side effects and have been consuming clean water ever since the DEP began installing filtration systems on contaminated residential properties in 2021.[13] But they were certainly exposed to PFAS, which Lawrence said showed up in tests of their manure until the filter was running.

When asked who would be responsible for maintaining those filters long-term, David Madore, a DEP spokesperson, said in an April 2024 statement that "subject to funding availability," the agency would continue to do so.[14]

While Penny would prefer not to think about their pollution problem, PFAS permeate every part of her daily routine—rendering burdensome the very things that used to bring her happiness.

"Well, my flower gardens, for one thing. They've just gone to weed. I lost joy doing that," she said. "At our age, it's kinda tough because it's not like we can just start all over again," Penny added, noting that they were both turning seventy that year.

Their initial plan had been to leave the land to their three children, divided equally among them. The two girls, she said, are already established—one lives in Fairfield and the other in the adjacent town of Benton. Their son, Kevin, however, had expressed interest in living in this house, but that was before PFAS was on everyone's radar.

"I don't think he should," Lawrence said. "Why would anybody want to build a house here?"

Fred Stone, a multigenerational farmer about a hundred miles to the south, was asking the opposite question—why *wouldn't* anyone want to build a house here?—that is, before decades of sludge spread decimated his dairy operations.

"My grandfather purchased the farm," Fred said, presenting a logo of Stoneridge Farm that boasts its existence "since 1914."[15] His grandfather's acquisition was a relic of the World War I era, and was eventually conferred to Fred's father.

The history of the white colonial house that sits on the property, however, extends far beyond 1914—to the late eighteenth century, in fact. Yet although the house has retained its narrow stairwells and creaky wooden floorboards, it has benefited from some noticeable modern upgrades, including the eventual installation of indoor plumbing and electricity. And in 1997, Fred and his wife Laura decided to transplant the entire structure about a thousand feet downhill to its current road-side position.

Guarding the rocky dirt driveway on an August 2023 Saturday morning was a navy-blue Ford pickup truck, its giant grill hovering over a Maine farming license plate with registration number "DAIRY·0." Fastened onto the bumper behind the official plate was a saffron-shaded sign shouting "BEWARE OF COW" in all black caps.

The automotive accoutrements were a perfect match to the many posters and placards adorning the walls of the historic home's ground-floor office: "Cow Country: Watch Your Step!," "Some days you step in it; some days you don't," and "Manure Happens." Even the pencil cup on Fred's mother's antique desk—now used by Laura—bore the face of a cow.

Born in 1922 and educated as a teacher, Fred's mother spent the Second World War in a naval shipyard drafting room—after which, she began working at a local one-room schoolhouse and ultimately earned her master's degree and took on administrative roles.

"She was ahead of the curve," Fred said. "You think I'm sharp-tongued? You oughta hear her."

At first, Fred had his sights set on studying veterinary medicine at the University of Maine. But during his junior year of high school—when he was waking up at 5:00 a.m. for farm work—his parents told him they'd have to sell the cows if he went to college, as his father was aging out of his career. So Fred changed his mind, opting to take over the farm upon graduating and marrying his on-again, off-again high school sweetheart a year later.

"Laura and I met showing cows," Fred said, referring to their mutual penchant for competitive livestock exhibitions. "It was all well and good when I was beating her, but when she started beating me, we had to get married."

From a lawn chair in the unfinished basement garage that serves as Fred's headquarters, the sixty-seven-year-old sat under a string of cobwebs and wires dangling from exposed ceiling beams. Across from him, a dusty bookshelf bore agricultural titles dating back to 1839, a detailed history of World War II, and reference volumes on cattle diseases. Fred reminisced, with resignation in his voice, about how his family legacy had crumbled. His dirt-caked fingernails occasionally rattled as he spoke—a symptom of the Parkinson's disease that he takes pains to hide.

Fred and Laura bought the farm from his parents on February 18, 1977. While at the time their county had about sixty-three dairy farms, Fred lamented that "now there's just a handful left."

Even if the farm had not been polluted by PFAS, its future wouldn't have been certain, as his daughter and son-in-law are teachers, not farmers. His son, who lives only about a mile from him, is working for an area contractor and pulling the family's derelict gravel pit "out of mothballs, because that's the only thing on this farm that's not contaminated."

"I can't touch any of the fields that you came by," he sighed.

For Fred, the precise date on which he received the news of his property's demise is always at the tip of his tongue: November 3, 2016.

On that date, a letter from Kennebunk, Kennebunkport & Wells Water District alerted him that PFAS concentrations in the aquifer that fills the property's well were more than double the EPA's health advisory at the time.[16]

A makeshift "management team"—Fred and his wife, children, a veterinarian, and an attorney— came up with two choices: stay quiet, since the state wasn't widely testing for PFAS, or alert the state and Oakhurst Dairy, where they were shipping milk, that there was a problem.

"Obviously, we did the latter," Fred said.

When asked if this was a difficult choice to make, Fred's unequivocal response was "no."

After Oakhurst sent a milk sample to a certified lab in California for tests—which came back with sky-high PFAS numbers—Stoneridge was immediately "suspended from shipping milk," Fred recalled.

At that point, the Stones were on a mission to salvage their dairy business and decided to install a $23,000 filtration system in May 2017. Fred recalled how, before DEP officials became familiar with PFAS, an inspector recommended that he exterminate his herd.

"I said, 'I'll do that. We'll take them all down there. I'll put on my show whites. And I'll stand in front, and I'll take the first bullet and then you can slaughter the rest of them.' A week later, I get a letter from the state of Maine about suicide prevention. You can't make this shit up," Fred recounted, noting that many of these cow lineages date back forty to fifty years.

By the first week of June 2017, Fred continued, the agency issued a report that "clearly stated that the contamination was from the sludge spreading that we had done from '83 until '04."

But as it turned out, that spreading had been conducted by none other than Fred Stone. At the state's bidding, he had slathered his fields and others on an annual basis with what he had assumed was a nutritious soil amendment.

He later learned that such assumptions couldn't have been further from the truth. As a clearer picture of Maine's contamination crisis began to emerge, the DEP began testing all the legacy sites that at one point had sludge-spreading licenses. Such sampling was able to occur due to what Fred acknowledged as the state's "excellent job" in maintaining records—evidence that made a contamination map of Maine "look like it had smallpox."

Fred was shocked to find that the soil concentrations were still 750 ppt when the issue was discovered, as he had stopped spreading there about a decade and a half prior. On one early occasion in which an inspector showed up for a visit, Fred had both choice words for her and decades-old documents to justify his anger.

"Because I am a complete a-hole, I walked over to my filing cabinet and pulled out a permit from '86," he said. "And it is on the Department of Environmental Protection's masthead. It states that this material will not contaminate any waters in the State of Maine. This material will not present a health hazard—there's a whole laundry list it goes through."

The letter does, in fact, conclude that such operations will neither "pollute any water of the state" nor "create a nuisance," with the signature of former DEP commissioner Kenneth C. Young Jr.[17]

"And just because I'm really 'go for the gold,' I also included the letter from Kennebunk Water," Fred continued. "And game-set-match: I'm positive that the poor girl from DEP did not know that those documents existed."

The Kennebunk Water letter, signed on November 3, 2016, by then superintendent Normand R. Labbe, alerted Fred about "a water quality concern"—that the likely source of a regional PFAS plume was on his property. A series of tests had revealed that the highest combined result "was detected in excess of 140 ppt" and came from a monitoring well adjacent to their domestic well. Expressing concern for the family, Labbe offered to test their domestic well "on a one-time basis."[18]

Asked how the DEP had arrived at approving sludge spread, the agency's spokesperson, Madore, said that the 1983 license was issued decades "before DEP had standards in place for PFAS." However, he noted that farms had to meet certain thresholds for other contaminants such as "heavy metals, nitrogen loading rates, and dioxins," according to waste management laws at the time.[19]

Maine's regulators are hardly alone in dealing with the fallout: the federal EPA has also acknowledged the presence of PFAS in sewage sludge but has yet to launch substantial mitigation efforts.[20] Currently, national rules that govern sludge focus only on a few specific pollutants, including mercury, lead, and arsenic. And while the agency has taken some initial steps toward addressing the issue, such as conducting a 2024 risk assessment, for many Americans, the response is too little, too late.

For example, a group of Texas farmers in June 2024 sued the EPA with the aim of compelling the agency to regulate PFAS in sludge. In their suit, the plaintiffs alleged that their water became contaminated with "exceedingly high levels of PFAS" after their neighbor's property was spread with sludge in 2022. They said that they suffered multiple medical issues, while also citing the deaths of several animals, including a stillborn calf. Because the calf was stillborn and its liver was rife with PFOS, the suit concluded that the compound traveled from the mother to her offspring.[21] Mainers, too, are joining the federal fray, with the Maine Organic Farmers and Gardeners Association indicating in May 2024 that it intended to sue the EPA.[22]

In the meantime, there's also some evidence that PFAS can move from the sludge-laden soil into food. A 2016 study from Spain found that PFAS, and particularly PFOA, could be absorbed by carrots and lettuce from the soil.[23] Meanwhile, in 2018 the US Food and Drug Administration (FDA) sampled produce from an area in Fayetteville, North Carolina, that is known to have PFAS contamination, and found the compounds in sixteen out of twenty samples.[24]

But back in 1983, when Fred received his initial sludge spread permit from Maine's DEP, no such knowledge was available to farmers who engaged in the practice. However, Fred said he views that very permit as "the key that unlocked" the door for future action because it "put the state on the hook." Although he noted that it was his "civic duty" to take the sludge, Fred acknowledged that he had received payment for loading and spreading the material with his machinery onto other properties.

Throughout his years of spreading, Fred said he mostly worked with Kennebunk Sewer District—from which Stoneridge ended up taking on about half of the district's sludge. This system, he recalled, was working "fine for a bunch of years," until Kennebunk hired an intermediary company to coordinate the spread—which Fred described as an interloping "slipshod operation" and "a disaster waiting to happen."

"That's when we bailed," he said.

The middleman, he explained, had a reputation for spreading in the height of the summer, while Fred preferred working in late fall— just before the first frost but when windows were closed to block out the stench.

After learning about Stoneridge's contamination, Fred decided in January 2017 to switch the cows to clean feed, and after eighteen months their PFAS levels were low enough to ship milk to Oakhurst. But the tables turned once again, when Fred discovered that one of their feed products came from locally sourced corn—which was also contaminated.

"The numbers started to go back up," Fred said, musicalizing this surge with an ascending whistle. And when the Stones lost their milk license for the second time in spring 2019, their lenders made clear that the investment was no longer worth the risk.

"My wife and my daughter took our farm sign off," Fred recalled, gesturing toward a giant placard that now sits collecting dust in the basement, rather than welcoming customers.

"I have the one that I would take when I would go to the shows," Fred continued. "It says that Stoneridge Farm produces quality milk for Oakhurst Dairy."

Many of the former milk-producing cattle now have health problems, which Fred said has included a malignant growth around one cow's stomach. While he believes other cows may have had cancer, he noted that this is impossible to diagnose without a postmortem examination.

Regardless, Fred described the symptoms as "just weird stuff that you wouldn't ordinarily see on a dairy operation."

"I wish snow wasn't cold, I wish rain wasn't wet, and I wish I still didn't love my cows. And the more people I meet, the more I love my cows," Fred said.

Not only were the animals at Stoneridge Farm exposed to copious amounts of PFAS, but so, too, were the humans. The last time the Stones had their blood levels tested was in August 2023, when Fred and Laura's PFOS levels were more than twelve and nearly nine times the national average, respectively.

"I have full blown Parkinson's," Fred said. "And I've been told I do an awful good job of hiding it, but every now and then it rears its ugly head."

In December 2023, Fred's doctor, PFAS specialist Rachel Criswell, sent him two papers that she said might "suggest a possible connection between PFAS exposure and neurological disorders," while stressing that these are only associations, rather than cause.

One of the studies explored connections between PFAS contamination and Parkinson's disease as a cause of death in Italy—but only identified an elevated mortality rate in females.[25] The other, however, cited evidence that PFAS exposure could be connected to "an increased cause of death from Parkinson's disease" in elderly populations.[26]

Criswell, a primary care physician at Skowhegan Family Medicine and public health researcher,[27] said she typically offers tests to firefighters, military veterans, paper mill workers, residents of legacy farmland with private wells, and those who live near contaminated water sources. While she doesn't have a cookie-cutter approach toward checking a patient's PFAS levels, Criswell consults the National Academies of Sciences, Engineering, and Medicine's Guidance on PFAS Exposure, which provides advice on blood tests and other clinical care tools.[28]

In addition to suffering from Parkinson's, Fred reported in an April 2024 follow-up call that his heart had recently been "starting to act crazy" and that he had cardiovascular imaging scheduled for the next month, followed by an ablation procedure—which involves scarring some of the heart tissue to help control an irregular heartbeat. In the meantime, he was monitoring his vitals on a daily basis.[29]

Aside from these physical ailments, it was clear that Fred was also suffering from the mental anguish of losing the dairy operation that had been the lifeblood of his family for three generations.

"For the last 100 years and—since 1914—this is the first year those fields have not been cut," Fred mourned.[30]

When asked whom he blames for the entire sludge-spreading debacle, he comes up with an answer immediately.

"That's easy. I blame myself," he said. "One of my biggest regrets over this mess is that at some point in time, hopefully not tomorrow, I'm going to have to tell my father and my grandfather what happened to the farm that they entrusted me with."

But Fred expressed even more empathy for others across the state who have endured an incalculable toll from the PFAS-laden sludge-spreading. The businesses "that really got nailed," in Fred's mind, were the organic farms run by "kids that were starting out."

He voiced particular concern about a young man named Adam Nordell, who together with his wife, Johanna Davis, had started up the organic Songbird Farm in recent years.

"He's got customers calling him up wanting to know what the hell's going on here—where it's supposed to be certified organic, and what's this industrial contaminant doing on your farm?" Fred mused. "He, for whatever reason, credits me for saving his life. I thought he would've credited me for torpedoing his farm."

Adam and Johanna, in fact, managed their Central Maine farm for about twelve years—the last seven of which included a property they had purchased, as well as an adjacent parcel they were leasing from a local land trust.

"We sort of hit our stride as farmers," Adam said.[31]

As state officials began pulling milk from store shelves, Adam recalled that in November 2022, one of his customers came in with news about a deer-hunt advisory stemming from PFAS contamination. While Adam assumed that the issue wasn't relevant to his farm, an eventual look at the DEP's map of sludge-spread map proved otherwise. Lo and behold, there was a pin right on Songbird Farm.

"That was the start of our farm tragedy," Adam said, noting that their soil sample results arrived just before Christmas. "We had a big problem."

Adam and Johanna learned that almost their entire property—a former cornfield—had been spread with sludge in the early 1990s, below where their house, barn, and toddler's sandbox were ultimately built.

"This experience has been the most traumatic thing that I've gone through," he continued. "It felt like the ground dropped out from underneath us."

In the fall of 2023, Adam and Johanna finalized the property's sale to Maine Farmland Trust, which plans to conduct agricultural research at the site.[32] As of April 2024, they were renting an apartment in the next town over—having moved three times since the crisis began.

Asked whom he blames for the hardships his family has endured, Adam pointed his finger at the PFAS manufacturers, describing them as "grossly negligent." But he also questioned how authorities could have ever considered promoting food production on waste-laden land. He noted that in 1981, long before there was even mention of PFAS, Cornell researcher Donald Lisk had warned of the dangers linked to spreading sludge, which contains "a galaxy of dangerous chemicals, depending on the spectrum of industries in the area."[33]

"You've distilled all the toxins from society, and then you're going to put that at the base of the food chain. That is an insane policy," Adam declared.

He said he doesn't fault the farmers, like Fred, who actually spread the sludge—in fact, precisely the opposite.

"It's thanks to Fred Stone that anyone in Maine knows that there's an issue of PFAS contamination," Adam said. "So I try to remember never to miss an opportunity to thank Fred. He's the hero of the story in Maine."

CHAPTER 9

First in the Nation

F RED STONE LIKES TO TELL PEOPLE THAT "this PFAS thing is like quick-sand—when you get involved in it, it sucks you in."[1]

Shortly after he understood the magnitude of his pollution problem, his attorney connected him with two activists who at the time were affiliated with the group now known as Defend Our Health. After the activists propelled him toward the media in March 2017, Fred found himself thrust onto a legislative stage where he suddenly had to play a lead role.

It was hardly a position he expected. "We're not organic—we're conventional—and so we do not fit the mold of what you'd call an environmentalist," Fred said. Yet to him, the issue was not about labels or partisanship.

"It doesn't matter whether you're Republican or Democrat, what you are—it's very hard to vote against public health and food safety," Fred said on a Saturday morning in August 2023.

When asked if he was the owner of the Trump sign on a lawn adjacent to his property, however, Fred's increasingly persistent response was a vehement "No, no, no no, NO, NO, NO." Rather, he said he supports former vice president Mike Pence due to his religious values.

As Fred was discussing his unconventional views, his neighbor, Democratic state senator Henry Ingwersen, appeared at the door of the dusty basement garage. Ingwersen, a retired teacher-turned-beekeeper, objected to his neighbor's self-appraisal, noting that he does, in fact, match the "typical political leanings of Maine farmers."[2]

"Something rare that you did was to courageously stand up," Ingwersen said. "It has really made a difference in crossing party lines and getting people of all stripes to really pay attention."

When Ingwersen first took office as a Maine legislator in 2018, Fred invited him over to the farm to learn about the contamination, and the unlikely duo worked together to advance early PFAS-related laws. Among the first was the June 2019 Safe Food Packaging Act, which paved the way for prohibiting PFAS in certain products but did so with the caveat that a ban could only take effect two years after the Maine Department of Environmental Protection (DEP) identified a safer alternative.[3] The DEP adopted a final rule on the subject in spring 2024, and the prohibition will take effect in 2026.[4]

In March 2020, Ingwersen sponsored an initial attempt to amend Maine's six-year statute of limitations for PFAS-related lawsuits with a discovery clause that would give people more time to sue.[5] Although his bill stalled in committee, a new version earned legislative and gubernatorial approval in June 2021.[6] That same month, Maine's legislature set interim drinking water limits for six different types of PFAS, while mandating that all public water systems, schools, and daycares sample their water for these compounds.[7]

By July 2021, lawmakers had passed a bill that required the state to test for PFAS at more than 500 former sludge spread sites.[8] Another pioneering law that summer made Maine the first state to pass a prohibition on products containing intentionally added PFAS[9]—stipulating that a near-full ban would take effect by 2030.[10] Additional legislation led to the elimination of PFAS-containing firefighting foams as of January 1, 2022.[11]

Just a few months later, farmers saddled with sludge received welcome news from Democratic governor Janet Mills: a $60 million "PFAS Fund" that would primarily support state buybacks of polluted agricultural land.[12] The five-year program, finalized in 2024,[13] also received an additional $5 million from the US Department of Agriculture.[14] Fred, who served on an advisory panel for the fund, boasted that he "only walked out once" in frustration during related discussions.

Lawrence and Penny Higgins, in Fairfield, were disappointed when they learned they couldn't qualify for the program, after finding out that they would be ineligible. While their property value had plummeted because of PFAS, the alpaca business they run there does not constitute official farmland.

Confirming that residents like the Higginses do not qualify, David Madore, a spokesperson for the DEP, explained that the fund serves to "purchase eligible properties at fair market value," stressing that only the owners of commercial farms could qualify.[15]

In his garage-turned-office in August 2023, Fred expressed general approval of Maine's legislative outcomes, remarking that PFAS discussions have largely stayed "out of the political minefield" and have had "close to unanimous support."

"Whether you're Republican, Democrat, conservative, liberal, whatever you are, pink, blue, purple," he said, "it doesn't matter."

While Fred was instrumental in creating Maine's PFAS Fund, he's "not too keen" about the idea of participating in a buyback due to the historic nature of his farm.

Although he still maintains between thirty-five and forty cows at Stoneridge, Fred "slaughtered over 100 head" when he could no longer afford to sustain them. The monthly feed bills for his remaining animals come to about $6,000–7,000, which Fred pays via state-subsidized agriculture grants.

The Stones were working on various business plans with the state, including the possibility of selling show calves, establishing an ice cream "micro-dairy," or housing solar panels. But such decisions, he cautioned, might end up in someone else's hands.

"My wife and I have been fighting this thing since '16, so there's not a whole lot of lead in our pencils," Fred said.

Fred's ideal solution to the current predicament would be to engage in a conservation easement, in which he would get to retain ownership of his multigenerational farm but would refrain from selling food products in exchange for payment from the state. Yet although he favored this type of "restitution for the contaminated land," Maine's government was only offering direct buyouts.

Jim Britt, a spokesperson for Maine's Agriculture Department, emphasized the state's significant support for Stoneridge Farm, citing various PFAS tests and reimbursements for clean feed, water filtration, income replacement, and associated administrative costs. While Britt stressed that the agency is prepared to buy Stoneridge's "real property at fair market value as if it were not contaminated," he confirmed that current rules prohibit the purchase of easements.[16]

As he waits to see what happens next, Fred has been allowing a club of remote-control "bush pilots"—hobbyists who operate model aircraft—to run a miniature airport on his property, free of charge. Fred does derive some joy, if not money, from this venture, describing the planes as "the cutest thing."

His son has also been operating a sand and gravel venture at the farm because PFAS do not attach themselves to these materials.

Taking a bird's-eye view of his family's finances, Fred credited a somewhat random corporate tax decision—made more than two decades ago—for digging them out of an otherwise bottomless pit. That move involved shifting Stoneridge Farm Inc. from sole proprietorship to an "S Corp"—an entity through which owners pay themselves a "reasonable salary"[17] and include earnings on their personal returns rather than owing federal corporate taxes.[18]

At a certain point, Stoneridge Farm Inc. could no longer pay those requisite reasonable salaries—which ostensibly "put Fred and Laura Stone in a bad position," as Fred described it. Yet because the Stones had invested most of their assets into the corporation—aside from their car, which they own, and their house, which is financed separately— they had nearly nothing to their names. Fred and Laura were therefore able to qualify for food stamps and government-subsidized healthcare, as well as file for Chapter 12 bankruptcy on their house.

As he mourned the passing of his multigenerational home, Fred was still standing—or, at the very least, sitting in a basement lawn chair— even as the dusty, eighteenth-century walls crumble around him.

"I may not look it, but I am a raging volcano on the inside," Fred declared.

Fred has pushed Maine forward, dragging it out of the muck and setting the bar high for other states—and for federal government agencies—as they struggle to wade through uncharted waters.

In addition to approving funds for the buyback program, Maine became the first state to require that sludge be tested for PFAS and then to ban the material's spread. In April 2022, Mills signed into law a bill that banned the application of PFAS-containing sludge on farmland.[19] As of mid-2024, Maine was the only state to have prohibited the presence of PFAS in sludge entirely, although at least sixteen other states were either implementing or considering solutions to this problem. However, these solutions were not necessarily all-out bans and instead included actions like requiring testing, labeling fertilizers, and providing resources for farmers who discover contamination.[20] In January, Michigan began enforcing PFAS thresholds for biosolids, while also requiring users to sample wastewater sources for any sludge that surpasses certain limits.[21]

Reluctant to take anything at face value, Fred identified possible complications that have developed due to state-level restrictions on sludge. There might be fewer places to put the sludge in Maine, but it still must go somewhere—and sometimes, that destination is across international boundaries. For example, the Canadian Broadcasting Corporation reported in March 2023 that Casella Waste Systems—a private company that also runs some of Maine's public landfills—was shuttling "130 truckloads per month of biosolids across the border."[22]

Jeff Weld, a spokesperson for Casella, pointed to two "diametrically opposed bills" that Maine's legislature passed in 2022. The first banned the spread of biosolids,[23] while the second eliminated an escape clause that had let Maine dumps accept minimally processed out-of-state waste.[24] As a result of that legislation, in-state sites could no longer receive sufficient thickening materials to absorb liquid sludge, creating what Weld described as "a well-documented urgent situation" in which wastewater facilities faced a problem finding places to send these biosolids. But subsequent relief measures, he explained, enabled the sludge "to be temporarily bypassed to Canada," he confirmed.

Prior to the 2022 legislation, PFAS-laden sludge crept across the state of Maine—creating a patchwork of pollution that has refused to stay put. Ending up in aquifers, PFAS have also befouled the fauna that inhabit the region's watersheds. Chief among the affected species are fish of critical importance to the Penobscot Nation, whose reservation abuts the Penobscot River.

Dan Kusnierz, who has managed the tribe's Water Resources Program since 1993, said he remembered when Fred Stone's situation first appeared on the news. PFAS had been vaguely on his radar, but he was neither familiar with its properties nor envisioning any impacts on an island about sixty miles northeast of Fairfield, near the city of Bangor.

However, the region's history is intertwined with the promulgation of paper mills, which began thriving in the colonial era. European settlers were drawn to the "massive white pines," which they would tag "to indicate that those were property of the king," Kusnierz explained.[25] To get pine logs to England—to create masts for ships—the settlers would float them down the river, to be collected at mills along the way.

In the modern era, six paper mills persisted along the Penobscot River, several of which discharged dioxins—highly toxic, persistent organic pollutants, used in bleaching, that are known to cause cancer.[26] By the early 1990s, officials began issuing do-not-eat advisories for the river's fish, which had major impacts on the sustenance rights on tribes—whose average daily fish consumption is nearly nine times that of the general Maine population.[27]

It was a combination of dioxins and dams that caused tribal leaders to find out about PFAS—and mostly by chance. Following the removal of two dams and the renovation of a third on the Penobscot, the tribe welcomed the return of the waterway's anadromous fish, ocean dwellers that migrate upriver to spawn. Yet they remained uncertain as to whether the fish were safe to consume.

Partnering with the EPA in 2017 and 2018 to investigate possible contaminants,[28] Kusnierz suggested adding PFAS to the list. The results, released in 2021, showed not only high levels of dioxins and other legacy chemicals, but also of several types of PFAS[29]—high enough that the CDC's toxics agency warned of potential adverse health effects from fish consumption. The biggest offender was PFOS, particularly affecting American shad females and their eggs— as well as blueback herring, striped bass, and sea lamprey.

"That's when PFAS became real to us," Kusnierz said.

Recent research has shown that consuming just a single serving of freshwater fish each year could have the same impact as drinking PFAS-polluted water for a month.[30] But Kusnierz said he had assumed this would not apply to fish that spend most of their lives in the ocean.

After running through many different possible explanations, the Penobscot team considered the state-owned Juniper Ridge Landfill, situated northwest of the reservation, as a possible PFAS source. Asked whether the site accepts PFAS waste, Jeff Weld from Casella—the dump's operator—acknowledged that "the waste that the facility accepts does contain PFAS chemicals." Yet because the landfill doesn't receive materials such as used water filters, which are known to have high PFAS content, Weld said he could not consider the debris to be "PFAS waste."[31]

From its opening in 1993 until transitioning to the state in 2003, Juniper Ridge went through a series of proprietors connected to today's Nine Dragons Mill.[32] The paper manufacturing facility, located in the Penobscot-adjacent city of Old Town, was first established as a sawmill in 1860 and regularly changed hands over the years,[33] until its most recent shift to ND Paper, a US division of Chinese containerboard producer Nine Dragons Paper (Holdings) Limited.[34] An on-site treatment facility at the mill not only processes the facility's own trash but also receives leachate—liquid that passes through a solid waste dump—from Juniper Ridge.

Standing in August 2023 in a prickly overgrowth of roadside weeds, Kusnierz gestured toward a wall of bushes that he said were planted as "a visual barrier to the landfill." As a swarm of eager mosquitoes buzzed at the ready nearby, he expressed concern about the landfill's wastewater, which he said undergoes secondary processing[35]—eliminating suspended biosolids, but not PFAS—at Nine Dragons and then "goes into the river." Despite the landfill's location downstream, Kusnierz noted that potentially contaminated anadromous fish can move both up- and downstream.

Four state-commissioned samples of Juniper Ridge's leachate taken in 2021 and 2022 showed collective levels of six regulated PFAS that were as much as 131 times greater than the state's thresholds for drinking water at the time—not that Mainers were directly consuming dump drainage.[36] The EPA, meanwhile, has found PFAS present in the wastewater of more than 95 percent of 200 landfills surveyed nationwide.[37]

Weld, from Casella, said that "because waste is a byproduct of society's existence, and PFAS are ubiquitous in society . . . the waste that is accepted at Juniper Ridge Landfill contains PFAS." He noted, however, that "landfills do an outstanding job of sequestering the chemicals." When asked where the landfill sends its leachate for treatment, Weld responded that "Juniper Ridge has contracts with multiple facilities for treatment."

As far as Nine Dragons is concerned, Brian Toth, general counsel for ND Paper, said in an email that PFAS "were not intentionally used" in the manufacture of packaging or paper products.[38] Confirming that ND Paper's Old Town Mill was "on extended downtime" as of mid-2024, Toth stressed that "plans to reopen continue to be evaluated" and that the on-site wastewater treatment facility was being managed in the interim. Asked if the treatment plant receives leachate from Juniper Ridge and whether that waste only undergoes secondary processing prior to release into the river, he responded in the affirmative, adding that "the Old Town Mill's wastewater treatment facility continues to receive and treat leachate from the Juniper Ridge facility."

Even in areas of the country without a clearcut paper trail of paper mills, PFAS are appearing in the ground, whether in a remote village in Michigan's Upper Peninsula[39] or in supposedly pristine parts of Florida's Everglades.[40] In a 2022 study, scientists observed unexplained PFAS pollution in parts of New Hampshire—uncovering the compounds wherever they looked.[41]

While the reason behind this pervasiveness remains uncertain, project chief Andrea Tokranov believes that the compounds can travel through the atmosphere and fall as rain. Asked whether this means that all of New Hampshire likely has PFAS, Tokranov said that this would be a "logical conclusion." Their study, she added, targeted places that didn't have an obvious PFAS source and still came across the compounds at "fairly high" levels.[42]

Back in central Maine, which does have an obvious PFAS source—in the form of sewage sludge—Kusnierz wondered how anyone would ever support spreading waste products on people's property to begin with.

"It seemed like it was really encouraged—like this is a great thing that you should be doing," he said, referring to former policies that encouraged sludge spread. "It doesn't sit right."

Kusnierz's skepticism about the soundness of sludge-spreading rings true for the Higginses, the Stones, and so many other Mainers for whom the putrid practice also doesn't sit right.

Soon after the Higginses learned about their contamination, gossip began brewing about the burgeoning community crisis. But Lawrence expressed frustration that state officials weren't taking any tangible action at the time.

"They weren't doing anything," he said. "All they were doing is—"[43]

"Complaining," Peggy interjected.

With nothing to lose, Penny raised the idea of reaching out to famed activist Erin Brockovich, simply because she had seen the 2000 Oscar-winning film about her story and had heard about her ongoing environmental advocacy efforts. Brockovich, whose story was portrayed by Julia Roberts, emerged in the public eye after she identified hexavalent chromium contamination in a rural California town's drinking water in the early 1990s.[44]

"She told me to call Erin. Well, I didn't know who Erin was. But I emailed her," Lawrence said. "I emailed to her on a Sunday, and that Sunday night, she replied to me, and said, 'Yeah, absolutely I want to help you.'"

After their successful appeal to the celebrity environmentalist, Lawrence and Penny amassed a "core group" of neighbors on Facebook—a group that was created at Erin's suggestion—who decided to launch litigation together. Erin then connected the Fairfield residents to Texas-based attorney Russ Abney, who partnered with a local team to represent them.

For Abney, timing was key: he waited patiently until summer 2021, after Governor Mills signed the law adding a discovery clause into PFAS-specific personal injury litigation. Now that his clients would have six years to sue from the moment they discovered harm, rather than six years from the moment of contamination, Abney filed suit on behalf of about a dozen households against numerous paper companies and waste disposal services.[45] The filing, which was transferred from county to US district court, sought both financial compensation and medical monitoring for the plaintiffs due to their persistent exposure to PFAS.[46]

At the top of the defendant list was Finnish company Huhtamaki, Inc.,[47] whose factory in nearby Waterville supplied molded fiber food trays and disposable plates.[48] After undergoing many revisions, the list in March 2023 had dwindled to Huhtamaki and three chemical companies: Solenis, BASF, and 3M. The document alleged that Huhtamaki "intentionally and recklessly discharged those toxins" into the water supply, in concentrations more than "1,300 times the safe level established by the State of Maine." As for the chemical corporations, the plaintiffs accused them of failing to warn Huhtamaki "that their PFAS chemicals were toxic."[49]

A mid-April response from the paper company confirmed its purchase of PFAS-containing products from the three manufacturers, while denying "any other allegations directed at or relating to Huhtamaki."[50] After a judge rejected a motion to dismiss from the chemical companies in October 2023,[51] Solenis and BASF filed documents disputing most of the allegations against them.[52]

3M, meanwhile, refuted any "causal connection" between exposure to PFAS at typical environmental levels "and any human health effects," while rejecting a description of the firm as a purveyor of "toxic PFAS chemicals for profit to Huhtamaki." The company admitted "that it has, at times, sold certain PFAS-containing products to Huhtamaki and/or its predecessor(s)."[53]

Addressing the ongoing lawsuit, an April 2024 statement from BASF discussed coordination with regulators about PFAS, potential cleanup action, and "scientifically sound communications." The statement added that "BASF does not believe the allegations have merit, and it intends to defend the case vigorously."[54] Solenis, meanwhile, did not provide comment. A statement from Huhtamaki—in response to this case and another suit— acknowledged past usage of FDA-approved PFAS, while noting that its "processes no longer use any intentionally added PFAS chemicals in its paper-based products made in Waterville."[55] 3M did not directly respond to requests for comments about this litigation.

Abney, the attorney for the plaintiffs, said that while Huhtamaki is responsible for about 60 percent of the wastewater going to the local treatment plant and is "the only large PFAS user we could identify on that stream," he expected that a different defendant would be held accountable.

"I suspect when the jury sees the evidence they will place most of the blame on 3M," Abney said in a mid-2024 email.[56] While noting in a follow-up text message that the discovery process had just begun, Abney explained that his suspicions were rooted in concerns over transparency between the companies.

"I would be surprised if the documents show that 3M was transparent with Huhtamaki about the contents or hazardous nature of the chemicals it was supplying to Huhtamaki," Abney said.

As for Lawrence and Penny Higgins, the alpaca enthusiasts are on the fence as to who is at fault for the crisis. With nothing left to lose, Penny said they are planning to ride out the lawsuit and see if they "come up with a miracle."

⌒

A few miles up the road from the Higginses' abode, the gabled roof of a white, Cape Cod–style cottage emerges along a ridge bedecked in greenery. Outside the hilltop property, sixty-two-year-old Nate Saunders marveled at the "beautiful day."[57] Yet in the same breath, he gestured across the street to a distant line of trees, behind which about "2,350 dump trucks of wastewater sludge" were spread over vast acreage owned by several families.

While Nate now manages Maine's Radiation Control Program, he previously worked for the state Drinking Water Program. Although he has no evidence that sludge was spread on his side of the street—which at one point was all cornfields—Nate also has no other explanation for the massive contamination on his property.

"I literally have their PFAS in my bloodstream and a lot of it," he said, noting that so, too, does the land nearby. State soil samples updated in 2022 for fields adjacent to his property confirm that claim.[58]

Meanwhile in June 2023, Nate's well water clocked in at 17,800 ppt for a sum of six types of PFAS, he said, noting that this was nearly 900 times higher than Maine's drinking water standards at the time.

Until 2021, Nate had no idea that his property was chock-full of PFAS. That February he received a surprising phone call from the Maine CDC's state toxicologist, asking if he lived on this particular street.

"I said, 'Yes, it's a beautiful place to live. What can I tell you about it?' He said, 'Well, your neighbor had tested pretty high in PFAS.'"

Like the Higginses, Nate and his family received a drinking water filtration system from the DEP soon after the contamination on their property was discovered. But a new clean water supply didn't make up for the decades of damage. As Nate investigated possible health impacts of PFAS, he considered his wife's 2010 battle with kidney failure and began to connect the dots.

Initial blood samples taken from Nate in 2021 revealed PFOS

concentrations that were 471 times the national average. His PFOA and PFHxS levels were hardly low either, clocking in, respectively, at 896 and 27 times the national averages for these compounds.[59] Separate tests taken by his doctor at around the same time revealed similar results.[60]

That same spring of 2021, Nate stopped drinking the contaminated water—and the changes were noticeable in future blood tests. By March 2023, his PFOS levels were a mere 172 times the national average, while his PFOA and PFHxS levels were 493 and 24 times their respective norms.[61] Separate tests that had indicated abnormal kidney function—a particular risk since Nate gave one of his own kidneys to his wife—had also improved since the filter installation.[62]

Although the shifts in Nate's lab results were dramatic, his PFAS levels still surpassed those of almost the entire US population.[63] His results even eclipsed those of Americans who lived or worked in settings most notorious for their PFAS problems. Among those individuals were 3M workers tested in the year 2000,[64] DuPont workers assessed in 2004, and Northern Alabama residents evaluated in 2010 and 2016.[65]

As Nate grappled with these findings, he decided to seek justice for the havoc he believes that PFAS has wrought on his family. In 2022, his attorneys filed a personal injury suit, which was still ongoing in mid-2024, against Huhtamaki—which, after a few transfers, landed in Maine's business court.[66] Huhtamaki provided a collective response to this litigation and the Higgins case, noting that, like several other paper mills in Maine, the company used the compounds in its past operations at the site but that it no longer does so.

While Nate has no idea what the outcome of his case will be, he is certain that the PFAS in his well isn't disappearing anytime soon. Starting with a 2021 average monthly reading of 14,200 ppt, Nate created a model to project just how long it would take to get his well down to 20 ppt, Maine's drinking water standard at the time. The answer? Another seventy years.

"I'll be 140," he laughed.

With an uncertain future ahead, Nate in August 2023 looked forward to the federal drinking water regulations that would arrive the next year—and require water systems to monitor the substances under the 1974 Safe Drinking Water Act. But he identified an inherent disconnect between these rules and his neighborhood: the fact that "half of the state of Maine is private wells."

Because the Safe Drinking Water Act applies only to public utilities, water tests on wells for legacy contaminants like arsenic usually occur as part of real estate transactions, Nate explained. When it comes to PFAS, he stressed, the onus is on the consumer—creating a "buyer beware" situation, in which potential homeowners need to track down data independently.

But Nate had a few other bones to pick with the federal government. When he tried to tabulate how many facilities were releasing PFAS nationwide, he came up empty-handed. Nate later learned that this was because the federal government had opened a gaping loophole in a new reporting program. That oversight, however, was just one of a series of delays for measurable action on PFAS.

CHAPTER 10

A Premature Victory Dance

Americans plagued by PFAS—like Nate Saunders in Maine, Mark Favors in Colorado, or Brenda Hampton in Alabama—might be forgiven for asking why these forever compounds are *their* problem. Why must they file lawsuits, or fight for congressional inquiries, or push state officials to pass laws that protect constituents? Isn't the federal government supposed to oversee this?

Those would be reasonable questions—and today, the answer is yes: the US Environmental Protection Agency is charged with protecting Americans and the environment from toxic chemicals. However, that wasn't always the case. In fact, legacy PFAS even predate the creation of the EPA itself, which wasn't established until 1970, though the Food and Drug Administration (FDA) did have some authority over PFAS use in food-related products.

Even when the nation's first major law to govern chemicals passed in 1976, preexisting compounds were automatically presumed safe—enabling not only PFAS but also many other dangerous substances, like asbestos, to remain on the market and go largely unchecked for decades. In short, federal oversight has hardly been a panacea for dangerous chemicals. The long-standing struggle between regulators and industry begs the question: Who wields the real power over Americans' exposure to these toxic substances?

In the early days of PFAS manufacture, its makers were able to largely stave off government interference. But in 1998, 3M encountered a problem so big and widespread that it could not be swept under the rug: the company could not find any human blood that was free of PFAS. Seeking a "human blank"—a clean sample—for research purposes, the company tried a blood bank to no avail, according to former EPA staffer Charlie Auer. Turning back to historical blood samples from 1969 and 1976, 3M scientists found PFOS there as well. Even in parts of China that had no recorded use of PFOS technologies, specimens still came back positive for the substance. Eventually, the company realized it needed to alert the EPA.

In May 1998, 3M filed a "substantial risk notification" to the agency, claiming that although PFOS didn't pose a significant risk, the alert would serve as a "precautionary measure."[1] While PFOS's ubiquity was new information to the EPA, the finding wasn't completely novel, as university researchers had told 3M all the way back in 1975 that fluorine was "widespread" in human blood. Additionally, 3M apparently had come forward about PFAS once before—in the early 1980s. When 3M researchers linked PFOA to birth defects in rats, the company sent the study to the EPA, with the caveat that its records did not show any human health effects related to PFAS.

Neither 3M nor EPA provided details on what became of the company's 1981 notification to the agency, if anything. The EPA declined to comment on the handling of the birth defect finding, as it occurred so long ago, though it noted that it was not yet aware of PFAS's omnipresence at that time. A former EPA official, who was not yet at the agency in 1981 but was aware the studies, said that the EPA was "heavily involved" in follow-up research to the birth defect finding. According to the official, scientists determined that while initial studies indicated PFAS exposure could result in a congenital eye issue, the results were misleading and, in fact, the problem "turned out [to] be an artifact" of how the researchers sliced the eye tissue during the studies. 3M likewise said that follow-up analysis found that PFOA was not causing the birth defects, and that it told the EPA as much.

3M declined to comment on why it did not share information on PFAS's prevalence prior to 1998, other than to say that some of its own findings had been published in scientific journals as early as the 1980s.[2] But two years after the company told the EPA that PFOS was everywhere, 3M agreed to stop making the substance, as well as PFOA. It was this episode that shook up manufacturing in Decatur, where the plant that previously made PFOS shifted toward adhesives for the back of Post-it notes and for reflective strips worn by firefighters. While 3M publicly maintained that there was no evidence that its products posed long-term health problems,[3] the EPA issued a press release saying that 3M's data showed that the substance is "very persistent in the environment," accumulates in people and the environment, and "could potentially pose a risk to human health."

Charlie Auer, then at the EPA, also decided to alert foreign governments, including South Korea, France, and Australia—as well as officials with the European Union and Organisation for Economic Cooperation and Development—writing in emails in 2000 that PFOS "appears to combine persistence, bioaccumulation, and toxicity properties to an extraordinary degree." He also warned them about PFOA, calling it "closely related structurally to PFOS."[4]

The EPA may have started to sound the alarm on the two most notorious types of PFAS, but the agency still faced an uphill battle, especially as far as PFOA was concerned.

Auer recalled reaching the conclusion "that this was a pretty significant issue that needed to be dealt with in some way pretty promptly." And at the same time, he understood the importance of doing so "before it became politicized."

To try to address the PFOA issue, the EPA in 2006 convened a "Stewardship Program" made up of eight chemical companies: 3M (and its subsidiary Dyneon), DuPont, Arkema, Asahi, BASF, Clariant, Daikin, and Solvay Solexis. The program's goal was to reduce PFOA emissions by 95 percent no later than 2010, and to stop releasing the substance entirely by the end of 2015. All the companies reported that they met these targets, and the EPA's website states that PFOA manufacturing has been phased out—with a caveat: existing stockpiles of the chemical could still be used, and some imported items could also contain PFOA.

A source familiar with the matter, granted anonymity in order to speak freely, said they felt that, in negotiations over programs like the PFOA Stewardship Program, industry had more power than the EPA, since the companies could just walk away.

The agency itself now admits that, at the time, it was dealing with a weaker set of regulatory tools than it has today. Nevertheless, a spokesperson said that the "EPA used the authority it did have to take action on the PFAS we understood to be hazardous to human health and the environment."[5]

Auer, meanwhile, described these early efforts as a major win in the fight against PFAS. He pointed to data showing that levels of PFOS and PFOA in Americans' blood have declined significantly—by more than 70 percent for PFOA and 85 percent for PFOS—since 1999 and 2000.[6]

Had the EPA not implemented these steps, Auer believes, blood levels of PFAS in the population "would have continued to rise and then would have been at a higher base level when EPA got around to dealing with it a decade or fifteen years later."[7]

In addition to organizing voluntary programs, the EPA did push back against the companies' somewhat loose interpretation of its reporting requirements. In fact, in the early 2000s, it pursued legal action against both 3M and DuPont for allegedly failing to report key information. Mark Garvey, a former EPA attorney, said that the case against DuPont revolved around the company's 1981 finding of PFOA in the umbilical cord of an exposed employee—showing that the chemical could move between a pregnant woman and her baby.[8]

Garvey described this discovery as "one of those 'Oh my God' moments."

The EPA ultimately won $16.5 million from DuPont in the ensuing settlement, which at the time included the largest civil administrative penalty the agency had ever collected under an environmental law.

While the federal government still hadn't cleaned up the PFAS that was already out there, some EPA officials thought that the phaseouts of PFOA and PFOS meant that, at the very least, they had turned off a titanic tap of toxic chemicals.

"We thought: Problem solved, that was the end of that issue," said Betsy Southerland, whose lengthy EPA career eventually led her to lead the agency's water science and technology office. Little did she know, however, that this was only the beginning.

The EPA may have started clamping down on PFAS in the early 2000s, but the George W. Bush administration was meanwhile staying cozy with DuPont. In 2002, President Bush named DuPont CEO Charles Holliday Jr. to the National Infrastructure Advisory Committee, and the next year, the president awarded DuPont the National Medal of Technology for its work to mitigate the environmental impact of substances that depleted the ozone layer.[9] During a 2007 tour of DuPont's Experimental Station, Bush spoke about reducing US dependence on oil—and mentioned the importance of being "wise stewards of the environment."

In early 2009, with PFOA and PFOS on their way out of commerce but still lingering in the environment, the EPA made its first attempts to inform communities around the nation about what concentrations would be unsafe—deciding that more than 200 parts per trillion was an unacceptable level of PFOS while more than 400 parts per trillion of PFOA was dangerous.

Yet beyond these standards—which were simply advisories without any regulatory teeth—PFAS was left on the back burner. Even with the shift in administrations from Bush to Obama, PFAS regulation and investigation continued to slip through the cracks, with PFAS becoming a matter of bipartisan indifference. Once the PFOA Stewardship Program wrapped, top officials at the EPA turned their focus to what they viewed as more pressing health problems.

Jennifer Orme-Zavaleta said that around 2011, when she became director of the EPA's National Exposure Research Lab, PFAS wasn't seen as a priority by some of the agency's leadership. She recalled how the toxics branch of the agency didn't list PFAS "as a priority contaminant for further research."[10]

"They were basically saying, 'We've got what we need, we're done,'" said Orme-Zavaleta, who would later go on to serve as a top official in the EPA's Office of Research and Development.

Two agency sources, who were granted anonymity to speak freely about the EPA's inner workings, said they were told explicitly to stop working or focusing on PFAS by their managers during the early Obama years. They didn't characterize this push as insidious suppression of science, but rather as a more typical ebb and flow of scientific interest in a subject.

Nevertheless, some research continued, and key findings about replacements for PFOA and PFOS revealed that the PFAS issue was far from over. EPA researchers found in 2012 that a range of other PFAS, including the PFOA replacement GenX, were present in North Carolina's Cape Fear River.[11]

Orme-Zavaleta said that the finding "really opened the door on the fact that even though PFOA and PFOS were no longer in commerce, there were replacement compounds that were being used that were found in the environment." Further investigations, published in 2016 by both internal and external researchers, found GenX to be not only in the river, but also in the water supply of nearby Wilmington, a port city along North Carolina's southeastern coast.

An agency source said that these GenX findings "did a lot to get [the] attention of managers and public health officials across the country"—raising concerns that this problem was bigger than just PFOA and PFOS: their replacements could also be toxic and persistent.

"The big victory dance we were all doing back in 2008 is really—that was way premature and in fact totally unrealistic," said Southerland, the former water official.[12]

Auer, the point person on PFAS in the EPA's first decade of dealing with the chemicals, defended the agency's early efforts, noting that he and his colleagues "did the best we could with the understanding that existed at the time."[13]

While there was already "good evidence" in the early 2000s that PFOA and PFOS had an "accumulative tendency," it was not yet clear that the same is true of other PFAS, Auer added.

Toward the end of the Obama administration, the EPA updated the levels that it considered safe for PFOA and PFOS, bringing them down to 70 ppt. This more stringent threshold informed utilities around the nation that water they previously thought was safe to give their customers was in fact poisoning them. It sent water managers, like those in Colorado, scrambling, but federal officials say the shift was important for keeping the public safer from the deadly substances.

Linda Birnbaum, a toxicologist who at the time was the director of the National Institute of Environmental Health Sciences, described the 2016 move as simultaneously a huge step in the right direction but also not good enough. As someone who believed that PFOA and PFOS were carcinogens, Birnbaum felt "there's really no safe level."

She recalled the head of the EPA's Office of Water at the time phoning her with news of the new threshold. In her memory, the official told her, "Linda, I know you're not going to be happy with this, because I know you'd like it stricter."[14]

But Birnbaum was not disappointed. "I'm a pragmatist, and this makes me happy," Birnbaum told him. "You've dropped the number from 400 to 70.'"

A month after the EPA updated the PFOA and PFOS safety thresholds, President Barack Obama signed a major overhaul of the nation's chemicals law, the 1976 Toxic Substances Control Act. The 2016 amendments marked a major change in how the agency handled new chemicals—which would need to be proven innocent to enter the market, rather than proven guilty to be eliminated.

Previously, certain chemicals "would go out onto the market" unregulated if EPA toxicologists couldn't come up with data as to why they shouldn't, said Maria Doa, who directed the EPA's Chemical Control Division at the time.

But thanks to the 2016 updates, the agency at least now had a better suite of tools to deal with new chemicals, especially the law's requirement for evidence demonstrating that a chemical was safe—*before* it could be approved.

Noting the ramp-up in scrutiny that followed, Doa joked, "There was a voodoo doll that the industry people had with my face on it."[15]

But this upswing in regulation was relatively short lived, as the Trump administration came to power in 2017.

"January came and then we were still kind of going along," Doa said, "until the new folks came on board—the new political folks—and then things got more complicated."

When Trump took office in 2017, the EPA had just seen a resurgence of attention on PFAS—especially as the GenX issue entered the public eye. In 2018, the agency put forward a four-step plan:

1. Evaluate whether it should set a drinking water limit for PFOA and PFOS.
2. Take steps toward proposing to designate PFOA and PFOS as "hazardous substances"—a move that could obligate historic polluters to clean them up.
3. Develop groundwater cleanup recommendations for these two chemicals.
4. Assess the toxicity of GenX and another PFAS, called PFBS, which was used as a replacement for PFOS.[16]

In practice, however, activists, Democratic politicians, and many career EPA staffers raised concerns about how the Trump administration went about tackling the chemicals. Critics complained that the administration took years to evaluate whether to set drinking water limits—instead of actually doing so—and thereby delayed the rollout long-term.[17]

Radhika Fox, who led the EPA's water office for three years under the Biden administration, said that the Trump administration had used an "unnecessarily drawn-out process."[18]

Officials also alleged that the Trump administration took a similar approach to cleanup. Jim Woolford, a former EPA official, said that in April 2019, his office was charged with urgently writing a rule that would designate PFOA and PFOS as hazardous substances. While his staff wrote the rule in a matter of a few months and he was told the administrator's office received it that autumn, he lamented that it was like "waiting for Godot, because it just sat there."

Although he asked the political officials who oversaw his work about the rule "every couple weeks," all Woolford got in response was that it was under review. By the time he retired in April 2020, the rule still hadn't come out. And the version that the agency did ultimately publish in January 2021 had a key difference. Instead of issuing a proposed rule, as had been drafted by Woolford's staff, the EPA released an alert about its future intentions to do so—meaning, rather than moving one step forward, it took a giant step back.*

Those delays in regulation, Woolford contended, had the potential to cause further harm to communities struggling with the impacts of PFAS contamination.

Under the agency's scoring system—which determined the sites included on the federal government's priority cleanup list—the only chemical releases that were eligible for inclusion were those officially deemed hazardous. Therefore, a site's PFOA and PFOS contamination could not score it any points—making cleanup less likely.

Steven Cook, a Trump appointee, said that career staffers were the ones hesitant to move forward because such action "hadn't been done before."[19]

He contended that the agency ultimately landed on issuing a notice that it could propose a rule—rather than actually proposing one—because the agency had not yet publicly laid out all of the pros and cons of pursuing a hazardous substance designation. The very creation of the advance notice could "create that record," while floating some ideas and getting feedback from members of the public, according to Cook.

In terms of timing, Cook attributed the holdup to the 2020 election, since the matter made its way to the White House for review during the height of campaign season. He also described an agency that was trying to solve a problem but also maintain its corporate-friendly and "deregulatory" political stance.

---

* A Freedom of Information Act request corroborates Woolford's story, proving that a proposed rule to designate PFOA and PFOS as hazardous substances was drafted, and dated 2019, even if it was never released.

Whatever the reason for the delay, sites around the country were anxiously awaiting the "hazardous" designation. Peterson Space Force Base in Colorado, for example, could not qualify for the agency's priority cleanup list until PFAS were formally declared a health hazard.[20] While installed personnel bided their time, cleanup activities were limited to preliminary efforts, and nearby families still contended with contamination. Sean Houseworth, spokesperson for the Air Force Civil Engineer Center, said in May 2023 that the air force was "prepped and ready" to move forward, but was simply waiting on the EPA.[21] Once the final regulations were available, the air force would collaborate with the state of Colorado to formulate a plan of action.

When it came to determining whether and how severely newer PFAS were toxic, Trump-appointed officials have been accused of straight-up changing the science—particularly when it came to assessing the risks of substances like PFBS. Instead of following career staff recommendations to assign PFBS with just one number to reflect a toxicity-related value, Orme-Zavaleta said that political officials offered a range of numbers.

"That's a pretty unfounded approach," she stated, noting that such a range could allow bad-faith actors to cherry-pick the most favorable number and leave often good-faith actors like states with less precise information about the substance's degree of toxicity.[22]

In response, Trump official David Dunlap has argued that this was not a science-integrity issue, but instead was a "compromise."[23] (The Biden administration later rescinded the Trump-era assessment.)

Under Trump, political appointees tried to repeat this behavior with an evaluation for GenX, recalled Betsy Behl, who worked on risk assessments at the agency.

"We were facing exactly the same issues . . . rewriting of things and the push to provide a range of numbers, not a single number," she said.[24]

Behl noted that the GenX assessment was further behind the PFBS evaluation process-wise, so the imprecise range of numbers was never actually finished. Had the assessment been completed, GenX levels in North Carolina's Cape Fear River could have been much higher and caused even worse health outcomes for exposed populations, she said.

Not only was the Trump administration's EPA interfering with scientific endeavors and failing to limit exposure to existing PFAS chemicals, the agency was also approving new ones.

While the Toxic Substances Control Act requires new chemicals to undergo safety reviews, the law contains a loophole called the Low Volume Exemption, which allows chemicals produced in small amounts to undergo a less rigorous review. EPA career officials said the Trump administration was able to use this escape clause to approve additional—and potentially dangerous—PFAS.

"Most of those [chemicals] didn't even get much of a review at all. They just rubber-stamped them," said Southerland, who retired in 2017.[25]

Garvey said that when the agency began approving new PFAS, he was "just screaming bloody murder about 'how can we approve new chemicals to go out on the market while we're saying that every time we turn around everything's worse and worse? That we're finding it in more places. That it's more toxic than we thought. That it's reacting differently.'"[26]

In 2018, the EPA used this exemption to approve a type of PFAS for use in ski wax[27]—despite "uncertainty" as to whether the substance could waterproof a person's lungs—making the organ's air sacs unable to infuse oxygen into the blood.[28]

In total, more than 600 different PFAS were approved under the exemption.[29] Twenty-nine of those took place under Trump, while the others occurred over the past several decades.

At the same time, the agency was also apparently obstructing the reporting of existing compounds. In 2020, Congress passed legislation that required companies to report their PFAS discharges to the EPA.

However, a technicality built into that law allowed firms to avoid these requirements if the chemicals in question were released in small enough concentrations.

Because so many sites used tiny but still highly toxic quantities of PFAS, little reporting occurred at the time and no clear picture evolved about contaminants released. Ultimately, surveys showed that in 2021, just forty-four facilities across the United States reported PFAS discharges to the EPA that year.[30]

Yet this glaring omission wasn't just a case of congressional neglect. Internal EPA correspondence showed that career staff members tried to notify legislators that they were about to write the loophole into law, but that they felt their attempts were thwarted by top officials, including a key political appointee.[31]

One staffer complained that he and his team "had tried to tell" Senate colleagues about the problem, but that he couldn't get authorization to do so. Chief among those whom the staffers blamed for preventing the message from getting to its destination was Nancy Beck, a Trump appointee who previously had worked as an executive at a chemical industry lobbying group.

When the EPA staffer's team finally did get approval to include the matter in materials that were sent to Beck, who could have relayed them to the Senate, he said that "we knew she wouldn't send them."[32]

Beck, who as of early 2024 worked for the law firm Hunton Andrews Kurth LLP, told *The Hill* that she did not have time to comb through the communications. She noted that in January 2019, another individual was appointed to the position directly above her.

"She was the decision-maker, not me," Beck said.[33]

Nate Saunders, from Maine, described the lack of reporting as "a travesty," having suspected that something was awry when he asked an EPA contact in August 2022 if anyone had, in fact, disclosed discharges.

"It turns out that no one in the country has reported PFAS release, except for the companies that make it and handle it as a waste," the contact told Nate.[34]

While the rule would ultimately be updated in fall 2023[35]—a prospect Nate anticipated a few months prior—he stressed that the revision would still give companies space to postpone reporting for several years.

"What is the cost of that? The cost is the American public for three years will not know the extent of PFAS contamination across this entire nation. That is a dramatic public health issue," he said. "That is criminal, in my opinion."

☞

After the presidential transition in 2021, the Biden administration saw itself inheriting a massive chemicals problem, not only from its predecessor, but also from decades of inaction.

"As a country, there was sort of this collective failure to think about the unintended consequences of the way we were making and using chemicals," said Michal Freedhoff, the EPA's top chemicals official under the Biden administration. "Catching up to that collective failure is something that's going to take time," she continued. "But this administration has, under any objective standard, done more to fix those problems than any administration ever has."[36]

When President Biden won the election in 2020, his administration decided to take PFAS head-on—setting out a "PFAS Strategic Roadmap" in October 2021 that focused on three areas: researching PFAS, reducing their use, and cleaning them up. And it did make some significant strides.[37]

Among the tangible actions was the closure of the loophole that had enabled companies to avoid reporting PFAS releases. In December 2023, the EPA announced that it had finalized a new rule to eliminate the exemption.[38]

Then, in April 2024, the agency took the boldest step to date in the history of PFAS: putting forward national limits on how much PFOA,

PFOS, GenX, PFHxS, PFBS, and another PFAS called PFNA (perfluorononanoic acid) could be in drinking water for people on public water systems. While this action officially tackled just six out of thousands of chemicals, many available technologies capable of removing these compounds could also be effective at eliminating others. However, water providers won't be required to actually install such equipment until 2029.

Though the impacts may not be immediate, Fox, the former head of the EPA's water office, described the rule as "historic."

"There are 100 million people in this country who may have a drinking water source with PFAS in it," Fox said. "So if we implement this rule well, the lives saved, the disease prevented, is really, really significant."[39]

The Biden EPA also officially designated PFOA and PFOS as hazardous substances under the nation's legacy pollution cleanup law—making it easier to either force polluters to clean up historic contamination or foot the bill for the EPA's cleanup work. At the same time, the agency was working to evaluate lesser-known types of PFAS to gain more knowledge about the substances and inform further action.

Despite these considerable steps forward, there is still a long road ahead in the national quest to unravel decades of damage. One challenge the Biden administration faced involved clawing back the number of PFAS approved under the Low Volume Exemption, which gave a less rigorous review to new chemicals expected to be produced in small quantities.

With hopes of reversing past damage, the agency asked companies to voluntarily rescind these approvals of their chemicals. As of April 2024, around sixty approvals—out of more than six hundred—were voluntarily withdrawn. The administration also proposed to exclude future PFAS from the future Low Volume Exemptions. Under this rule, the EPA would still okay some new PFAS through its normal review process—if manufacturers can show that they're being used in a "closed system" in which they're unlikely to flow into the environment, Freed-hoff explained.

For at least one major manufacturer, the changes appear to have made a difference. In 2022, 3M announced that it would exit its PFAS business completely by 2026, citing "accelerating regulatory trends" as well as "changing stakeholder expectations."[40]

However, environmental activists say there's much more to do. Scott Faber, the Environmental Working Group's senior vice president for government affairs, called for limits on how much PFAS industry can discharge into the environment. Although the EPA in 2021 indicated intentions to propose a rule that would limit such releases into water, the agency had yet to do so as of May 2024.

It's also not clear whether the changes instituted by the Biden administration's EPA would survive in a Republican administration. Democrat Dan Kildee, then a congressman from Michigan, expressed concern that at least some of these achievements, like the drinking water limit, could be fleeting. "I worry that these protections will only last as long as an administrator does, and we need law on the books that's permanent, that protects Americans from dangerous chemicals," he said.[41]

On the other hand, Kildee did express confidence that Congress would eventually take more action—even though the issue currently faces a partisan divide—given the prevalence of the substances. He voiced hopes that Congress would codify drinking water limits, require the EPA to limit PFAS releases, and set up health benefits for military veterans who were exposed on the job.

"PFAS is ubiquitous in the environment and every member of Congress, all 435 house members and all 100 senators, sooner or later are going to have a constituent come to them and ask them what they're doing about the contamination right here at home," Kildee said. "But what I worry about is—that will take a lot of time, and people who are continually getting exposure don't have time."

CHAPTER 11

The Next Generation

For Emily Donovan, June 7, 2017, started off like any other day, until she looked at the newspaper.

A front-page article warned that a toxic chemical was contaminating drinking water in the nearby city of Wilmington, North Carolina.[1]

"At the time, my concern was 'Is this in my tap water as well?'" said Emily, who lives in a Wilmington suburb called Leland, which is served by a different water utility.[2]

In the months that followed, she learned that it was. As it turned out, GenX, the next-generation PFAS compound that was supposed to be safer than its predecessors, was now flowing through the taps of thousands of residents.

"It was heartbreaking, and it was scary. We raised my children on this water, and we are heavy water drinkers," said Emily, a mother of boy-girl twins.

She began asking questions: Was her husband's brain tumor related to the water? Is this why so many people she knows have cancer?

"There was a lack of information. That was the hard part. There was plenty of stuff online about PFOA and PFOS. There was hardly anything on GenX," she said.

When the PFAS problem became apparent, Emily was the youth director at a local church. On Sunday evenings, her students would hold a prayer circle, where they described problems that no child should have to face.

"Half of the students were asking for some really heavy prayers: prayers for parents that were sick and terminal or for siblings that were suffering and hospitalized. It was not normal. Not what I remembered growing up," she said.

⌒

The sheer fact that the public even found out about GenX in Wilmington's water was "completely serendipitous," said Vaughn Hagerty, the reporter who broke the story in the *Wilmington Star-News*.[3]

But he was quick to temper expectations with a disclaimer about the scoop: "It's not exactly a 'meeting some guy in a darkened parking lot who has a porn star codename slipping me the information'" type of story, Hagerty said.

Instead, he came upon the finding while undertaking a freelance project that focused on regional levels of a range of chemicals, including PFOA and PFOS. Hagerty wanted to make sure the story hadn't been written already, so he did some Googling.

That led him to a university professor's presentation about chemicals in North Carolina waterways, including GenX, which had been found in the Cape Fear River. This sparkling, blue-brown channel flows for about 200 miles from the middle of the state all the way to the Atlantic Ocean, providing drinking water for numerous communities along the way, including Wilmington.

Hagerty called the professor, Detlef Knappe, to try to get some answers. That helped him piece the story together: the previous year, the EPA and outside scientists published a study showing GenX in Wilmington's taps, but this information seemed not to have found its way to local residents. (The regional EPA office did not respond to a question about whether there had been any community outreach.)

Hagerty recalled that "next to nothing" was known about GenX at the time. Nonetheless, he knew that it was being made to replace PFOA, and what he learned about PFOA "certainly . . . bore looking into." While US information was limited, the National Institute for Public Health and the Environment in the Netherlands classified GenX as a suspected carcinogen. Meanwhile, Knappe estimated at that time that 250,000 people could be impacted.[4]

One of those people, Jessica Cannon, stopped working after her third child was born. It was also around this time that the Wilmington resident and former OBGYN became very interested in politics, at both the local and national level.

When Donald Trump was elected in 2016, she started a Facebook group for local women who were upset by the result. She said that the group "snowballed" into an advocacy and volunteer organization that worked on political campaigns and acted as a "watchdog" for what was going on in North Carolina's general assembly and for holding the local congressman accountable.[5]

By the time Hagerty's story hit the presses, Jessica's group was already a "cohesive unit."

"We were just poised to act," she added.

Joining forces as a unified front, Jessica, Emily, and local politician Harper Peterson Jr. sat around Peterson's table just days after Hagerty's story broke and established a group dedicated to fighting the contamination.

"We developed Clean Cape Fear pretty much right away," she said.

The new group sought to both inform their neighbors about GenX by holding public meetings and seek justice from the manufacturer of that chemical, a company called Chemours.

About five years before the kitchen-table campaign, the world started catching up to DuPont. At the time—in 2012—EPA scientists had learned about GenX's presence in the Cape Fear River, where DuPont's

Fayetteville Works facility was discharging PFAS-laden waste about eighty miles northwest of Wilmington. That same year, the C8 Science Panel (the team of scientists that assessed PFOA's potential health impacts because of Bilott's class action lawsuit in Parkersburg, West Virginia) had linked PFOA to kidney cancer, testicular cancer, thyroid disease, ulcerative colitis, and diagnosed high cholesterol—in addition to preeclampsia, which had been identified the year before. And about two dozen personal injury lawsuits had started rolling in, with thousands more to follow.[6]

But DuPont came up with a creative solution: in 2013, the company announced that it planned to spin off its PFAS business—and the liability that came with it.

"They're trying to isolate themselves legally," said David Larcker, director of Stanford University's Corporate Governance Research Initiative. "It's kind of a strategic maneuver that probably helps the shareholders of the existing company."[7]

Larcker described the situation as "pretty terrifying," noting that if companies can do this, they may be less motivated to treat the environment responsibly. The resultant "ability to walk away from this legally or from a regulatory standpoint" could create some "pretty bad incentives" with regard to protecting the climate and water, Larcker added.

In the summer of 2015, DuPont separated from the PFAS-manufacturing segment of its company, calling the new corporation Chemours. By the end of that year, DuPont estimated that it was facing 3,500 lawsuits related to PFOA in Ohio and West Virginia. Most of them were personal injury claims, while thirty-seven were alleged wrongful deaths. When it spun off its PFAS business to Chemours, DuPont projected that the new company would be taking on legal responsibility—amounting to about $291 million.[8] Of that total, DuPont estimated that Chemours would have to pay up to $128 million for the 3,500 PFOA suits alone.[9]

Change remained in the air, and in 2017, DuPont merged with fellow chemical giant Dow, becoming DowDuPont. Just two years into their marriage, Dow and DuPont called it quits. In doing so, the corporations carried out their plan of becoming three companies: Dow, DuPont, and Corteva—and neither Dow nor DuPont left the divorce with exactly the same assets it came in with. After the split, DuPont took on a slightly different name. Before the merger, its full government name was E. I. du Pont de Nemours. The new DuPont dropped the first part, formally being called just DuPont de Nemours (though its friends—and enemies—still called it DuPont for short).

Since the split, DuPont has claimed, both legally and to journalists asking questions, that it is no longer the same company that pumped PFOA into Parkersburg's water.[10] It also maintains that it's no longer the same company that spun off Chemours, since it's now a Frankenstein, made up of parts of the former DuPont and pieces of the former Dow. As of early 2024, the CEO of the new DuPont was Ed Breen, who was also the CEO of the old DuPont, assuming that role in late 2015 after the Chemours spinoff.

Larcker, from Stanford, said it's a "legitimate argument" that that the new DuPont may not necessarily be the exact same company as the old DuPont but stressed that "somebody's got to be responsible" for the contamination.

DuPont declined to answer a lengthy list of questions, contending that it is neither the same company responsible for the contamination nor the one that spun off as Chemours. "In 2019, DuPont de Nemours was established as a new multi-industrial specialty products company. DuPont de Nemours has never manufactured or sold PFOA, PFOS, GenX or firefighting foam," spokesperson Dan Turner said in an email.[11]

"There's a clear difference between DuPont de Nemours and legacy E. I. du Pont de Nemours [sic]," he added. "Every event and action described in your questions relates to E. I. DuPont de Nemours. DuPont de Nemours was not established at the time of any of these matters."

The company also did not address questions posed about subsequent or ongoing litigation.

Chemours also declined to comment on events that occurred prior to its spinoff from DuPont, saying that it didn't exist yet.

In 2019, Chemours sued what was then DowDuPont, alleging that DuPont created and spun off Chemours as "part of a plan to try to off-load its historical environmental liabilities." Chemours also alleged that DuPont significantly underestimated the potential liability it was facing—noting that the 3,500 Ohio and West Virginia cases ultimately settled for five times DuPont's estimated maximum.

Chemours said if it had to face unlimited liability for DuPont's historic actions, despite DuPont's inaccurate projections as to how much those actions could actually cost, then DuPont "is admitting that the entire spin-off process was a sham." Chemours also alleged that it received a disproportionate percentage of Dupont's problems, compared to how much of the company's profitable business it got.

"Chemours received only 19 percent of DuPont's business lines, but was saddled with approximately two-thirds of DuPont's environmental liabilities and 90 percent of DuPont's pending litigation," the lawsuit said.

The spinoff company also accused its former owner of considering an investment of $60 million to end PFAS discharges into the Cape Fear River, but ultimately deciding against doing so. "Why bother spending money to fix the problem, DuPont apparently reasoned, when it could be conveniently passed on to Chemours?" the lawsuit said.[12]

The case was ultimately dismissed in 2020, after DuPont again separated from Dow. A Delaware judge ruled that the issue was subject to arbitration rather than to adjudication by the court.[13] In 2021, Chemours and Dupont—as well as Corteva, an agriculture chemicals company that spun off from DowDuPont—announced a cost-sharing agreement. Under that deal, DuPont and Corteva together were to take on 50 percent of expenses related to PFAS-related litigation for up to $2 billion.[14]

Meanwhile, for others working to hold DuPont (and Chemours) accountable for the pollution, the corporate maneuvers presented an additional hurdle.

"It certainly delays things," said Mark Garvey, a former EPA lawyer who had worked on the agency's PFAS cases. "The delay of having to remove a chemical from the market and delay from having to pay a penalty—that's profit for these companies."[15]

He noted that personnel with both Chemours and the new DuPont denied responsibility and knowledge of the actions of the old DuPont.

"Trying to get answers about 'what did you know in 1990, when you did X?' . . . the response comes back, 'We can't respond to that because that is prior to the existence of this organization,'" Garvey said. "It made it difficult for us to trace back previous decisions that the company had made."

"It's just so frustrating to have a company that's called DuPont, and they're pretending not [to be] the same company," he added.

Chemours has taken a similar position, Garvey said.

"There's a certain magical date that Chemours became Chemours, and at that point, the employees at Fayetteville and Parkersburg, they became Chemours employees," he said.

"They keep on telling us how they cannot speak to what happened before X date," he added, recalling a particular meeting after the spinoff between multiple Chemours employees and EPA officials.

Frustrated, Garvey finally asked the Chemours officials for a show of hands: "How many people in this room worked for DuPont before they worked for Chemours?"

It was every single one of them, he said. His next question was, "How long? How long did you work for DuPont?"

"These people had worked for DuPont ten, fifteen years before they started working for Chemours, and they're there in the room with us telling us how they can't speak to what happened," he recalled.

Following these conversations, in May 2024, DuPont announced plans to separate into three companies, with its electronics and water divisions expected to split off from the larger company eighteen to twenty-four months later.

☞

Eight days after Hagerty's article was published, Chemours held a closed-door meeting with local and state officials—including Michael Regan, who was then the head of North Carolina's Department of Environmental Quality (DEQ), but who would later lead the federal EPA in the Biden administration. One journalist, the *Star-News*'s Adam Wagner, was allowed in the room.[16]

At the meeting, Chemours product sustainability director, Kathy O'Keefe, told the officials that the company did not believe it was releasing an unsafe level of GenX.

"Our belief is that the GenX level in the drinking water coming from the Cape Fear River is safe and it does not pose any harm to human health. We have that belief; we're confident in that belief," she was quoted as saying in Wagner's notes.[17]

O'Keefe's confidence notwithstanding, the EPA has since concluded that there is suggestive evidence that GenX might cause cancer.[18]

But regardless of the health impacts of the compound, O'Keefe also cited a regulatory loophole that allowed the company to dump GenX into the river in the first place. She said that while Chemours doesn't release the GenX it makes on purpose, when it's created as a byproduct of a separate substance, that byproduct can be discharged.

The discharges that ended up in the river came "from this unregulated byproduct," O'Keefe said, later adding that the ability to manufacture the byproduct is "not regulated by any regulatory agency."

Woody White, who was the chairman of the New Hanover County

Board of Commissioners—the county that includes Wilmington—protested the assertion that the *byproduct* GenX was allowed to enter the environment if the *manufactured* GenX was contained.

"That does not meet the commonsense test," he said during the 2017 meeting.

A spokesperson for the state Department of Environmental Quality similarly pushed back in a May 2024 email, saying that the department viewed Chemours's discharges of GenX as "unpermitted discharge" and a violation of its permit.[19]

Mike Johnson, the environmental manager of the Fayetteville Works plant, also told the officials that the byproduct GenX had been being released into the river since 1980. He added that in 2013, the company installed pollution control technology to prevent 80 percent of it from going into the river.

Over the course of the forty years that Chemours and its predecessor, DuPont, had released GenX into the Cape Fear River, residents were consuming contaminated water. And while it can be difficult to link a specific person's illness to the substance, area residents who drank the tap water have wondered if the health effects they and their family members experienced were a result of the toxic exposure—and whether more diseases could develop among their loved ones as a result.

Emily Donovan is one of those people. A few years after moving to the Wilmington area, her husband, David Donovan, started to experience worsening vision.

"It was so gradual that I don't think he put much thought into it," Emily said on a January 2024 phone call.

But one day, she was walking around and noticed the sheer quantity of different reading glasses her husband, who was only in his forties, had amassed. She told him: "I don't think this is normal. You should probably go get your eyes checked."

He went to the doctor, who suggested an MRI. "It was a brain tumor the size of a golf ball," Emily said. Desperate to save David's vision, the couple scrambled to find a neurosurgeon.

"It was very stressful. We had two young kids," she said. "The twins were just turning four while he was having surgery. I know we missed their birthday because he was in the hospital."

Ultimately, though, they were lucky: a world-class surgeon was in the area at Duke University, and David's surgery was successful.

Emily believes the cause of her husband's cancer was environmental rather than genetic: David's twin brother, who lives in another part of the state, has not developed a similar illness.

Another Wilmington resident who was among the "lucky" ones is middle school teacher Chris Meek, whose gallbladder rupture may have saved him. Chris had "probably the scariest moment" of his life when he was rushed into hospital in 2013. After an emergency surgery, the doctors did a CAT scan and asked the educator what his plan was to deal with the mass on his kidney. Chris didn't know about any mass—but as it turns out, he had kidney cancer. Fortunately, however, the doctors caught the cancer early enough that it hadn't spread, so he was able to have the kidney removed after recovering from his gallbladder surgery.

Since learning about the pollution that has long plagued the region's water, Chris said he has become "90 percent sure" that this is what caused his cancer.

"When corporate greed and shareholders' wants and needs are more important than the communities that you're dumping your shit into, yeah, that's not cool," he added.[20]

But unlike Chris and David, some Wilmington residents never recovered. Amy Shands, originally a New Yorker, brought "all the stereotypes" with her to the South, according to her husband Jonathan. She didn't lose any arguments, and even if she did, she would never admit it.

"I love how strong she was," Jonathan said, adding that Amy was a fighter for her speech pathology patients. The couple met online in 2002, right after Amy received her graduate degree and was preparing to move to Wilmington for work.

"She always drank water," Jonathan recalled, noting that he was "stuck on soda."[21]

When Amy went in for an MRI related to her multiple sclerosis around early 2020, the doctors detected a tumor in the speech pathologist's head. After she endured a course of radiation that summer for what turned out to be sinus cancer, the family thought the nightmare was behind them.

But their brief respite was over the next year, when Amy developed an issue that caused the left side of her face to droop. The cancer had returned. Doctors removed the cancer from behind her sinuses, but, because Amy had a bad reaction to some of the medicines, they could not fully remove the part closest to her brain, Jonathan said.

When she was told in 2021 that she had only two years to live, Amy made it clear that she had a lot of dreams. One of them was to spend a weekend in upstate New York to watch her favorite artist: the Dave Matthews Band. That year, Amy and Jonathan made it to four Dave Matthews concerts in a four-month span. But Amy had another big goal—to attend her daughter Isabella's high school graduation. Unfortunately, this was one argument the New Yorker wasn't able to win.

Amy took her last breath at 11:01 p.m. on January 9, 2022—on Dave Matthews's birthday. She was forty-three, Isabella was fourteen.

"To us, my daughter and me, we still think she's on a trip and that she will come home," Jonathan said, noting that he doesn't like to talk about his wife in the past tense. "She's the mediator when we get into arguments. We'll still talk to her like she's still here. We know that [she's] not, but it helps us cope."

Jonathan said he believes contaminated water "has to be" a factor in what happened to his wife. The family first learned about the issue when Amy went to see the premiere of the film *Dark Waters* in Wilmington in 2019. The next day, they switched to getting their water delivered. He said he wants to see the manufacturers of the chemicals put in prison.

"You killed people. That should be a life sentence," he said.

Chemours pushed back on the notion that its PFAS discharges were contributing to illnesses in the region.

"While we sympathize with anyone experiencing or impacted by health issues, much of the available data doesn't support the conclusions some individuals have drawn," Cassie Olszewski, a spokesperson the company, said in a May 2024 emailed statement.[22]

Olszewski pointed to a 2017 analysis by the state of North Carolina finding that pancreatic, liver, uterine, testicular, and kidney cancer rates in four impacted counties were similar to statewide levels, with a few exceptions. New Hanover County, which includes Wilmington, had an elevated rate of testicular cancer in comparison to that of the rest of the state between 1996 and 2015 and a high rate of liver cancer between 2006 and 2010. However, Brunswick County had periods of lower rates of pancreatic and uterine cancer compared to the state average, and Bladen County, northwest of Wilmington, had a lower rate of kidney cancer.[23]

Regardless, Wilmington families are still contending with a chemical that the federal EPA now says can impact the liver, kidneys, and immune system and has an association with cancer.[24] And with so much at stake, local environmental advocates have sued to try to put a stop to the contamination and achieve justice for area residents. In 2018, a local group called Cape Fear River Watch, which seeks to protect the channel from pollution, sued the state of North Carolina to push the agency to take further action against Chemours—with the goal of getting the agency to force the company to stop dumping GenX into the river.[25]

Asked about the environmental group's lawsuit, a spokesperson for the Department of Environmental Quality pointed to North Carolina's 2017 decision to order Chemours to stop discharging PFAS and the agency's 2018 legal action seeking to get the company to stop discharging its wastewater until the state issues it a permit with "appropriate limits."[26]

The River Watch suit ultimately led to a 2019 "consent order"—a legal agreement that required Chemours to reduce its PFAS discharges into the Cape Fear River, cut its releases of GenX into the air by 99.99 percent, and test local residents' private wells for contamination. Chemours also has to provide alternate water sources for private well owners whose tests show high levels of contamination.[27]

Dana Sargent, Cape Fear River Watch's executive director, said that this agreement simultaneously "does a lot of things . . . to get the company to clean up the mess" while also emphasizing that it is "not enough." Specifically, she noted, the deal only requires Chemours to provide alternative supplies for people whose drinking water is contaminated with at least one of 12 specific PFAS—leaving some compounds, and some people, excluded.

In the May 2024 response, Olszewski said that Chemours's Fayetteville Works site has eliminated more than 97 percent of its water emissions of PFAS and has achieved 99.99 percent efficiency with its technology meant to control air emissions.

⌒

As it turns out, the GenX debacle was not North Carolina's first run-in with PFAS or the Fayetteville plant, which was owned by DuPont until the 2015 spinoff. The company started making PFOA in North Carolina in 2002.[28]

In 2001, DuPont applied for a permit to produce PFOA at the Fayetteville plant, writing that it had been using the substance "for more than forty years with no observed health effects in workers"[29]—despite its findings from decades past.

Hope Taylor, the leader of local environmental group Clean Water for North Carolina, said that the United Steelworkers union contacted her around 2003 to let her know about the new PFOA operations—and about groundwater contamination.

Luckily for Hope, the union at the time had been working with an environmental consultant, Richard Abraham, who was investigating the PFOA issue. That work led him to Fayetteville, where the substance had recently started being manufactured.

"At the time, no one was really paying attention to it as the place where this stuff was being made," he said. "It was . . . supposedly a new state-of-the-art facility which, by the time I got there, was already leaking and contaminating groundwater and surface water."[30]

"There were reasons for significant health concerns for the workers, as well as the general public," Hope added in a November 2023 phone call.[31]

While regulators eventually set up groundwater monitoring systems near the facility, contamination levels continued to increase for the year or two that followed, Hope recalled. The rising numbers prompted them to start speaking with the area's residents, who she said "were reporting some anomalous things in their livestock and then of course they were worried about their water."

During Fayetteville's first time in the ring with PFAS and its producers, there was at least one state official who tried to put up a fight, but he recalled feeling like he got nowhere. Tom McKinney, who was an inspector with the state's Division of Air Quality, said that in 2004 he visited the then-DuPont facility for work. He learned that not only was PFOA getting into the air, it was also leaching into the groundwater.

While McKinney didn't know much about PFAS at the time, as Rob Bilott's cases and the EPA were just beginning to bring the issue to light, he did know that chemicals containing halogens (a group of elements that includes fluorine), could be persistent in the environment.

And so he wrote in notes on the meeting that the groundwater finding was "quite surprising."[32] But he found that his reports were not well received within the state government, which he described as succumbing to "corporate capture."

Hope, with the clean water group, recounted similar inaction from the state.

"We had a meeting with the heads of several divisions," she said, referring to the state's environmental agency. "They sat and listened and asked a few questions and did absolutely nothing to further investigate the problem."[33]

While the agency was dismissive of the PFAS issue at the time, federal authorities did take some actions—and DuPont pledged to curtail its PFOA emissions as part of the EPA's stewardship program, which sought voluntary commitments from PFOA producers to stop making the substance. Little did Hope know, however, that the issue would crop up again in about a decade as the plant made different chemicals—chemicals that were also toxic.

"We were naive in thinking that . . . agreement with EPA was going to result in a much better situation," she said.

CHAPTER 12

Whac-A-Mole

WHEN THE NEWS ABOUT WILMINGTON'S WATER WOES broke in 2017, one of Emily Donovan's first concerns was for her kids—and about what, exactly, was in the water that they and their friends were drinking at school.

In a bid to minimize any future exposure, her Clean Cape Fear group approached local water provider, Brunswick Regional Water & Sewer H2GO, with a request to install PFAS filtration devices in the four schools that the utility serves. H2GO agreed—making plans to equip all of the buildings with reverse osmosis systems.

"It is just the right thing to do," Bob Walker, H2GO's executive director, told local news in August 2017.

The company, he stressed, could bring "an immediate impact to the customers that are most vulnerable, and that's our children."[1]

And for the town's youngest residents, the circumstances were dire: the schools didn't have clean water.

As Parent Teacher Associations (PTAs) around the nation were asking parents for help with things like snacks, Emily recalled that, at her kids' schools, the requests were instead for bottled water.

"That was our reality," she said.

But officials in Brunswick County—which does not include Wilmington but does include Leland, where Emily lives—apparently didn't share her perspective. In a joint statement at the time, the county manager and the school district superintendent said they had "full confidence that the Brunswick County water supply—including at our schools—is absolutely safe to drink."

"If alternative treatment methods are deemed to be the best way forward in the future, it is something that will be best implemented on a countywide basis," the statement continued.[2]

County spokesperson Meagan Kascsak said in a May 2024 email that back in 2017, local officials were waiting for state-level guidance.

"Obviously, this letter is now more than six years old and was written without the information we now have from the EPA and NC DEQ [North Carolina Department of Environmental Quality] concerning PFAS," Kascsak said.[3]

By September 2017, just weeks after H2GO's director had pledged to provide the filters, the county formally decided it would not accept the company's $200,000 donation.[4]

"The school district actually did a shitty thing," said Emily, who only learned about the decision in November of that year. "The superintendent at the time received a letter from the county manager telling them that they were not authorized to receive the donation, and the superintendent just sat on it for a couple of months."

The letter, she explained, was essentially arguing that "it's not fair to give filling stations to a couple of schools and not all the schools." But to Emily, county officials were just letting more kids drink contaminated water.

"Not once did that county lift a hand to try and find filling stations for the rest of those schools," she recalled.

Brunswick County eventually agreed to bring safe water to all students in 2020, at which time the district announced that it would install a reverse osmosis system in each of its schools. That decision occurred after a sample taken from the local Belville Elementary put Brunswick County's PFAS levels higher than any of the forty-three other sites sampled from around the country.[5] Nonetheless, she stressed, bureaucratic delays left many students drinking contaminated water for three years longer than they needed to be.

A spokesperson for the school district did not respond directly to questions about the episode, but instead shared a timeline detailing its installations of reverse osmosis systems, the earliest of which were at two schools, including Belville, as a trial.

In 2012, the same year that scientists detected GenX in the Cape Fear River, a major Wilmington-area water utility had just undergone a major renovation.

"We were a perfect testbed to see, 'All right, what does advanced water treatment do in terms of . . . sources contaminated with GenX?'" said Kenneth Waldroup, the executive director of the Cape Fear Public Utility Authority (CFPUA), a water utility that serves Wilmington.[6]

As it turned out, the new system didn't do very much, as became apparent after the 2016 study—in which both EPA and outside scientists found the substance in Wilmington's drinking water. Waldroup, who himself only joined the utility in 2021, credited the 2016 research and Vaughn Hagerty's 2017 article for spurring action from the city-owned CFPUA. While only limited information on GenX was available at the time, the utility pressed on toward a solution.

"There was a perfect window of community concern and interest and political desire to address it," Waldroup said, adding that the utility chose to say, "Yes, we're going to remove these chemicals. We don't know whether they're harmful or not, but we know they're related to things that are harmful."

That turned out to have been a wise choice—as the EPA would later declare that scientific evidence was strong enough to suggest that GenX might cause cancer. While seeking out a long-term solution, the utility's managers implemented two temporary fixes. First, they began filtering out about 40 percent of the GenX that it encountered, Waldroup said. In parallel, CFPUA set up free drinking water stations to provide clean, on-demand supplies to members of the community.

By 2022, the utility finished installing a more lasting solution that could remove PFAS to non-detectable levels: massive granular activated carbon filters.[7] Waldroup likened the technology to a larger-scale Brita pitcher—although Brita products are neither designed nor marketed for PFAS removal.

"We have 3 million pounds of that," he said, referring to the carbon and noting that each year, the material gets cleaned out and reused.

While effective, these efforts have come with significant costs. The water treatment plant's annual budget has also nearly doubled, adding $4 million onto what was already a $4.9 million operation, plus the $43 million upfront cost to build it. The utility is currently suing Chemours and DuPont to try to recoup its costs.

"Our neighbors up the river have been putting PFAS in the river, unpermitted, for what, four decades now? That's why these were built," said Hagerty, the former reporter who is now a CFPUA spokesperson, during a tour of the site. "Let's just say you . . . have a daughter and she likes to play baseball and she's practicing batting the ball and she's breaking your neighbors' windows all over the place. Well, have you solved the problem if you give her a batting cage? Well, no—you've got all these broken windows you've got to take care of."

Hagerty stressed that the chemical companies should repay "the millions of dollars it costs us every year," not to mention the millions spent on testing—adding that the fees "only occurred" because of the pollution.[8]

Other water providers in the area, which also get their water from the Cape Fear River, have taken similar steps. Brunswick County, where Emily Donovan lives—though she's on a different water system—was in the process of installing a reverse osmosis plant, similar to the one in Brenda Hampton's region of Alabama. The county says that this project was slated for completion in late 2024.

Meagan Kascsak, the county spokesperson, said that since 2017, Brunswick "has been committed to finding a water treatment solution to benefit all our water customers." She added that as of May 2024, the reverse osmosis plant was 78 percent complete. However, the county does not appear to have done anything to provide its general population with clean water in the meantime. Asked what, if any action, the county has taken, Brunswick County Public Utilities director John Nichols described efforts to distribute educational materials, advise residents on in-home treatment systems, and provide PFAS test results—but made no mention of efforts to secure clean water.[9] Kascsak noted that neither the state nor the federal government provided any sort of interim solution.

Wilmington-area residents served by private utilities, meanwhile, have also had to contend with contamination, and in some cases, apparent inaction. When Ann Truett moved to Wilmington in 2022, she was hoping it was where she would stay. But an accidental discovery of contamination in her new town caught her by surprise. The seventy-two-year-old immigration lawyer, who was on the verge of retiring at the time of a March 2024 conversation, was looking for a new environmental cause to support when she came across the region's PFAS problem.

"When we moved in, I started to look at articles because one of the things I wanted to volunteer for was to become a proponent . . . for the environment, to prevent climate change, and most of all to help wildlife," Ann said.[10]

It was during this quest that she found some "super concerning" articles about PFAS. With the help of Dana Sargent at Cape Fear River

Watch, Ann was able to get her water tested, and it came back positive for what the EPA considers to be unsafe levels of PFOA, PFOS, and GenX. Prior to getting her water tested, Ann had started drinking bottled water, but she still used her tap water for showering, washing the dishes, and even for making ice cubes.

"We had been exposed for about eighteen months," Ann said, referring to herself and her husband. She expressed particular concern about her husband, as he already had health issues before moving to Wilmington, having suffered three strokes and undergone triple-bypass heart surgery. Ann herself has autoimmune issues.

She remains frustrated about the fact that her real estate broker never informed her of the contamination when she sold her the home. She said she recently called the broker and asked, "Why didn't you tell me about the chemicals?" The realtor's response, she recalled, was simply, "I did not have to."

While Ann installed a reverse osmosis system for her kitchen sink and a whole-house carbon filtration system, she was planning to leave the area and return to Massachusetts. And even though the house is now equipped with these filtration systems, she intends to inform the next buyer.

"I would never do what was done to me," Ann said.

However, she continued, it seems that other people would.

"I have a next-door neighbor who just moved in in December," Ann said, noting that the neighbor's ten-year-old daughter has a medical issue and should not be drinking the water. "No one told them about the fact that there's dangerous levels of PFAS in the water." Ann's water was provided by a utility called Aqua NC, a branch of the national brand Aqua, an Essential Utilities company, which is a private company.

"They're not providing any information, let alone filtration to their customers," Dana Sargent said. "It's appalling and dangerous for people." She noted that the company does publish some information on its website but added that customers are unlikely to actively seek out a water quality report without prompting.

Asked about whether the utility treats water for PFAS in Wilmington, a spokesperson for Aqua did not directly respond, instead noting that the company is pursuing funding for PFAS treatment through state programs and lawsuits. However, the utility's sampling of Ann's system showed significantly lower levels of GenX than the sampling she had completed. The reason for this difference is not clear.

And the issue doesn't just pertain to people who get their water from a utility. Many people in the area get their water from private wells that they pump themselves. And not all of those people were aware of the 2017 news, or if they were, they didn't think that it necessarily impacted them.

"We did our best to try to educate people. It's just really hard. It's a complicated issue," Dana Sargent said in an April 2024 phone call. "Even after all these years, I still have people contacting me [saying], 'I didn't know.'"

However, many would learn in the years that followed just how much pollution was in the water that they, their families, and their friends and neighbors were consuming.

In Betty Newkirk's small circle of houses alone, she could name nine neighbors who had died of cancer.

"The man [who lived] behind me, Alfred Bennett, had cancer, died. Mr. Rufus James, cancer, he died. His son, Rufus Jr. Cancer. Died. Across the street, James Whitted. Cancer. Died. On the side of me was Ms. Evelyn Grady. Cancer. Died. Behind them was [Ezekiel] Robinson and his wife Margaret. Cancer. Died. And that was just in that little area," Newkirk said, during a March 2024 visit to the neighborhood.[11]

And the death tour continued: Vernita Grady across the street. Lois Dutton, whose house was in front of hers. In a follow up email, she added Martha McGuire next door and Rosa Moore across from the church to the list. A few weeks later, her count was up to twenty-eight community members who had died of cancer, including breast cancer, bladder cancer, and lung cancer.

Betty hasn't lived on the street since 2008, but after tallying just how many families were torn apart by disease, she came face to face with her own mortality.

"I could have been gone if I stayed," she said.

Betty's friends and family members were living in a district just outside of Wilmington, known as Rock Hill—a predominantly Black community about a fifteen-minute drive from downtown. Rock Hill, today dotted with stand-alone, ranch-style houses, was built on the site of a plantation, and is home to many descendants of the slaves who worked the lands centuries ago.

Most of the homes are not attached to a water utility, and instead pump water from private wells—often covered by pump houses, which look like small doghouses sitting on property lawns. Many residents are also not hooked up to the municipal sewage system, using their own septic tanks instead.

"It's a country area, and people live back up in the dirt roads. You know, we don't even have streetlights," said Janice Gaines, vice president of the Rock Hill community organization. It's also generally seen as an older community.[12]

Brother and sister Terrel and Donna Allen, who are from Rock Hill, described the house they grew up in as something of a revolving door of death. Their mother died of dementia. Their father died of bone cancer. Then a renter, Beverly Williams, died too, of throat cancer. It turns out, the Allen house would eventually test positive not only for relatively high levels of PFOA and PFOS, but also for an alphabet soup of other PFAS initialisms: PFBS, PFO2HxA, PFO3OA, and most of all, perfluoro-2-methoxyacetic acid (PFMOAA). However, availability of testing, or even general awareness of PFAS, didn't start in Rock Hill until around 2022.

"It's just unbelievable that this was going on and that we didn't know . . . about it," Donna said, adding that the information "could have saved some lives."[13]

Janice, who grew up in the neighborhood but no longer lives there, said she was generally familiar with North Carolina's PFAS problem from the media, but didn't realize that her childhood neighborhood was affected—it simply "didn't register." But things changed around 2022, close to the time she became vice president of the Rock Hill community organization.

Emerson Whitted, an outspoken octogenarian and former president of that group, has claimed responsibility for alerting the community about their possible predicament. After hearing about PFAS on the news, the former middle school social studies teacher decided to call up Chemours for more information. Eventually, the company came and tested his well—and gave him back a list of numbers and chemicals that included PFOA and PFOS.

When she learned about the issue, Janice contacted just about every authority she could to try to get both answers and clean water.

"We went to the health department, we went to New Hanover County and talked to the commissioners, we talked to Cape Fear Public Utility, we talked to River Watch, we went to different meetings with scientists," she said, noting that everyone was listening, but no one was acting.

Eventually, though, several members of the community got their wells tested. Some of them qualified for Chemours-funded water, but some of them did not. Many people whose tests turned up some PFAS—just not the right kind or amount to qualify for complimentary water—ended up paying for it anyway out of their own pockets. Others obtained supplies from the local church, for which the county funded a water line after the neighbors started making noise.

Janice's parents, who are in their eighties, still live in Rock Hill. Like so many others in the community, her family has also been plagued by illnesses. Her mother had a thyroid issue, while her father and brother have both had prostate cancer—with her brother diagnosed at a young age. After going dormant for many years, her father's cancer returned, Janice said in March 2024. But she didn't put the pieces together until she learned about the contamination. And despite her efforts to bring clean water to her community, Janice said she feels like she has let people down.

"The older generation really took care of making sure that things got to where they were now, the younger generation just let things fall by the wayside," she continued, blaming herself and her peers for failing to be "on top of things" as sickness spread. "It's all cancer, cancer, cancer, cancer—you know, lightbulbs should have went off."

Janice herself also experienced a type of cancer that she found very surprising: skin cancer, on a part of her body where the sun doesn't shine. After being diagnosed with skin cancer in her rectum in 1998, at age thirty-three, she had to get a very painful laser surgery.

Janice remains in disbelief about her diagnosis, noting that she was never a person who spent much time in the sun—and she "sure didn't throw that up at it." While she doesn't live in Rock Hill anymore, she did for thirty-three years, and has less-than-fond memories of the well water she drank there.

"It had like an egg taste to it," she said. "So we didn't drink a whole lot, but we did make Kool-Aid and all that to take the taste away."

For some of Rock Hill's old-timers, like Emerson and Bernard Williams, the PFAS issue is the latest battle in a long-term fight for the community to get access to public utilities that serve wealthier and Whiter communities nearby.

They said they've been fighting for decades, long before they knew about PFAS, to get hooked up to public sewage utilities, too.

"New Hanover County had a whole slew of chemical plants," Emerson said, adding that there also used to be a fertilizer factory. "And many of our people worked in those places."[14]

In 1984, he said, the county was supposed to extend water and sewer services to the people of Rock Hill. But there wasn't enough money, and ultimately, the cash went to protect estuaries on the local intercoastal waterway. County spokesperson Alex Riley said in an email that the planning and land use department doesn't have records "related to requests for water and/or sewer installation" from the early 1980s.[15] However, Bernard, the community organization president, corroborated Emerson's account, saying that they "were slated to have clean water and sewer and sidewalks." Yet by virtue "of being low-income, or a Black area, a lot of times this stuff gets sidetracked."[16]

The community renewed its push for water and sewage connections in 1996, Emerson recounted, noting that they still don't have these services today.

To Emerson, the devastation that their neighborhood has endured from the PFAS problem is "a real affirmation of the fact that [the] government doesn't protect you." He described the area as one with a "political process that doesn't respond to things until they become a crisis."

The Whitted family, too, has endured the tragic effects of cancer—including the death of Emerson's wife, LaVerne Whitted, who succumbed to breast cancer in 2007 in her late fifties.[17]

"I have no way of knowing what the exact cause was," Emerson lamented.

Nonetheless, with the surge in PFAS pollution has also come a strengthening of neighborhood bonds and advocacy efforts. Lena Williams, who is married to Bernard, said that PFAS comes up at every monthly meeting held by the community organization. Another difference between past and present has been the increasing drive in recent years to come together as a unit to fight for the population's needs.

"I just regret that it has taken this long for voices to be heard," she said during a visit to her backyard garden. "The noise was made, but not as a collective group. . . . When we took on the task of trying to be accountable for what is being done . . . then we were heard."[18]

As of that March 2024 conversation, at least some progress was underway to get the people of Rock Hill hooked up to clean water. After community members spoke out, New Hanover County directed funds to connect twenty-four homes that are close to existing water lines. Riley, the New Hanover spokesperson, said that the county's fiscal year 2024 budget allocated $500,000 toward connecting households close to the water main.

While these incremental steps only help a portion of the community, a broader solution may also be on the horizon. There's a proposal on the table—supported by community leaders like Janice and Bernard—to require CFPUA to connect all Rock Hill residents to the water line. Bernard said, however, that it's important for residents to get tested regardless, fearing the funds might get diverted elsewhere.

Although Rock Hill has "been out front" in its fight for clean water, Bernard stressed that he and his neighbors are well aware that other communities also need aid.

After all, Rock Hill isn't the area's only community of private well users—and its residents are not the only ones who have tried to get their homes connected to city water. Despite the community fears, CFPUA says it doesn't plan to stray from its decision to deliver assistance to the neighborhood.

Waldroup, with the CFPUA, said that the county has 19,000 private wells overall. One-fifth of those, he said, merited protection under the consent order with Chemours and an even greater number tested positive for PFAS, but did not qualify for protection.[19]

With more testing came more demand for municipal water, but because local utilities only have so many resources, they have had to make tough choices as to where they can extend their water lines. In 2023, North Carolina's state legislature gave CFPUA $18 million dollars to connect underserved and contaminated individuals to city water,[20] but Waldroup said he anticipates needing much more to fix the entire Wilmington-area issue—estimating that the cost could exceed $100 million.

In deciding whom to connect, Waldroup noted that there are several approaches that CFPUA can take: trying to mitigate health risks by connecting people whose wells are most contaminated or trying to reach the maximum number of residents by prioritizing households that are located closest to existing water infrastructure. The third method, he said, could involve accounting for both health impacts and the population's socioeconomic status. That's the approach that CFPUA appears to be endorsing—and the one that might at least get the residents of Rock Hill some reprieve.

Residents have continued to tally names of friends and relatives who suffered from various cancers on Rock Hill's two main streets. By May 2024, the list of such cases grew from Betty's initial 28 to more than 130—people who suffered from cancers of the breast, lung, throat, prostate, stomach, pancreas, colon, cervix, and kidney. And some of the names were familiar ones: four Allens, a Gaines, six Whitteds, and seven Williamses.

In April, Bernard wrote a letter appealing to the county health director for assistance and possible intervention. Specifically, he called upon the county to investigate whether there's an unusually high cancer rate, to connect Rock Hill to a medical research team, and to create an education plan to help residents live healthy lifestyles

Reiterating the dire circumstances Rock Hill is facing in a subsequent phone call, Bernard stressed that such a high incidence of cancer in a single community indicates that "something's wrong."[21]

While there are some solutions on the horizon, the story in Wilmington and other towns along the Cape Fear River is far from over.

As the community has mobilized to stop Chemours, the company has doubled down. The company announced in 2022 that it wanted to expand its production of PFAS at the Fayetteville plant—without a projected increase in its "overall" PFAS emissions. However, local activists oppose the expansion plans.

"When Chemours submitted their plans to expand . . . everybody freaked out," Emily Donovan said. "We don't think Chemours can really be trusted."[22]

Emily even reached out to the United Nations because "our human rights are getting violated"—and the UN agreed, expressing "grave concern" in a statement about the planned expansion. Chemours said that it has taken a "broad and unprecedented set of actions, costing hundreds of millions of dollars, to eliminate almost all PFAS discharges" from the Fayetteville Works plant.[23]

Olszewski, the spokesperson for Chemours, stressed that the company is committed to "health, safety, and reducing our environmental footprint," but did not directly respond to questions asking for elaboration on its expansion plans.[24]

As far as state government is concerned, a DEQ spokesperson said that the department "continues to conduct a comprehensive review" of Chemours's proposal, including a request for additional information from the company as well as holding public hearings and considering public comments.[25]

Meanwhile, scientists at North Carolina universities have sought to figure out what all this forever chemical exposure means, so they launched the "GenX Exposure Study," examining the blood of people from Wilmington and Fayetteville, as well as from Pittsboro—a town fifty miles northwest of Fayetteville that draws its water from the Haw River, which flows into the Cape Fear. Curiously, their first set of findings—blood samples taken from Wilmington-area residents in 2017 and 2018, didn't show any GenX. Instead, it found three "brand-new" PFAS in almost everyone's blood—new PFAS with new acronyms: perfluoro-3,5,7,9-tetraoxadecanoic acid (PFO4DA), per-fluoro-3,5,7,9,11-pentaoxadodecanoic acid (PFO5DoA), and Nafion byproduct 2, with the latter named for a Chemours product.[26]

Nonetheless, not finding GenX doesn't mean that people weren't exposed to it, according to lead investigator Jane Hoppin. Different from some legacy PFAS like PFOA and PFOS—which were found in the people of Wilmington in the study—GenX doesn't last very long in human beings.

"They don't have it in them today, but they did have it in them," said Hoppin, an environmental epidemiologist at North Carolina State University. "We know that some people in Wilmington who lived there for forty years probably drank 700 parts per trillion GenX for forty years, but it doesn't accumulate in the body, so we can't measure that long-term."[27]

But GenX can still have had an impact—even if it's no longer inside a person's body. Hoppin gave a boozy metaphor: "You could drink a drink every Saturday night for forty years and I could measure you the following week and you wouldn't have any alcohol in your body. Doesn't mean that the exposure didn't leave its mark." She also noted that while GenX doesn't last forever in humans, it still builds up in the environment.

It's not totally clear what the health impacts are, if anything, of the PFAS detected in the blood of Wilmington's residents, though a 2022 study in rats found that Nafion byproduct 2 is toxic to fetal development. When fed to the mothers in high doses, the byproduct caused stillbirths, decreased rat pup survival shortly after birth, reduced weight in the pups, and caused liver damage in both pups and mothers. The mothers also showed lower levels of thyroid hormones. The authors concluded that the compound's impacts were slightly less powerful than those of PFOS, but more so than those of GenX.[28]

Wilmington's water woes have become an unremitting match of Whac-A-Mole—every time one type of PFAS is knocked out, another kind rears its ugly head. And despite the city's monumental investment in new treatment facilities, some of those PFAS are managing to break through the filters. Shortly after the massive granular activated carbon system went online in 2022, the utility discovered that certain types of PFAS were sneaking into the water.

These compounds have become known as "ultra-short chain" PFAS, named for how many carbon atoms are found in their chemical structure. With eight carbon atoms, PFOA and PFOS are considered "long-chain," while GenX is considered "short-chain," with six carbon atoms. The "ultra-short-chain" compounds, however, have three or fewer carbon atoms.

The two PFAS that are slipping by are perfluoro-2-methoxyacetic acid (PFMOAA)—the substance that appeared in particularly high levels at Terrel and Donna Allen's childhood home in Rock Hill—and perfluoropropionic acid (PFPrA). As is typical of most emerging compounds, the scientific research on these substances is limited. And yet, as of early 2023, PFMOAA had actually become more common than GenX in the Cape Fear River and was the fourth most prevalent PFAS found in the state's well water, according to a presentation from North Carolina's Department of Environmental Quality (DEQ).[29]

Waldroup, with the CFPUA utility, said that water managers were unaware of Chemours's ultra-short chain discharges when they were choosing a design for their filter.

"We were looking at five or six contaminants," he said.

Research on PFPrA and PFMOAA is limited, but a 2024 rat study conducted by EPA scientists linked PFMOAA to liver damage, deficiency in thyroid hormones, and death of rat pups.[30] Meanwhile, with scant information available about PFPrA, the EPA described evidence of health impacts as "limited"—noting, however, that the lack of data does not equal safety.[31] One study out of China did find that PFPrA exposure was linked to decreased blood sugar levels,[32] while the EPA cites a 2002 study from Japan that found liver damage in rats.[33]

Between PFMOAA and PFPrA, Waldroup said that the utility has particularly focused on the latter, which has been appearing in the community's treated drinking water at a higher rate. Yet from Waldroup's perspective, this news may not be entirely dire—in March 2024, he said that all available data indicates that if this substance poses a public health threat, it only does so "at levels much higher than we are seeing."

"So we feel pretty good that we don't need to adjust our treatment technology just yet, but we are researching that," Waldroup added.[34]

But for Emily Donovan, the discharge of a previously unknown type of PFAS is nothing less than a scandal: another new contaminant for residents to figure out, in the wake of the horrors presented by the GenX compounds that she says have already ravaged her community.

"We should absolutely be outraged about GenX," Emily added. "And we should absolutely be outraged about PFPrA—because we know absolutely nothing about it."

CHAPTER 13

The Real Fix

Emily donovan is not the only one confounded by the Whac-A-Mole nature of the PFAS plague. As scientists rush to understand the threat—and develop solutions—a central challenge is the sheer number of different compounds out there.

Chris Higgins, a professor of civil and environmental engineering at Colorado School of Mines, recalled in January 2024 that fifteen years before, when he first began working on contamination from firefighting foam with Defense Department officials, their initial response was to "just start cleaning stuff up."[1] But he and his colleagues stopped them in their tracks, explaining that they didn't even understand what was in AFFF at that point.

"There's a lot of different chemistries in the foams, particularly the 3M foams," Higgins said. And not all of them show up in standard screenings.

Using a new method in a 2024 study, Higgins and fellow researchers were able to identify eighty-eight types of PFAS in groundwater historically contaminated by AFFF—many of which were novel variations, including precursor compounds. These chemicals, Higgins explained, actually generate other compounds, transforming into PFAS after they are released into the environment. The scientists' conclusion? The risk from the myriad types of PFAS "is likely to be underestimated."[2]

"That's why we're trying to understand that diversity of chemistry," Higgins said. "DOD is well aware of this, and they are, in evaluating treatment technologies, wanting to make sure they're not just addressing the PFOS and PFOA, but everything that we can measure."

Jens Blotevogel, a principal research scientist at Australia's Commonwealth Scientific and Industrial Research Organisation,[3] is likewise on a mission to identify as many kinds of PFAS as possible. And with 10,000, maybe 15,000, out there, that's a lofty goal.

But Blotevogel, who also is affiliated with Colorado State University, is harnessing the best possible technology—(ultra)high-resolution mass spectrometry[4]—to accomplish this ambition. Mass spectrometry is a tool that converts individual molecules into ions and then sorts them by their mass-to-charge ratio: in this case, with the purpose of identifying and quantifying particular kinds of PFAS with utmost precision.[5]

"Let's use the highest-resolving mass spectrometer that we have on this planet to cover as much as we can and maybe settle this," Blotevogel said.[6]

In the endless world of emerging PFAS, it's becoming increasingly clear that the ultra-short-chain subtypes are a troubling new facet of the forever chemical problem, due to their ability to break through filtration barriers. These tiny substances, which are now appearing in Wilmington's water, have just three or fewer carbon atoms—as opposed to the eight or more carbons in longer-chain PFAS or the in-between makeup of short-chain compounds like GenX.

Similar to other PFAS, these ultra-short compounds are beginning to show up in the water—and the blood—of the general population. In a 2023 study of eighty-one people in Indiana, for example, researchers found PFPrA in the blood of 99 percent of participants. Another ultra-short-chain compound, trifluoroacetic acid (TFA), turned up in the blood of 74 percent. The study also detected both compounds in 95 percent of participants' drinking water.

The ultra-short-chain PFAS were not only ubiquitous, but they also made up between 66 and 92 percent of the total PFAS detected in most of the samples taken. As a result, the researchers suspect they may now be "abundant" in humans—though their sources remain unknown.

"Our findings warrant urgent research focused on the ultra-short-chain [PFAS] to elucidate their sources, potential human exposure pathways, and the effects of these exposures on human health," the scientists concluded.[7]

With so many types of PFAS showing up in human bodies, scientists around the world are on a mission to demystify exactly how the compounds are affecting our health. And unfortunately, they're discovering that the consequences are much broader than initially understood. Data has accumulated to show that PFAS can impact a whole host of organs and body systems, including—but not limited to—the brain, gastrointestinal tract, heart, lungs, kidney, and immune function, according to Linda Birnbaum, former director of the federal government's National Institute for Environmental Health Sciences (NIEHS).

"If somebody tells you that they think they have this effect, I think it becomes incumbent to say, 'Well, it could be,'" unless there's clear evidence to the contrary, Birnbaum said.[8]

One scientist researching these effects is Vaia Lida Chatzi, a professor at the University of Southern California's Keck School of Medicine. To Chatzi, the future of PFAS research centers around unraveling the molecular mechanisms that propel these compounds: their modus operandi, so to speak.

By examining "biomarkers," or pinpointing what effects PFAS have on, say, metabolism or inflammation, scientists may be able to get ahead of diseases triggered by the compounds.[9]

"If we manage to have these molecular signatures of PFAS effects in human studies, perhaps you don't have to wait for the disease to manifest—you can have these earlier markers of effects," Chatzi said.[10]

And with the widespread use of big data and machine learning tools, Chatzi expressed confidence that scientists would be able to identify some of these early biomarkers within the next decade. Reducing contact with contaminants while detecting underlying issues through biomarkers, she explained, could stop the illness in its tracks.

At USC's Center for Translational Research on Environmental Health, where Chatzi serves as director, she said that researchers are now exploring potential PFAS impacts by using "organoids"—three-dimensional clusters of organ-specific cells that form microscopic models of actual organs. Her team has been giving their "3D liver organoids" PFAS doses that would be physiologically relevant to humans, with hopes of deciphering the resultant effects on the liver.

As she started to explore potential connections to liver injury, Chatzi recalled feeling "really struck by reviewing the literature," which indicated that studies from thirty years ago had already linked PFAS exposure in mice to such effects. Among those studies were various investigations undertaken by researchers within DuPont, back in the 1960s and '70s.

Chatzi said she is confident in declaring that there is a link between PFAS exposure and nonalcoholic fatty liver disease,[11] although certain elements of the mechanism behind that link are unclear. With that association now established for the non-alcohol-related condition, Chatzi is also exploring whether there is a kind of "synergistic exposure" between PFAS and alcohol consumption.

Since PFAS are already associated with fatty liver disease, she found it natural to pose the question: What about other types of liver disease?

John Adgate, a professor of environmental and occupational health at the Colorado School of Public Health, said that he, too, believes that the link between PFAS exposure and liver disease is a promising research avenue—citing strong animal studies, in particular, that have already established some solid epidemiology on the subject.

Adgate said he was currently applying for a grant to conduct an active human study on this issue, focusing on the El Paso County residents (like Liz Rosenbaum) whom he and his colleagues have sampled and observed via CO SCOPE.[12]

When it comes to diagnosing real-life patients with PFAS-related liver conditions, Chatzi, who is also a physician, explained that clinicians are generally aware of illness that stems from exposure to toxic substances. "So if you have, let's say, a patient with fatty liver disease, and it's not based [on] diet or physical inactivity, then they need to think about environmental drivers of fatty liver disease," Chatzi said.

While Chatzi has long been delving into the destructive potential of PFAS on human health, she expressed some optimism about the future—because of the power of collaboration among scientists, clinicians, and communities.

"Ten years ago, these were emerging chemicals," Chatzi said. "Now we have lots of knowledge—everybody's talking about PFAS, but we didn't know a lot about them."

"What is important for me is that we empower the communities that are impacted by PFAS exposure and advocate for solutions," she continued. "It's important that any new data that we generate, any new research that we do on PFAS, is focused more on the needs of the community."

Another physician-scientist who embodies that drive for community involvement is Rachel Criswell in Maine, who has long been treating patients like Fred Stone and the Higginses, but who also is involved in several research initiatives on PFAS.

Criswell has already completed several community-based studies about PFAS, and as of March 2024, she and Abby Fleisch, a

Portland-based MaineHealth pediatric endocrinologist, were in the middle of new research project. They had recruited and enrolled 150 participants and sampled their blood, with the goal of understanding how PFAS from sludge in farming communities makes its way into residents' bodies. Criswell and Fleisch also intend to study the mental health effects caused by the ongoing crisis. Beyond problems brought on by stress, they are investigating whether PFAS can cause physical changes that affect mental health.

For instance, might PFAS exposure change the bacteria and viruses in the gut? A wide body of research has already established a link between such changes and conditions like depression and anxiety. They have therefore taken fecal samples from participants, to see what, if any, relationship PFAS exposure might have with this inner microbiome.

Criswell's earliest research on PFAS exposure was tied to breastfeeding, exploring whether the compounds affected nursing milk and could possibly be passed to infants.[13] But this type of research comes with complications, as it's impossible to do a randomized or controlled clinical trial. Instead, scientists need to locate so-called exposure cohorts—nursing individuals who live in high-risk areas.

Stressing that she remains "so pro-lactation," Criswell said she has yet to advise against breastfeeding—although she also hasn't yet had any patients who were exposed to high levels of PFAS and were also nursing. But if she did, she said she would discuss the risks and benefits with the parents and set their babies up with a pediatric endocrinologist for future monitoring.

"It's really needed, especially for these kids with high levels of exposure," she said, noting her interest in understanding the differences between standard, while unsafe, levels of PFAS versus extreme exposure.[14]

Criswell is also looking at reducing the body's PFAS burden in a procedure similar to donating blood. An April 2022 study of Australian firefighters showed that routine plasma removals could reduce PFAS blood levels by 30 percent.[15] Removals of blood were effective as well, but less so than those of plasma. Meanwhile, a 2023 report from Jersey—a Channel Island off the coast of northwest France—similarly recommended a "phlebotomy" service that would take a pint (US units) of blood from firefighters exposed to PFAS.[16]

Along these lines, scientists are also exploring the ways menstruation can provide "a unique route of elimination," according to Suzanne Fenton, director of North Carolina State University's Center for Human Health and the Environment and a former researcher at the National Toxicology Program.[17] Already in 2014, scientists found that menstruation might be responsible for a considerable difference in male and female PFAS blood levels.[18]

"Some PFAS bind strongly to proteins in blood, and when women menstruate, they lose those blood proteins linked to PFAS," Fenton said.[19]

PFAS are not only coursing through the blood vessels of virtually every American, but they are also percolating in the plumbing of every US household. While pipes cannot benefit from the cathartic capabilities of phlebotomy or menstruation, the country's water systems are responsive to three main types of purification technologies. Reverse osmosis, the setup in Brenda Hampton's area of Alabama, involves pushing water through a semipermeable membrane, which removes contaminants like PFAS and prevents them from passing into the resultant clean water stream.[20] While effective, this technology is expensive and also consumes a lot of energy and water.[21]

A second method of filtering out PFAS is called ion exchange, the system of choice in El Paso County, Colorado. Although the specific ions used can vary, this region relies on a "resin" dotted with positively charged beads and soaked in saltwater, from which the material attracts negatively charged chloride ions. Once PFAS-polluted water is added to the system, negatively charged PFAS ions swap places with chloride, which binds to sodium in the water to regenerate the non-harmful byproduct of salt[22]—along with a PFAS-laden resin that eventually must be discarded.[23]

Granular activated carbon (GAC), the system of choice in Wilmington, North Carolina, uses spongy, carbon-based materials like coal to trap and remove contaminants. When raw water rushes through the system, PFAS are attracted to the material and end up filling in vacant spaces in the coal.[24] Once those caverns are clogged, the carbon then needs to be replaced.

While all three of these mechanisms—reverse osmosis, ion exchange resin, and GAC—effectively remove PFAS from drinking water, the compounds don't evaporate into thin air. In fact, they often become someone else's problem, in a toxic waste dump across state lines or festering in the flames of an incineration site. And yet—scientists are now making the impossible possible, finding viable ways to break apart and finally eliminate a monster that humans created.

David Trueba, president and CEO of the PFAS destruction company Revive Environmental, likened the prospect of breaking up "the strongest bond in chemistry" to "playing Red Rover with these molecules"—referencing the childhood game in which a player must run toward the opposing team's lineup with hopes of rupturing their human chain. Tearing PFAS molecules apart, Trueba explained, requires both direct access to the compounds and sufficient energy to break a bond as strong as "The Rock and John Cena holding hands."[25]

Some of that work has started occurring at sites like Peterson Space Force Base. Although years of lag in federal regulation of PFAS slowed the pace at which the site's official cleanup could progress, movement on the issue didn't stop them entirely. Sean Houseworth, of the Air Force Civil Engineer Center, highlighted the on-site research potential of the base, which has played host to some twenty different treatment and remediation studies.

"In a general sense, okay, you clean it, but what do you do with the byproduct?" Houseworth asked.[26]

Numerous researchers are exploring what to do with that byproduct—including academic laboratories, such as that of Chris Higgins at the Colorado School of Mines, as well as companies like Battelle and Noreas. And many of these efforts have been engaged in PFAS destruction.

"There's a lot of activity and there's a lot of, I would say, optimism—at the end of day, it is going to come down to cost," Higgins said. "There are off-the-shelf technologies that work for removing PFAS from water—what everyone wants to do is take it to the next stage and not just remove them from water but also destroy them."

Blotevogel, the scientist in Australia who has been working to identify thousands of PFAS compounds, is also researching ways to demolish them. Noting that industry has thus far largely focused on breaking them down via incineration, Blotevogel said that this approach is inefficient when battling a problem as large as PFAS.

From a technical perspective, incineration does degrade PFAS, as these compounds "do break down thermally," according to Blotevogel. As of May 2024, however, the United States had a moratorium on such activities, awaiting the Defense Department's publication of final safety guidelines.[27] Incineration of PFAS results in byproducts like carbon monoxide, carbon dioxide, water, hydrogen fluoride, and sulfur molecules.[28]

"People are concerned [about] what comes out of the smokestack," Blotevogel said.

And then there's the sheer amount of PFAS all over the world, making the idea of burning it all a formidable and inordinately expensive task, Blotevgoel explained. He described all the biosolids and PFAS-impacted solid waste as "the big elephant in the room."

But scientists in laboratories across the world are rising to the challenge, with several innovative techniques for breaking down PFAS—some of which are market-ready.

One is electrochemical oxidation, the process by which voltage is applied to break down organic compounds in wastewater.[29] As electrical current passes between submerged, conductive metal plates called electrodes, the influx of current "breaks all these bonds," Blotevogel explained. Once the voltage is high enough, the PFAS give up an electron to the positive electrode—triggering a chain reaction that transforms pollutant into harmless fluoride and trace amounts of carbon dioxide.

Blotevogel and his colleagues in a 2019 study tested the effectiveness of electrochemical oxidation on degrading GenX, after the compound was filtered out of a wastewater stream. They found it was effective—and more efficient when applied to filtered GenX rather than raw water.[30] While costs still remain high, Blotevogel said that certain smaller companies can already come with trailers to treat liquid waste streams with this breakdown method. Some of these startups, such as the Massachusetts-based Aclarity, are offering such services at industrial sites, municipal facilities, landfills, and airports.

The second of the three PFAS degradation methods flagged by Blotevogel, low-temperature plasma treatment, centers around the formation of plasma—matter created by either heating or applying voltage to a gas in such a way that the resultant positively and negatively charged ions have enough energy to separate from each other.[31]

By bubbling gas that contains these unhinged ions through a solution, the plasma treatment can bring the PFAS to what Blotevogel described as a "gas–water interface"—a no-man's-land where PFAS tend to gravitate because they "don't like to be really in water or in gas." At that interface, the highly energetic, charged particles within the plasma bubble are able to rip apart the tightly bound molecules that make up PFAS.[32]

The third technique Blotevogel mentioned, sonolysis, involves using ultrasound at specific frequencies to generate "cavitation bubbles"—essentially "small holes in the water"—that engulf the PFAS and then collapse. The energy consumption for this approach is greater than that of other technologies, but the method results in a complete breakdown without producing persistent byproducts.[33]

Although his research has largely focused on electrochemical oxidation, Blotevogel said that he doesn't believe that one type of PFAS degradation is superior. Rather, due to the scope of the PFAS problem, he stressed the need to develop "as many technologies as we can."

One of the institutions that has long been trying to eradicate PFAS is Battelle Memorial Institute—an independent, nonprofit applied science and technology organization.

In January 2023, Battelle launched Revive Environmental, a company dedicated to PFAS destruction and headed by Trueba.[34]

Revive might be a new venture in name, but Battelle's work with PFAS is not. The organization has been doing PFAS testing since about 1998 and ended up working with Rob Bilott to do the medical tests and data aggregation for Wilbur Tennant's landmark case in West Virginia. While Battelle has long worked with a spectrum of government entities and companies, including 3M, to track PFAS, Trueba said that it wasn't until 2018 that a research group recognized the need "to close this recycle loop that's in the industry."

"You can put it in a landfill, you can deep-well inject it. You can incinerate it, but it goes in the air," he continued. "How do we stop PFAS from being in the water, but then if we take it out, we don't put it back somewhere where it gets back into the water?"

Revive's PFAS Annihilator technology is powered by a chemical reaction in "supercritical water"—water that is neither in a liquid nor gas state but has properties of both, under specific high-temperature and high-pressure conditions.[35] At that point, gases that don't typically dissolve in water can do so, creating what Trueba described as a "super solvent fluid."

Because supercritical water is highly expandable and compressible, chemical reactions and the transfer of mass can occur with fewer restrictions. The technology incorporates readily available oxidants—compounds, such as air or hydrogen peroxide, that accept electrons from other substances—to catalyze the breakdown of the formidable carbon-fluorine bonds and leave behind PFAS-free water, carbon dioxide, and inert salts.

The thirty- to forty-five-second process takes place in a reactor that can be housed in a twenty-foot container and that keeps water in that high-temperature, high-pressure state, Trueba noted. And if the PFAS arrives in concentrated form, following filtration, the reactor can treat the equivalent of a half a million gallons of raw wastewater per day.

As of March 2024, Revive had seven commercial systems built—four of which would be operational by the middle of April, while the other three would be running within six months. The company has the supply chain capability to build one every twelve weeks if there is enough demand for such a rollout, Trueba said.

Revive deployed its first commercial-scale PFAS Annihilator in May 2023 at a wastewater treatment facility in Grand Rapids, Michigan. The plant was working with multiple area landfills at the time to transport, separate, and concentrate their wastewater—with the ultimate goal of processing between 300 and 500 gallons per day, stemming from a total of 300,000 to 500,000 gallons of raw water prior to concentration.[36] This amounts to between a third and a half of the state's total landfill leachate, as of 2019.[37]

Among the filtration technologies that work together with the PFAS Annihilator is Revive's own granular activated carbon system, called GAC Renew. Trueba said he estimates that by 2030, about 60–70 percent of water treatment systems will be using granular activated carbon as a low-cost, high-flow way of removing PFAS. But because most of these devices are single-use, PFAS-filled filters often end up in landfills, he noted. With GAC Renew, Revive can remove the contaminants from the carbon—and thereby use the carbon repeatedly—and then transfer the residual PFAS to the Annihilator for destruction.

Despite these and other technological advances in the quest to break down PFAS, Trueba said he still views PFAS as essentially "forever" substances. "What we're talking about now is not a generational chemical," he said. "We're talking about a societal systemic problem that, if we do nothing, we will have a societal issue very soon."

But with the evolving technologies emerging on the market, Trueba also found some room for hope. And he stressed that no single company will be acting alone—there are all the startups and scientists developing the technologies that Blotevogel detailed, as well as a major Tacoma, Washington–based innovator Aquagga, which is also deploying trailers nationwide.

"Candidly, we're only a drop in the bucket of the solution," he said, noting that many companies with diverse toolsets will need to work together. "There are real solutions that are going to make a huge difference. And not just in five years. We're ready now."

Scientific strides and regulations notwithstanding, experts remain uncertain as to whether the end of the road for PFAS is approaching.

Birnbaum, the former head of the NIEHS, was hopeful that the EPA's action to regulate PFAS in drinking water would allow the United States to "dramatically reduce the levels of all PFAS."[38] Nonetheless, she still expressed concerns about the evasive, ultra-short-chain compounds that are capable of breaking barriers and that "won't be removed by the filtration systems."

Likewise, former EPA official Betsy Southerland was optimistic about getting contamination out of drinking water. But she was less convinced about the prospects of cleaning up other sources of PFAS pollution,[39] given that drinking water only accounts for around 20 percent of exposure for the general population.[40]

"They're in so many products—that's where this becomes really complex from a regulatory standpoint: cosmetics, dental floss, food packaging, cookware, clothing, all kinds of special industrial-use products," Southerland said, specifically referring to short-chain PFAS.

Even though such compounds don't last as long, they still pose a threat because "our bodies are bombarded with them by so many different sources," she added.[41]

The "real fix," from Southerland's perspective, would be for the EPA to stop "all new PFAS from coming on the market," while also banning or restricting existing ones—or a congressional ban. Yet even if such action occurred today, Southerland stressed that minimizing the PFAS "that are already out in the environment" would also be a formidable task.

Contemplating the tremendous toll that PFAS have taken on the global population, Adgate, from the Colorado School of Public Health, emphasized the need to assess "the whole picture." Rather than looking at one individual or disease at a single moment, he suggested "following people over time," while acknowledging that such a pursuit could take decades.

"We're planting trees that other people are going to harvest, so to speak," he said.

And in Colorado Springs, one of the roots of those trees maintained her resolve as she tabulated the sprawling set of tattoos along her arms. The shit-stirring spoon was deliberately "blue for water," while the cherry blossoms were emblematic of "getting laws passed" in Washington, DC. A steaming mug atop a stack of books? Her belief that "you can solve everything over a cup of coffee." Liz Rosenbaum then gestured toward a recent addition: a phoenix "coming out of the ashes" with an envelope—which she said could be a ballot, or PFAS data.

Lamenting that she's "running out of room," Liz was determined to make space on her body to ink one of her many three-ringed binders: the treasure troves that bear witness to her journey for justice.

As scientists, regulators, and activists fight for solutions, PFAS are coursing through the bloodstream of virtually every American—and inflicting damage as they spread. But ordinary people are opening their eyes to this contamination crisis. They're taking pains to avoid PFAS-polluted products, they're pressuring politicians, and ultimately, they're fighting back.

"My Life Won't Be in Vain"

IF ANYONE KNOWS WHAT IT MEANS TO FIGHT BACK, it's Brenda Hampton. Unwittingly stuck in the epicenter of an environmental disaster, she has suffered terrible consequences—and she is exhausted. But she keeps advocating for her community and does "see things changing," now that the crisis isn't just at her back door.

"Now it's at everyone's back door," Brenda said, over the phone in early April 2024.[1]

Stressing that these man-made chemicals had "gotten out of control," Brenda recognized that it took some time for the nation as a whole to recognize the gravity of the problem.

"At first, people didn't really understand," she said. "I had to educate myself about PFOS and PFOA. They didn't understand the depth of it and how a lot of things that we use daily contains these chemicals."

Despite sensing a palpable change in the air, Brenda reiterated the persistent power that these substances have over people as they linger in the human body. And the death toll has continued to rise in her immediate area. Brenda counted fourteen people in her community who had passed just in the previous four months.

Among those individuals were her sister Jacqueline—whom Brenda had left just a half hour before she died—and Buster Branham, the Wesley Acres resident whom she attended to regularly. Her "list" of people she visits and cares for has significantly dwindled in recent months, Brenda lamented.

The weariness audible in her voice, Brenda expressed her frustration at constantly feeling threatened as she has pursued this forever fight. She recounted getting held at gunpoint by an unfamiliar White man in a Walmart three weeks before, stressing, however, that she had no idea what his motive was.

"When he showed me his gun, I said, 'Oh, you've got a little Glock,'" Brenda recounted. "I said, 'I tell you what, I got a .357 Magnum in my handbag and I'm not fucking afraid to use it.' His eyes got real big. He said, 'You do?'"

Brenda did not actually have her gun in her purse that day, but the man didn't know that—and he darted away. She had stopped carrying it several years earlier, when things had calmed down.

"Now I'm back to carrying," she said.

Asked about her own health, Brenda replied that everything was "looking good," as her four-month-old granddaughter squealed in the background. Despite her low heart rate of 40 beats per minute and her stage 3a kidney failure, she reported a normal blood pressure of 97/63 and considered herself "on the straight and narrow." Yet when her nephrologist recently told her that she would likely need dialysis in the next five years, Brenda refuted his prognosis.

"I told him I probably won't even be here then, because I'm sixty-eight now," she recalled. "I've been fighting a long time, and I think it's time for my body to rest. I think God has just been blessing me."

Just a couple hours after that April 9, 2024, phone call, Brenda's world once again turned upside down. While still home alone with her baby granddaughter, she had a second heart attack. When she suddenly started feeling nauseated and her blood pressure rose to 169/149, she called her older granddaughter, a tenth grader at a high school nearby, to come and drive her to the hospital.

After an initial admission to Parkway Medical Center in Decatur, Brenda was transferred to Helen Keller Hospital in Sheffield, about forty miles northwest, and then to Huntsville Hospital. On Sunday, April 14, she relayed by text that she was "not doing well"[2] and that her blood pressure had dropped to 65/45 and her heart rate was still at 40. And because of her kidney failure, her cardiologist couldn't use contrast—a dye that helps doctors see heart issues in more detail.

"This is my second heart attack from these chemicals," Brenda wrote.

Although she was still having trouble walking on her own, Brenda was released soon after to her daughter's house in Decatur. She was equipped with a medical watch to track her blood pressure, heart rate, and oxygen levels, while receiving heart catheterization for a blockage and treatment for simultaneous pancreas and colon infections.

"I'm a wreck," she texted, noting that this experience was nothing like her first heart attack. "It indicates to me the chemicals are getting worse in my body."

Yet even in illness, Brenda was keenly observant, describing how she had noticed "the uncertainty the doctors have on their face."

"I feel God isn't through with me yet; he has something else for me to do," she wrote. "But I have to be real with myself."

As feelings of hope alternated with a sense of resignation and fear, Brenda acknowledged her teetering odds while also praying for a miracle.

"I can feel good knowing that the work and my life won't be in vain," she wrote. "That out of all this, if I can help just one person it will be worth it."

Acknowledgments

When Brenda Hampton endured her second heart attack, the bonds among America's PFAS activists community were clear, and perhaps even more formidable than the carbon-fluoride connections that make up the compounds themselves.

Liz Rosenbaum, who was with family in Alabama at the time, was quick to make a bedside visit to Brenda, who has become one of the core members of a cross-country PFAS family. But Liz stressed the fact that she wasn't alone—she texted that their "BIG coalition group chipped in money thanks to Emily Donovan coordinating it." Mark Favors, who also knows Brenda, made sure to check in as well.

These ever-expanding connections have shown us that the fight against forever chemical contamination could not have advanced without this diverse network of individuals, who have long understood that "it takes a village." As such, we would like to thank the members of our own personal and professional villages for their assistance with our book and support throughout the process.

We would also like to express our sincere appreciation for the community members who shared their time and often very personal stories with us—opening their doors and welcoming us into their homes and neighborhoods. It is our sincere hope that we have reflected your experience and endurance with accuracy and sensitivity on these pages.

Our utmost thanks to Emily Turner, our editor at Island Press, for believing that the PFAS story was one that needs to be told and that we were ones who should tell it. Her experience, thoughtful suggestions, and patience for us as new authors helped make this manuscript the best it could be. Thank you to Kim Lindman, our agent at Stonesong, for supporting our project from our initial query, remaining a fierce advocate on our behalf, and helping us to resolve initial differences in our vision.

We are also grateful to the Fund for Investigative Journalism, whose award enabled a great deal of our work, especially our on-the-ground reporting. In addition to providing funding, this grant connected us with Jen Nelson and Julia Dacy at the Reporters Committee for Freedom of the Press, who provided us with a generous amount of legal expertise.

Spoorthy Raman was an indefatigable fact-checker, whose thoroughness and willingness to work on an expedited schedule greatly improved our manuscript. Jamie DeWitt, Linda Birnbaum, and Robert Laumbach offered their toxicological expertise as we sought to understand the underlying science of PFAS.

Thank-you to our colleagues at *The Hill*, who encouraged us to pursue this project and understood as we juggled it with our day jobs. Particularly, we'd like to acknowledge Ian Swanson, Bob Cusack, Annika Neklason, Zack Budryk, and Saul Elbein.

We would also like to express our appreciation to all of our friends and family who stuck by us throughout this process. Sharon would like to thank her husband, Ravid Shaniv, for his unwavering partnership, and her children, Amit and Eden, for understanding why their mom was always at the computer on weekends. She is also grateful to her parents,

Iris and Gary Udasin, and brother Ronald Udasin for their lifelong support, and to all her in-laws for their encouragement from across the world. Rachel would like to thank her parents, Randi and Dan Frazin, her brother, Matt Frazin, and her grandfathers, Barry Shlissel and Bob Frazin, for constantly cheering her on and occasionally chastising her to get the book done.

As we put this work of rigor and resolve out into the world, we are grateful to all of the people, named in the book or not, who took time—and in many cases had the courage—to help us better understand the PFAS plague.

Notes

Introduction

1. Brenda Hampton, personal interview, January 7, 2022.
2. Erin Brockovich, personal interview, May 20, 2022.
3. Ryan C. Lewis et al., "Serum Biomarkers of Exposure to Perfluoroalkyl Substances in Relation to Serum Testosterone and Measures of Thyroid Function among Adults and Adolescents from NHANES 2011–2012," *International Journal of Environmental Research and Public Health* (May 29, 2015), https://www.mdpi.com/1660-4601/12/6/6098.

Chapter 1

1. Brenda Hampton, personal interview, March 26, 2023.
2. Brenda Hampton, personal interview, January 7, 2022; Sharon Udasin and Rachel Frazin, "Justice for PFAS exposure races a ticking clock," *The Hill*, January 25, 2022, https://thehill.com/policy/equilibrium-sustainability/590622-justice-for-pfas-exposure-confronts-ticking-clock/.
3. Brenda Hampton, personal interview, March 26, 2023.
4. Brenda Hampton, personal interview, June 2, 2023.
5. "Joan Rines Needleman" (1916–1997), Find a Grave, https://www.findagrave.com/memorial/128290892/joan-needleman, accessed November 14, 2024.
6. Brenda Hampton, personal interview, March 26, 2023.
7. Brenda Hampton, personal interview, February 16, 2022.
8. Brenda Hampton, personal interview, March 27, 2023.
9. "Roy J. Plunkett," Science History Institute, December 15, 2023, https://sciencehistory.org/education/scientific-biographies/roy-j-plunkett/; "Roy Plunkett | Teflon | Consumer Devices," Lemelson MIT, Massachusetts Institute of Technology, https://lemelson.mit.edu/resources/roy-plunkett, accessed November 14, 2024.

10. "Roy Plunkett and the Discovery of Teflon," Manchester University, YouTube, April 6, 2017, https://www.youtube.com/watch?v=_99DFRHS8SA.

11. "Monomers and the man: The origin of a legend," *Journal of Teflon*, 1963.

12. "Roy Plunkett and the Discovery of Teflon."

13. "Monomers and the man."

14. Anne Cooper Funderburg, "Making Teflon Stick," *Invention & Technology Magazine* 16, no. 1 (Summer 2000), https://www.inventionandtech.com/content/making-teflon-stick-1.

15. Funderburg, "Making Teflon Stick."

16. "Roy J. Plunkett," Science History Institute.

17. Alex Hutchinson, *Big Ideas: 100 Modern Inventions That Have Transformed Our World* (New York: Sterling, 2009).

18. Funderburg, "Making Teflon Stick."

19. Pierre Beccu, producer, "Tefal, Une Histoire Attachante," YouTube, March 21, 2013, https://www.youtube.com/watch?v=rgP-TZQ8yIs; Nicolas Truffet, director, *Une Histoire Attachante* (film), Bas Canal Productions, 2010, http://bascanal.fr/prodtestpb/portfolio/une-histoire-attachante/.

20. "Rumilly, the World Frying Pan Capital," Groupe SEB, May 4, 2024, https://www.groupeseb.com/en/webzine/rumilly-world-frying-pan-capital.

21. Funderburg, "Making Teflon Stick."

22. Jonathan Woodham, "A Dictionary of Modern Design," 2nd ed. (Oxford, UK: Oxford University Press, 2016).

23. Wikimedia Commons. "Amazing New Concept in Cooking," Happy Pan Poster, https://upload.wikimedia.org/wikipedia/commons/thumb/7/73/Happy_Pan_Poster.jpg/170px-Happy_Pan_Poster.jpg, accessed November 14, 2024; Teflon DuPont Original Advert 1971 (ref AD4676), The Nostalgia Shop, United Kingdom, https://www.thenostalgiashop.co.uk, accessed November 14, 2024.

24. Kate Collins, "Mad Men Monday, Episode 3," Duke University Libraries: The Devil's Tale, April 22, 2013, https://blogs.library.duke.edu/rubenstein/2013/04/15/mad-men-monday-episode-3/.

25. Alamy Limited, 1970s UK Teflon Saucepans Magazine Advert, https://www.alamy.com/stock-photo-1970s-uk-teflon-saucepans-magazine-advert-85334228.html, accessed November 14, 2024.

26. Jon Avise, "3M plant grew along with its home city," *Republican Eagle*, October 1, 2008.

27. Avise, "3M plant."

28. "3M Cottage Grove—3M Plant Locations in the United States," 3M, https://www.3m.com/3M/en_US/plant-locations-us/cottagegrove/, accessed November 14, 2024.

29. "Innovative Lives: Patsy Sherman, Go Ahead—Put Your Feet on the Furniture," Lemelson Center for the Study of Invention and Innovation, https://invention.si.edu/invention-stories/innovative-lives-patsy-sherman-go-ahead-put-your-feet-furniture, accessed November 14, 2024.

30. Brenda Hampton, personal interview, March 26, 2023.

31. For example, see: "John McMahon House," National Register of Historic Places Registration Form, NPS Form 10-900, National Park Service, Department of the Interior, October 27, 1987, https://npgallery.nps.gov/NRHP/GetAsset/NRHP/87001454 _text.

32. John Allison, personal interview, March 27, 2023.

33. Brenda Hampton, personal interview, March 26, 2023.

34. Brenda Hampton, personal interview, January 7, 2022.

35. "A Brief History of Decatur, Alabama," River City Kiwanis Club, 2004; O. S. Hagerman, "Locate in Decatur," Decatur, Alabama, Chamber of Commerce, January 1961.

36. Brenda Hampton, personal interview, March 27, 2023.

37. Patrice Stewart, "Phil Raths always puts his head in the mission," *Decatur Daily*, November 5, 2000.

38. William H. Jenkins and John Knox, "The Story of Decatur, Alabama," City of Decatur, 1970.

39. "Decatur Alabama: Where Industry Is Welcome," *Alabama Development News*, Alabama Development Office, Montgomery, AL, May 1976.

40. Hagerman, "Locate in Decatur."

41. Lucy Berry, "Shaken by International Paper Closure, Courtland Receives $32K Grant to Begin Long-range Recovery Plan," Alabama Media Group, November 18, 2014.

42. "Employment—Decatur city, Alabama," US Census Bureau, https://data.census.gov /profile/Decatur_city,_Alabama.

43. "Courtland town, Alabama" and "North Courtland town, Alabama," US Census Bureau, https://data.census.gov, accessed November 14, 2024.

44. Gloria Guzman and Melissa Kollar, "Income in the United States: 2022," US Census Bureau, September 12, 2023, https://www.census.gov/library/publications/2023 /demo/p60-279.html.

45. Brenda Hampton, personal interview, February 16, 2022.

Chapter 2

1. D. Kenwin Harris, "Polymer-fume fever," *The Lancet* (December 1951).

2. L. H. Cirker, internal DuPont memo to B. N. Epstein, September 2, 1959.

3. G. J. Mack, "Toxicity of Decomposition Products of 'Teflon,'" *Canadian Medical Association Journal* 85 (October 21, 1961); G. J. Mack, "Toxicity of Decomposition Products of 'Teflon,'" *Canadian Medical Association Journal* (December 16, 1961), https://pmc.ncbi.nlm.nih.gov/articles/PMC1848625/.

4. John A. Zapp Jr., *The Anatomy of a Rumor*, E. I. Du Pont De Nemours & Company, n.d.

5. Gordon Nordby and J. Murray Luck, "Perfluorooctanoic Acid Interactions with Human Serum Albumin," *Journal of Biological Chemistry* 219, no. 1 (March 1956), https://www.jbc.org/article/S0021-9258(18)65805-3/pdf.

6. B. S. Oppenheimer et al., "Further Studies of Polymers as Carcinogenic Agents in Animals," *Cancer Research* 15, no. 5 (June 1, 1955), https://aacrjournals.org/cancerres /article/15/5/333/473178/Further-Studies-of-Polymers-as-Carcinogenic-Agents.

7. Dorothy Hood, "Toxicity of Teflon Dispersing Agents," internal DuPont memo, November 9, 1961, EPA Administrative Record (AR) 226-1442.

8. G. W. H. Schepers, "Ammonium Perfluorocaprylate (C8APFC)," DuPont internal memo, February 9, 1962, AR 226-1442, 25.

9. "Surfactant," *Encyclopedia Britannica*, https://www.britannica.com/science/surfactant, accessed April 4, 2024.

10. John Barnes and Henry Sherman, "Effect of fluorocarbon dispersing agents on the livers of rats and dogs," Haskell Laboratory internal memo, August 19, 1965, AR 226-1443.

11. Francis X. Wazeter et al., "90-Day Feeding Study in the Beagle Dog," November 30, 1965, AR 226-2825.

12. Henry McNulty, letter to FDA, National Archives (College Park, MD), 1959.

13. A. J. Lehman, letter to Henry McNulty, National Archives (College Park, MD), February 1959.

14. A. J. Lehman, letter to Henry McNulty, National Archives (College Park, MD), March 2, 1959.

15. M. I. Bro, "FDA clearance for the use of TFE resin coated cooking utensils in domestic applications—visit with the FDA," DuPont internal memo, October 1, 1959, Hagley Library (Wilmington, DE).

16. C. F. Reinhardt Jr. et al., "Ninety-Day Feeding Study in Rats and Dogs with Zonyl RP," Haskell Laboratory, February 23, 1973, EWG PFAS timeline, https://static.ewg .org/reports/2019/pfa-timeline/3M-DuPont-Timeline_sm.pdf.

17. W. S. Guy, D. R. Taves, and W. S. Brey, "Organic Fluorocompounds in Human Plasma: Prevalence and Characterization," *ACS Symposium Series* (June 1, 1976): 117–34.

18. J. D. LaZerte, memo to L.C. Krogh, 3M, Office of Minnesota Attorney General Keith Ellison: 3M Lawsuit, August 22, 1975, https://www.ag.state.mn.us/Office /Cases/3M /docs/PTX/PTX2771.pdf; G. H. Crawford, "Record of a Telephone Conversation— August 14, 1975," memo, Office of Minnesota Attorney General Keith Ellison: 3M Lawsuit, August 20, 1975, https://www.ag.state.mn.us/Office/Cases/3M/docs/PTX /PTX1118.pdf.

19. "Blood Levels of RF/F in Selected Employees," 3M internal memo, June 20, 1978, AR 226-0479.

20. B. C. McKusick, "Discussion of Fluorochemicals with 3M," DuPont internal memo, July 23, 1979, AR 226-1459.

21. Sidney Pell, "Chambers Works Fluorosurfactant Study," DuPont internal memo, March 15, 1979, AR 226-1457

22. A. R. Behnke, memo to J. F. Hunt, DuPont, March 15, 1981, AR 226-1967.

23. Ibid.

24. George Hegg, "Section 8(e) Toxic Substances control act (TSCA) Perfluoroalkane Carboxylic Acids and Corresponding Ammonium Carboxylates," 3M, March 20, 1981, AR 226-1373

25. "Employee Communication", DuPont, March 31, 1981, AR 226-1374.

26. Bruce Karrh, memo to C. De Martino, "Ammonium Perfluorooctanoate (FC-143) C-8 Compounds," DuPont, March 25, 1981, AR 226-1375.

27. Lowell Ludford, 3M draft press statement: FC-143 Decatur, the office of Minnesota attorney general Keith Ellison: 3M Lawsuit, April 15, 1981, https://www.ag.state.mn .us/Office/Cases/3M/docs/PTX/PTX1253.pdf.

28. Joe Loschario, "C-8 Plant Staff Meeting," November 25, 1981, AR 226-1992.

29. Judy Walrath and Cherry Burke, "An Investigation into the Occurrence of Leukemia at Washington Works," DuPont, April 1989, AR 226-1308-1; H.A. Smith, "Washington Works Cancer Incidence and Overall Mortality Rates," DuPont, December 14, 1989, AR 226-1545.

30. "Organic Fluoride in the Blood," 3M internal memo, attached to letter from L. Zobel, 1987.

31. Carolyn LaViolette, email correspondence, May 6, 2024.

32. "Analysis of Selected Decatur Employee Serum for Sulfonic and Carboxylic Fluorochemicals," 3M, October 4, 1979, EPA Administrative Record (AR) 226-0034; James E. Gagnon, "Fluorochemicals in Tennessee River Fish," 3M, 1979, AR 226-0371; D. E. Roach and S. D. Sorenson, memo to J. Webster, "1983 Decatur Blood Fluoride Review," 3M, January 20, 1984, AR 226-0174; Geary Olsen et. al., "Fluorochemical Exposure Assessment of Decatur Chemical and Film Plant Employees," 3M, September 3, 1998, AR 226-0950.

33. Charles Reich, letter to US Environmental Protection Agency, "TSCA Section 8(e)— Perfluorooctane Sulfonate," 3M, 1998, https://static.ewg.org/reports/2020/pfas-epa -timeline/1998_3M-Alerts-EPA.pdf.

34. Geary Olsen et al., "An Epidemiologic Analysis of Episodes of Care of 3M Decatur Chemical and Film Plant Employees, 1993–1998," 3M, 2001.

35. James E. Gagnon, "Fluorochemicals in Tennessee River Fish," 3M, 1979, AR 226-0371.

36. "Daikin America Decatur Plant Monitoring," Daikin, January 15, 2004, AR 226-2353.

37. "Hydrogen Fluoride," American Chemical Society Molecule of the Week Archive, July 12, 2021, https://www.acs.org/molecule-of-the-week/archive/h/hydrogen-fluoride .html.

38. Christopher Barton, "The worst that could happen: Area companies describe their ultimate potential disaster, but they're highly unlikely to occur," *Decatur Daily*, November 14, 1999.

39. Dawn Kent, "3M diversifies, seeks wider product range," *Decatur Daily*, December 24, 2000.

40. Ibid.

41. "Fluorochemical Characterization of Surface Water Samples: Decatur, Alabama (W1979)," report prepared for 3M by Centre Analytical Laboratory, Revised: March 21 and 26, 2001, AR 226-1030a134 and AR 226-1030a140; "Fluorochemical Characterization of Sediment, POTW Sludge, and Landfill Leachate Samples: Decatur, AL (W1979)," Revised: March 28, 2001, AR 226-1030a146; John Giesy and John Newsted, "Selected Fluorochemicals in the Decatur, Alabama, Area," report prepared

for 3M by Entrix, Inc., 2001 and 2002, AR 226-1109 and AR 226-1364; Mark Ellefson, "Tennessee River Valley Samples," 3M, 2002 and 2003, AR 226-1365 and AR 226-1733.

42. "EPA Efforts to Reduce Exposure to Carcinogens and Prevent Cancer," US Environmental Protection Agency, updated March 20, 2024.

43. Giesy and Newsted, AR 226-1364.

44. Robert Laumbach, email correspondence, March 10, 2024.

45. "Fluorochemical Characterization of Sediment, POTW Sludge, and Landfill Leachate Samples, Decatur AL," Centre Analytical Research Laboratories report based on samples from the 3M Environmental Laboratory, March 28, 2001, AR 226-1030a146.

46. "Offsite Sampling PFOA Concentrations: Decatur, AL," Weston, AR 226-3722; Michelle Malinsky, "Analysis of PFBS, PFHS and PFOS in water, soil, sediment, fish, clams, vegetation, small mammal liver and small mammal serum," Interim Reports nos. 5, 15, and 18, 3M, 2005–2006, AR 226-3798a2, AR 226-3798a4, AR 226-3798a6; Susan Wolf, "Analysis of PFBS, PFHS and PFOS in water, soil, sediment, fish clams, vegetation, small mammal liver and small mammal serum," Interim Report no. 20, 3M, 2007, AR 226-3798a7.

47. Jackson Thornton, "West Morgan–East Lawrence Water and Sewer Authority Financial Statements," OCV, LLC, September 30, 2021, https://cdn.myocv.com/ocvapps /a77435609/files/WMEL-Final-Financial-Statements-2021.pdf.

48. Wolf, "Analysis of PFBS, PFHS and PFOS"; "Offsite Sampling PFOA Concentrations"; PFAS National Primary Drinking Water Regulation Rulemaking, Federal Register, 2024.

49. "Blood PFC Testing and Health Information Summary: Morgan, Lawrence, and Limestone Counties," Agency for Toxic Substances and Disease Registry (ATSDR), https://www.atsdr.cdc.gov/hac/pha/decatur/Blood%20PFC%20Testing%20and%20 Health%20Information.pdf, accessed November 14, 2024; Health Consultation: Exposure Investigation Report—Perfluorochemical Serum Sampling in the Vicinity of Decatur, Alabama, Morgan, Lawrence, and Limestone Counties," Agency for Toxic Substances and Disease Registry, April 1, 2013, https://www.atsdr.cdc.gov/hac/pha /decatur/perfluorochemical_serum%20sampling.pdf.

50. "Blood PFC Testing."

51. "How's My Waterway?," US Environmental Protection Agency, https://mywaterway .epa.gov/community/decatur,%20AL/overview, accessed November 12, 2024.

52. Evan Belanger, "3M underreported chemical output for years," Decatur Daily, November 30, 2017.

53. Carl Cole, personal interview, April 24, 2024.

54. Evan Belanger, "ADEM says it caught 3M error," Times Daily / Decatur Daily, December 11, 2017.

55. Eric Fleischauer, "3M idles some operations," Decatur Daily, September 20, 2019.

56. Eric Fleischauer, "EPA inspects 3M Decatur," Decatur Daily, September 26, 2019.

Chapter 3

1. Lamont Dupree, personal interview, March 28, 2023.

2. Katronica Jones, personal interview, March 27, 2023.

3. "Alabama Building Tries to Shake Swastika Shape," NBC News, March 14, 2008.

4. Howard "Buster" Branham, personal interview, March 26, 2023.

5. Brenda Hampton, personal interview, April 8, 2024.

6. Sharon Udasin and Rachel Frazin, "Justice for PFAS Exposure Races a Ticking Clock," *The Hill*, January 25, 2022; Brenda Hampton, personal interview, January 7, 2022.

7. Brenda Hampton, personal interview, March 26, 2023.

8. Brenda Hampton, personal interview, June 2, 2023.

9. Larry Hampton, personal interview, March 26, 2023.

10. Tom and Rose Adams, personal interview, March 26, 2023.

11. US Environmental Protection Agency, "Perfluorochemical (PFC) Contamination Near Decatur, AL," US EPA Archive, Spring 2012, via Wayback Machine, https://web.archive.org/web/20170210033138/https://archive.epa.gov/pesticides/region4/water/documents/web/pdf/epa_decatur_fact_sheet_final.pdf.

12. Brenda Hampton, personal interview, March 26, 2023.

13. Rebecca Renner, "EPA Finds Record PFOS, PFOA Levels in Alabama Grazing Fields," *Environmental Science & Technology* 43, no. 5 (December 24, 2008), https://doi.org/10.1021/es803520c.

14. "Wheeler: Facts & Figures," Tennessee Valley Authority hydroelectric, https://www.tva.com/energy/our-power-system/hydroelectric/wheeler, accessed October 20, 2024.

15. Scott Brooks, Tennessee Valley Authority, email correspondence, April 4, 2024.

16. "Alabama Fish Consumption Advisories 2023," Alabama Department of Public Health, July 2023, https://www.alabamapublichealth.gov/tox/assets/2023_fishadvisory.pdf.

17. "Warriors for Clean Water Reveal Test Results of Chemical Waste in River," WHNT, June 6, 2016.

18. Ronald Mixon, personal interview, June 2, 2023.

19. "Industrial Directory," Morgan County Economic Development Association, https://mceda.org/about-mceda/membership-directory, accessed October 20, 2024.

20. "WMEL and 3M Reach a Settlement Agreement," 3M News Center, April 26, 2019, https://news.3m.com/2019-04-26-WMEL-and-3M-Reach-a-Settlement-Agreement.

21. "*West Morgan–East Lawrence Water and Sewer Authority et al. v. 3M Company et al.*," Alabama Northern District Court, Public Access to Court Electronic Records (PACER), October 5, 2015.

22. Eric Fleischauer, "More chemicals in the river," *Decatur Daily*, June 23, 2019.

23. Anna Mahan, "WMEL Announces New Water System Is Up and Running," WAFF, May 24, 2021.

24. Carl Cole, personal interview, April 24, 2024.

25. Lamont Dupree, personal interview, March 28, 2023.

26. Larry Hampton, personal interview, March 26, 2023.

27. Brenda Hampton, personal interview, February 16, 2022.

Chapter 4

1. Pat Underwood, personal interviews, March 28 and March 30, 2023.
2. Catherine Godbey, "A Super Opportunity: Decatur's Pat Underwood to tour internationally with Marvel Universe Live," *Decatur Daily*, July 29, 2023.
3. Ward Webster, quoted in "Decatur officials mostly silent after chemicals found on former school, landfill properties," WHNT, December 11, 2019.
4. "Dr. James Ward Webster Obituary," Shelton Funeral Home, August 15, 2023.
5. "Decatur officials mostly silent."
6. Carl Cole, personal interview, April 24, 2024.
7. Mike Brown and Michael Wetzel, "3M, Decatur City Schools Reach Deal; 3M Buys Brookhaven Middle for $1.25 Million," WAFF / *Decatur Daily*, May 4, 2020.
8. "Here's what to know about the former Brookhaven Middle School Campus," 3M News Center, 2024, https://news.3m.com/brookhaven-fact-sheet.
9. Citizen Access Portal, Parcel # 0309302001002.000, Morgan County Revenue Commissioner; Amanda Scott, Morgan County Commissioner, email correspondence, April 15, 2024.
10. "3M Reopens Brookhaven Campus as Interim Green Space During Revitalization Project," 3M News Center, November 16, 2023, https://news.3m.com/3M-Re-opens-Brookhaven-Campus-as-Interim-Green-Space-During-Revitalization-Project.
11. "Conceptual Demolition and Interim Use Plan RTC Rev1 PFC 20-086," 3M, ADEM Laserfiche, October 6, 2021.
12. Dylan Hurst, Alabama Department of Environmental Management, email correspondence, April 18, 2024.
13. Woodtrail Estates LLC, Property Record Card—2022, Morgan County Commissioner County Parcel Viewer, Parcel Number: 1306140000004.001, PIN: 55360.
14. "'Alarming' chemical levels found at undisclosed dump site in Decatur, environmental group says," WHNT, February 19, 2020.
15. "Watchdog Group Says PFAS Chemicals Found at Former Dump Site," WAFF, February 19, 2020.
16. Business Entity Records: Woodtrail Estates, LLC, Alabama Secretary of State, Entity Number 000-635-496, June 24, 2020.
17. Woodtrail Estates, LLC, file no. 3100636, Delaware Department of State, Division of Corporations—Filing, June 22, 2020.
18. Parcels 1301110000002-4, Citizen Access Portal, Morgan County Revenue Commissioner, Tax Year 2023.
19. Pat Underwood, personal interview, March 28, 2023.
20. Jeff Parker, email correspondence, April 3, 2024.
21. Pat Underwood, personal interview, March 28, 2023.
22. Pat Underwood, personal interview, March 30, 2023.
23. Paige Bibbee and Charles Kirby, personal interview, March 27, 2023.
24. Ibid.; Paige Bibbee, personal interview, April 17, 2024.
25. Paige Bibbee and Charles Kirby, personal interview, March 27, 2023.

26. Rickey Terry, personal interview, March 27, 2024.

27. Mike Roman, quoted by Brian Lawson, "3M Decatur received federal grand jury subpoena related to unauthorized chemical dumping," WHNT, January 28, 2020.

28. Paige Bibbee and Charles Kirby, personal interview, March 27, 2023.

29. Ibid.

30. Barney Lovelace, email correspondence, January 15, 2020, screenshot shared by Paige Bibbee.

31. Barney Lovelace, screenshot of email message, forwarded by Paige Bibbee, Decatur City Council and City Board of Education, January 15, 2020.

32. John Seymour, email correspondence, April 20, 2024.

33. Bayne Hughes, "Council incumbents: Mayor, attorney trying to control election," *Decatur Daily*, July 26, 2020.

34. Ibid.

35. Barney Lovelace, personal interview, April 16, 2024.

36. Ibid.; Eric Fleischauer, "Election issues lead Decatur council to defund Chamber of Commerce," *Decatur Daily*, September 10, 2020,

37. Tab Bowling, "Fair Campaign Practices Act State of Alabama: Candidate & Elected Official Campaign Finance Report," Morgan County, Alabama—Probate Office, October 2019 and October 2, 2020.

38. Carlton McMasters, "Fair Campaign Practices Act State of Alabama: Candidate & Elected Official Campaign Finance Report," Morgan County, Alabama—Probate Office, August 21, 2020.

39. "Decatur–Morgan County Chamber of Commerce's Post," Decatur–Morgan County Chamber of Commerce, Facebook, August 4, 2020, https://www.facebook.com /decaturmorganchamber/posts/10157603078807741/.

40. Brian Lawson, "Decatur City Council races: Challenges to incumbents, questions on future of city's dealings with 3M," WHNT, August 24, 2020; "Eugene McNutt," LinkedIn, https://www.linkedin.com/in/eugene-mcnutt-58b05846/, accessed October 30, 2024.

41. "Willie LaFavor," LinkedIn, https://www.linkedin.com/in/willie-lafavor-69b37b16/, accessed October 30, 2024.

42. PRNewswire, "3M Reaches Agreement to Address PFAS With Several Parties Near Decatur, Ala.," 3M News Center, October 19, 2021; "Settlement Agreement," 3M, City, County, DU, October 2021, via DecaturPFAS.info, https://drive.google.com /file/d/1Ut3zs5ZjHu4Q5yHK7w-dWyLaj4FfLrv8/view.

43. City of Decatur, AL, "Special Called Meeting 10:26:2021," YouTube, October 27, 2021.

44. PRNewswire, "3M Reaches Agreement."

45. City of Decatur, "Special Called Meeting."

46. City of Decatur, AL, "March 9, 2020, Council Work Session," YouTube, March 9, 2020.

47. Sophia Schmidt, "Delaware Settles with PFAS-linked Companies to Fund Testing, Cleanup," Delaware First Media, January 22, 2022.

48. Ken Kolker, "3M paying Wolverine Worldwide $55M to settle PFAS suit," WOODTV, February 20, 2020.

49. City of Decatur, "Special Called Meeting."

50. Ibid.

51. Bayne Hughes, "Attorney: 3M settlement was best possible outcome under state law," *Decatur Daily* via Yahoo News, October 27, 2021.

52. Tab Bowling, email correspondence, March 24, 2024.

53. Stephanie Simon, email correspondence, August 28, September 22, and September 27, 2024.

54. "Managing Local Records in Alabama," Alabama Department of Archives and History, 2021, https://archives.alabama.gov/manage/docs/managing_local_records_guide.pdf; Rachel Laurie Riddle, "Resource Manual for Alabama Regulatory Boards and Commissions," Alabama Legislature, August 2023, https://alison.legislature.state.al.us/epa-resource-guide.

55. Local Government Records Commission, "Municipalities: Functional Analysis & Records Disposition Authority," Alabama Department of Archives and History, April 17, 2024, https://archives.alabama.gov/RDA/?id=21.

56. Carl Cole, personal interview, April 24, 2024.

57. Hunter Pepper, personal interview, March 19, 2024.

58. Paige Bibbee and Charles Kirby, personal interview, March 27, 2023.

59. Parcel # 0202030000001.000, Citizen Access Portal, Morgan County Revenue Commissioner; Amanda Scott, Morgan County Commissioner, email correspondence, April 2, 2024.

Chapter 5

1. Samuel J. Cox, "H-008-6: USS *Forrestal* Disaster, 29 July 1967," Naval History and Heritage Command, July 2017, https://www.history.navy.mil/about-us/leadership/director/directors-corner/h-grams/h-gram-008/h-008-6.html.

2. John McCain and Mark Salter, *Faith of My Fathers* (New York: Random House, 1999).

3. Richard Tuve and Edwin Jablonski, "Method of Extinguishing Liquid Hydrocarbon Fires," US Patent Office, Google Patents, June 28, 1966.

4. "Legacy Chemistries and Aqueous Film Forming Foam," 3M, 2024, https://pfas.3m.com/legacy-chemistries-and-aqueous-film-forming-foam.

5. R. L. Gipe and H. B. Peterson, "Proportioning Characteristics of Aqueous Film-Forming Foam Concentrates," *Naval Research Laboratory*, July 20, 1972, https://apps.dtic.mil/sti/citations/AD0747231.

6. D. J. DeYoung, "Seventy Years of Science for the Navy and the Nation (1923–1993)," *Naval Research Laboratory*, 1994, https://apps.dtic.mil/sti/citations/ADA277703.

7. Mark Favors, personal interview, May 5, 2023.

8. "Defense Development," Colorado Springs Chamber & EDC, January 11, 2024, https://coloradospringschamberedc.com/defense-military/defense-development/.

9. Lillian Favors Clark, personal interview, May 5, 2023.

10. "Dollmakers dedicate show to late fellow craftswoman," *Gazette Telegraph* (Colorado Springs, CO), December 3, 1991.

11. Vikki Lloyd, personal interview, April 23, 2024.

12. Mark Favors, "Official Testimony to the House Oversight Committee," Sierra Club, https://www.sierraclub.org/sites/default/files/uploads-wysiwig/Mark%20Favors%20 Testimony.pdf, accessed November 14, 2024.

13. "Are Toxic Chemicals at Air Force Bases Leading to Cancer?," *CBS Mornings*, You-Tube, January 8, 2018, https://www.youtube.com/watch?v=wKjqd6msAi4&ab_ channel=CBSMornings.

14. "6877 Metropolitan St, Colorado Springs," Google Maps, https://www.google.com /maps/place/6877+Metropolitan+St,+Colorado+Springs,+CO+80911/, accessed October 30, 2024.

15. "PFAS Concentration Map Series," Colorado Department of Public Health and Environment, Arc Geographic Information System (ArcGIS), February 16, 2024, https:// cdphe.maps.arcgis.com/.

16. Edward Lefebvre, "Biodegradability and toxicity of Light Water," Air Force Research Laboratory, November 1971, https://apps.dtic.mil/sti/trecms/pdf/AD1206791.pdf.

17. Edward Lefebvre and Roger Inman, "Biodegradability and toxicity of Light Water FC206, aqueous film forming foam," US Air Force Environmental Health Laboratory, EWG PFAS Timeline, 1974, https://static.ewg.org/reports/2019/pfas-dod-timeline /1974_Biodegradability-and-Toxicity-of-ANSUL-K74-100-Aqueous-Film-Forming -Foam.pdf.

18. L. M. Krasner et al., "Fire protection of large Air Force Hangars," Factory Mutual Research Corporation report for Air Force Weapons Laboratory, October 1975.

19. Curtis Cordell and Roger Nutter, "A review of fire fighting training in the naval education and training command," Navy Training Analysis and Evaluation Group, February 1980, https://apps.dtic.mil/sti/tr/pdf/ADA152977.pdf.

20. T. E. Higgins, "Industrial processes to reduce generation of hazardous waste at DOD facilities," CH2M Hill, report prepared for DOD Environmental Leadership Project Office and US Army Corps of Engineers, 1985; "Fire Fighter Trainer Environmental Considerations," Booz, Allen & Hamilton, report prepared for Advanced Technology Systems and Naval Training Equipment Center, 1981; Thomas Junod, "Gaseous Emissions and Toxic Hazards Associated with Plastics in Fire Situations—a literature review," NASA, October 1976.

21. Commander of the David W. Taylor Naval Research R&D Center, letter to commander of the Naval Ship Engineering Center, "Candidate Environmental Impact Statement Draft on Discharging Firefighting System Aqueous Film Forming Foam AFFF into Harbors, Status and Synopsis of," attached to report "Candidate Environmental Impact Statement: Discharging Aqueous Film Forming Foam (AFFF) to Harbor Waters During Tests of Machinery Space Fire-Fighting Foam Systems Aboard U.S. Navy Ships," David W. Taylor Naval Ship Research and Development Center, January 1978.

22. "Navy Hazardous Materials Management Guide," Navy Environmental Support Office, 1979.

23. "Fire Fighter Trainer Environmental Considerations," Booz, Allen & Hamilton, report prepared for Advanced Technology Systems and Naval Training Equipment Center, 1981.

24. William G. Fraser et al., "Installation Restoration Program Phase I: Records Search, Peterson Air Force Base Colorado," Reynolds, Smith and Hills, Inc., August 5, 1985, https://apps.dtic.mil/sti/tr/pdf/ADA168811.pdf.

25. Seshasayi Dharmavaram et al., "Hazardous Waste Minimization Assessment: Fort Campbell, KY," US Army Corps of Engineers Construction Engineering Research Laboratory, 1991; Seshasayi Dharmavaram et al., "Hazardous Waste Minimization Assessment: Ford Ord, CA," US Army Corps of Engineers Construction Engineering Research Laboratory, 1991; Dharmavaram Seshasayi, Douglas A. Knowlton, Bernard A. Donahue, and US Army Corps of Engineers Construction Engineering Research Laboratory, "Hazardous Waste Minimization Assessment: Fort Carson, CO," technical report, US Army Corps of Engineers Construction Engineering Research Laboratory, 1991.

26. Gregory Zagursky, William Jefferson III, and Robert D. Binovi, "Biological Analysis of Three Ponds at Peterson AFB, Colorado Springs, CO," Defense Technical Information Center report, November 1989.

27. National Part 139 CertAlert," Federal Aviation Administration, October 29, 2019, https://www.faa.gov/sites/faa.gov/files/airports/airport_safety/certalerts/part-139-cert-alert-19-02-AFFF.pdf.

28. "Per- and Polyfluoroalkyl Substances, Public Outreach Presentation, DOD PFAS, US Department of Defense, July 14, 2021, https://www.acq.osd.mil/eie/eer/ecc/pfas/po/docs/14JULY21/DOD-PFAS-JULY-14TH-PUBLIC-OUTREACH-PRESENTATION.PDF.

29. Meghann Myers, "New DoD specs for firefighting foam, now free of 'forever chemicals,'" *Military Times*, January 13, 2023; Ashley Murray and Jennifer Shutt, "Pentagon to halt use of firefighting foam that contains PFAS as cleanup costs mount," *Colorado Newsline*, March 16, 2023.

30. US Environmental Protection Agency, "PFOA & PFOS Drinking Water Health Advisories," report, November 2016.

31. "Revised Final Preliminary Assessment Report for Perfluorinated Compounds at Peterson Air Force Base, El Paso County, Colorado," Air Force Civil Engineer Center report, US Army Corps of Engineers, November 2016.

32. "Final Site Inspection Report of Aqueous Film Forming Foam Areas at Peterson Air Force Base, El Paso County, Colorado," Air Force Civil Engineer Center report, US Army Corps of Engineers, July 2017.

33. Arcadis U.S., Inc. "Final Preliminary Assessment and Site Inspection of Per- And Polyfluoroalkyl Substances: Fort Carson, Colorado," report prepared for US Army Environmental Command, US Army Corps of Engineers, January 2022, https://aec.army.mil/aec/6316/7813/6785/CarsonPASI.pdf; Steven J. Morani and US Environmental Protection Agency, "Investigating Per- and Polyfluoroalkyl Substances within the Department of Defense Cleanup Program," memo, Office of the Assistant Secretary of Defense, September 15, 2021, https://www.denix.osd.mil/derp/denix-files/sites/26/2021/10/Addressing-the-Investigation-of-PFAS_15Sep2021.pdf;

"Provisional Peer-Reviewed Toxicity Values," US Environmental Protection Agency report, February 5, 2024, https://www.epa.gov/pprtv; "Provisional Peer-Reviewed Toxicity Values for Perfluorobutane Sulfonic Acid (PFBS) and Related Compound Potassium Perfluorobutane Sulfonate," US Environmental Protection Agency report, April 2021, https://cfpub.epa.gov/ncea/pprtv/recordisplay.cfm?deid=350061; "Regional Screening Levels," US Environmental Protection Agency report, September 3, 2024, https://www.epa.gov/risk/regional-screening-levels-rsls.

34. Fort Carson spokesperson, email attachment, December 20, 2023.

35. Memo for Department of Defense Per- And Polyfluoroalkyl Substances Task Force, via EWG PFAS Timeline, Environmental Working Group, April 18, 2022.

36. Environmental Working Group, "More Than 600,000 Service Members Given 'Forever Chemicals' in Drinking Water," December 15, 2022, https://www.ewg.org/news-insights/news-release/2022/12/more-600000-service-members-given-forever-chemicals-drinking.

37. Ashish S. Vazirani, "Report to the Committees on Appropriations of the Senate and the House of Representatives: Perfluorinated Chemicals Contamination and First Responder Exposure," Under Secretary of Defense, October 30, 2023, https://www.health.mil/Reference-Center/Reports/2023/10/30/Perfluorinated-Chemicals-Contamination-and-First-Responder-Exposure.

38. "Evaluation of the Department of Defense's Actions to Control Contaminant Effects from Perfluoroalkyl and Polyfluoroalkyl Substances at Department of Defense Installations," Department of Defense Office of the Inspector General, July 22, 2021, https://www.dodig.mil/reports.html/article/2705951/evaluation-of-the-department-of-defenses-actions-to-control-contaminant-effects/.

39. Rachel Frazin, "DOD officials defend military's handling of toxic chemicals at tense hearing," *The Hill*, December 9, 2021; "Senate Hearing 117-515," US Government Publishing Office, 2022.

40. Dan Kildee, personal interview, March 5, 2024.

41. Sean Houseworth and Stephen Brady, personal interview, May 5, 2023.

42. Stephen Brady, email correspondence, May 1, 2024.

43. Sean Houseworth and Stephen Brady, personal interview, May 5, 2023.

44. Mark Kinkade, email attachment, February 26, 2024.

45. "PFAS Data: Cleanup of PFAS," Office of the Undersecretary of Defense for Acquisition and Sustainment, 2024, https://www.acq.osd.mil/eie/eer/ecc/pfas/data/cleanup-pfas.html.

46. "Progress at the 715 Installations Being Assessed for PFAS Use or Potential Release," Office of the Undersecretary of Defense for Acquisition and Sustainment, March 31, 2024, https://www.acq.osd.mil/eie/eer/ecc/pfas/docs/data/DoD-PFAS-Progress-as-of-31MAR24.pdf.

47. "PFAS Interim Action Locations," Office of the Undersecretary of Defense for Acquisition and Sustainment, February 2, 2024, https://www.acq.osd.mil/eie/eer/ecc/pfas/docs/data/DoD-PFAS-Interim-Action-Locations-List-02FEB24.pdf.

48. KOMAN Government Solutions, LLC (KGS), "Final Technical Memorandum

Annual Off-Base Water Well Sampling, December 2022," US Air Force Civil Engineer Center, partially redacted report shared by email, March 7, 2023.

49. Roy Heald and Brandon Bernard, personal interview, May 5, 2023.
50. John Hazelhurst, "Study: Local water contaminated," *Colorado Springs Business Journal*, January 14, 2016.
51. Tracie White, personal interview, February 6, 2024.
52. "USGS 384531104432200 WINDMILL GULCH @ BRADLEY," National Water Information System: Web Interface, US Geological Services—Water Resources, https://waterdata.usgs.gov/co/nwis/inventory/?site_no=384531104432200&agency_cd=USGS&, accessed November 14, 2024; "Q75G+CVX Security-Widefield, Colorado," Google Maps, 38°45'31.0"N 104°43'22.0"W.
53. Security Water District, "Important Information about Your Drinking Water," May 19, 2016, https://securitywsd.com/wp-content/uploads/2017/05/Security_Fact_Sheet_5-2016_Legal-FINAL.pdf.
54. "2024 Water Quality Report," Colorado Springs Utilities, City of Colorado Springs, https://39606065.fs1.hubspotusercontent-na1.net/hubfs/39606065/Document%20Library/2024WaterQualityReport.pdf, accessed November 14, 2024.
55. "Agreements Outline Air Force Commitment to Colorado Communities," Air Force Civil Engineer Center, April 18, 2018.

Chapter 6

1. "Princess Donetta Patterson," *Colorado Springs Gazette*, August 4, 2013.
2. Steve Patterson, personal interview, May 6, 2023.
3. Ibid.
4. Yazeed Saajid, personal interview, May 6, 2023.
5. Dustin Monke, "A Reshaped Life," *Dickinson Press*, January 31, 2008.
6. Dustin Monke, "Burnham a Productive Point Guard," *Dickinson Press*, February 5, 2009.
7. Yazeed Saajid, personal interview, August 3, 2023.
8. Steve Patterson, personal interview, January 16, 2024.
9. "VA Claims for Exposure to AFFF," *VA Claims Insider* (blog), February 23, 2024.
10. Ibid.
11. Steve Patterson, personal interview, May 6, 2023.
12. Najee Jackson, personal interview, May 6, 2023.
13. Mark Favors, personal interview, May 6, 2023.
14. "Frequently Asked Questions About the Southern Resident Endangered Orcas," The Whale Museum, 2024, https://whalemuseum.org/pages/frequently-asked-questions-about-the-southern-resident-endangered-orcas.
15. "Orcas (Killer Whales)," Animals | National Geographic, https://www.nationalgeographic.com/animals/mammals/facts/orca, accessed November 14, 2024.
16. Mark Favors, personal interview, May 5, 2023.
17. Wilbur Tennant, in video published by *The Intercept* / *Sharon Lerner* as part of a story titled "The Teflon Toxin, Part 2: Wilbur Tennant vs. DuPont," August 17, 2015.

18. Rob Bilott, *Exposure* (New York: Simon & Schuster, 2019), 50–53; Nathaniel Rich, "The Lawyer Who Became DuPont's Worst Nightmare," *New York Times Magazine*, January 10, 2016, https://www.nytimes.com/2016/01/10/magazine/the-lawyer-who-became-duponts-worst-nightmare.html.

19. Rob Bilott, personal interview, May 17, 2023.

20. Rob Bilott, *Exposure* (New York: Simon & Schuster, 2019), 54–58.

21. Nathaniel Rich, "The Lawyer Who Became DuPont's Worst Nightmare," *New York Times Magazine*, January, 10, 2016; "Judge OKs $107.6 million DuPont settlement," NBC News via the Associated Press, February 8, 2005, https://www.nbcnews.com/id/wbna7047037.

22. "C8 Probable Link Reports," C8 Science Panel, December 5, 2011, through October 29, 2012, http://www.c8sciencepanel.org/prob_link.html.

23. "Toxic, Forever Chemicals: A Call for Immediate Federal Action on PFAS," Hearing before the Subcommittee on Environment of the Committee on Oversight and Reform, US House of Representatives, Serial No. 116–72, Washington, DC: U.S. Government Publishing Office, November 12, 2019.

24. Emily Hernandez, "Air Force Must Pay $230 Million in Sutherland Springs Shooting Lawsuit," *Texas Tribune*, February 6, 2024.

25. "Toxic, Forever Chemicals."

26. Ibid.

27. Ibid.

28. Lauren Hitt, email correspondence, September 5, 2023.

29. Liz Rosenbaum, personal interview, May 6, 2023.

30. "Fannie Mae Bragg Duncan" (obituary), *Colorado Springs Gazette*, September 18, 2005.

31. William J. Dagendesh, "'Everybody Welcome': Colorado Springs Author Speaks on Fannie Mae Duncan Book to American Association of University Women," *Colorado Springs Gazette*, May 1, 2019; "Statue honors Fannie Mae," FOX21, October 25, 2019.

32. Marija Vader, "Rosenbaum shares food, 'Her Story' at 21c café," *Colorado Springs Business Journal*, December 16, 2015.

33. Liz Rosenbaum, personal interviews, May 5–6, 2023.

34. "Turning Anger into Action," Voices of Colorado, Conservation Colorado, February 11, 2022, https://conservationco.org/2022/02/11/voices-of-colorado-turning-anger-into-action.

35. Weixiao Cheng et al., "Integrative Computational Approaches to Inform Relative Bioaccumulation Potential of Per- and Polyfluoroalkyl Substances Across Species," *Toxicological Sciences* 180, no. 2 (January 23, 2021).

36. Suzanne E. Fenton, Alan Ducatman, et al., "Per- and Polyfluoroalkyl Substance Toxicity and Human Health Review: Current State of Knowledge and Strategies for Informing Future Research," *Environmental Toxicology and Chemistry* 40, no. 3 (December 7, 2020).

37. "Primary Hypophysitis," California Center for Pituitary Disorders, University of

California, San Francisco, 2021, https://ccpd.ucsf.edu/pituitary-disorders/inflam matory-conditions/primary-hypophysitis.

38. John Adgate and Chris Higgins, personal interview, January 25, 2024.
39. "PFAS Multi-site Study: Per- and Polyfluoroalkyl Substances and Your Health," Agency for Toxic Substances and Disease Registry (ATSDR), Centers for Disease Control (CDC), https://www.atsdr.cdc.gov/pfas/health-studies/multi-site-study.html, accessed November 14, 2024.
40. "Fountain Valley PFAS Study / PFAS Multi-Site Study Colorado: CO SCOPE," Agency for Toxic Substances and Disease Registry (ATSDR), Centers for Disease Control (CDC), June 14, 2022; "PFAS Exposure and Health Assessment Activities—El Paso County, Colorado," CDC, ATSDR, Colorado School of Public Health, September 9, 2020.
41. "PFAS Exposure Assessments," ATSDR, CDC, https://www.atsdr.cdc.gov/pfas/expo sure-assessments/, accessed November 14, 2024.
42. "Final Report: Findings Across Ten Exposure Assessment Sites," ATSDR, CDC, https://www.atsdr.cdc.gov/pfas/final-report/, accessed November 14, 2024.
43. "PFAS Exposure Assessment: El Paso County, Colorado," ATSDR, CDC, https://www.atsdr.cdc.gov/pfas/exposure-assessments/el-paso-county-colorado.html/, accessed November 14, 2024.
44. "Per- and Polyfluoroalkyl Substances (PFAS) Exposure Assessment," Security–Widefield El Paso County, Colorado, ATSDR, CDC, June 14, 2022.
45. "NHANES—About the National Health and Nutrition Examination Survey," CDC, May 31, 2023, https://www.cdc.gov/nchs/nhanes/about_nhanes.htm.

Chapter 7
1. Liz Rosenbaum, personal interview, May 5, 2023.
2. Caitlin Coleman, "Colorado Enacts Arsenal of Laws to Stop 'Forever Chemicals,'" Water Education Colorado, October 7, 2020.
3. "Protect Public Health Firefighter Safety Regulation PFAS Polyfluoroalkyl Substances," HB19-1279, Colorado General Assembly, June 3, 2019.
4. "Protect Public Health Firefighter Safety Regulation."
5. "Water Quality Control Commission Policy 20-1: Policy for Interpreting the Narrative Water Quality Standards for Per- and Polyfluoroalkyl Substances (PFAS)," Colorado Department of Public Health and Environment, July 14, 2020.
6. "Perfluoroalkyl and Polyfluoroalkyl Chemicals," HB22-1345, Colorado General Assembly," June 3, 2022.
7. Sharon Udasin, "Polis signs bill strengthening Colorado's 'forever chemical' product bans," *The Hill*, May 2, 2024; "Perfluoroalkyl & Polyfluoroalkyl Chemicals: Concerning measures to increase protections from perfluoroalkyl and polyfluoroalkyl chemicals," SB24-081, Colorado State Senate, May 1, 2024.
8. "States in the Lead: Alliance Impact," Policies for Addressing PFAS / Our Priorities, Safer States, https://www.saferstates.org/priorities/pfas/, accessed November 14, 2024.
9. "Consumer Drinking Water Notice," Wigwam Mutual Water Company PWSID

CO0121470," January 28, 2020; "Per- and Polyfluoroalkyl Substances (PFAS)," US EPA, April 10, 2024, https://www.epa.gov/sdwa/and-polyfluoroalkyl-substances-pfas.

10. John Adgate and Chris Higgins, personal interview, January 25, 2024.

11. Kristy Richardson, personal interview, February 6, 2024.

12. "PFAS Concentration Map Series: Dataset Descriptions," Colorado Department of Public Health and Environment, July 2022; "Story Map Series," Colorado Department of Public Health and Environment, Arc Geographic Information System (Arc-GIS), formerly accessible map data (https://cdphe.maps.arcgis.com/) confirmed via email correspondence with Shannon Barbare, Colorado Department of Public Health and Environment, August 12, 2024.

13. Sean Houseworth, personal interview, May 5, 2023.

14. Arcadis U.S., Inc. "Final Preliminary Assessment and Site Inspection Of Per- And Polyfluoroalkyl Substances," report prepared for US Army Corps of Engineers, November 2022.

15. "Rock Creek Near Fountain, Co.," Water Data, US Geological Services, https://waterdata.usgs.gov/monitoring-location/07105960/#parameterCode=00060&period=P7D&showMedian=true, accessed November 14, 2024.

16. Arcadis, "Final Preliminary Assessment."

17. Liz Rosenbaum, personal interview, May 6, 2023.

18. Greg Miller, personal interview, January 23, 2024.

19. Liz Rosenbaum, personal interview, May 6, 2023.

20. "Elect Liz Rosenbaum," Liz Rosenbaum campaign website, November 10, 2024, https://lizrosenbaumco.com/.

21. Stephanie Earls and Eric Young, "State House roundup for the Colorado Springs area: Democratic candidate may succeed Snyder," *Colorado Springs Gazette,* November 5, 2024, https://gazette.com/election-coverage/state-house-roundup-for-the-colorado-springs-area-democratic-candidate-may-succeed-snyder/article_b8eca926-9ad6-11ef-bc8b-7f7a430685d9.html.

22. "Liz Rosenbaum," Facebook, December 14, 2023, https://www.facebook.com/photo.php?fbid=10228087545148767&set=pb.1079005706.-2207520000&type=3.

23. "Class of 2017 Endowment," Colorado College, last updated February 8, 2023, https://www.coloradocollege.edu/us/giving/2017/.

24. Mark Favors, personal interview, May 5, 2023.

25. Sharon Udasin and Rachel Frazin, "Justice for PFAS exposure races a ticking clock," *The Hill,* January 25, 2022; "Toxic, Forever Chemicals: A Call for Immediate Federal Action on PFAS," Hearing before the Subcommittee on Environment of the Committee on Oversight and Reform, US House of Representatives, Serial No. 116–72, Washington, DC: U.S. Government Publishing Office, November 12, 2019.

26. Udasin and Frazin, "Justice for PFAS exposure."

27. Ibid.

28. "C8 Science Panel," The Science Panel Website, last updated January 22, 2020, http://www.c8sciencepanel.org/.

29. Udasin and Frazin, "Justice for PFAS exposure."

30. Paul Napoli, personal interview, January 20, 2024.

31. John Adgate, personal interview, January 25, 2024.

32. Kristy Richardson, personal interview, February 6, 2024.

33. Aqueous Film-Forming Foam (AFFF) Product Liability Litigation (MDL 2873), US District Court for the District of South Carolina, Master Docket No. 2:18-MN-2873-RMG, https://www.scd.uscourts.gov/mdl-2873/index.asp, accessed November 14, 2024; "Public Water System Settlements," PFAS Water Settlement website, last updated July 3, 2024, https://www.pfaswatersettlement.com/.

34. Sharon Udasin, "Federal court finalizes $1.2B 'forever chemicals' settlement involving major firms," *The Hill*, February 8, 2024; "DuPont PWS Settlement," Aqueous Film-Forming Foams (AFFF) MDL, US District Court for the District of South Carolina, Master Docket No. 2:18-MN-2873-RMG, December 5, 2023.

35. Sharon Udasin, "Federal court finalizes 'forever chemical' settlement between 3M, water systems for billions," *The Hill*, April 2, 2024; "3M PWS Settlement," Aqueous Film-Forming Foams (AFFF) MDL, US District Court for the District of South Carolina, Master Docket No. 2:18-MN-2873-RMG, December 5, 2023.

36. Sharon Udasin and Rachel Frazin, "Formidable legal bar shields military from PFAS lawsuits," *The Hill*, January 27, 2022.

37. "Doing Business with the House," Federal Tort Claims Act, House of Representatives, https://www.house.gov/doing-business-with-the-house/leases/federal-tort-claims-act.

38. Edward Richards, "Discretionary Acts," Public Health Law Map—Beta 5.7, LSU Law Center, April 19, 2009, https://biotech.law.lsu.edu/map/DiscretionaryActs.html; "Sovereign Immunity," Legal Information Institute, Wex Law, Cornell University, https://www.law.cornell.edu/wex/sovereign_immunity, accessed November 14, 2024.

39. "Giovanni Opinion," US Court of Appeals, Third Circuit, Case Nos. 17-2473 & 17-3196, Cuker Law, June 2019.

40. *Schaap et al. v. United States of America et al.*, US District Court District of South Carolina, November 21, 2019.

Chapter 8

1. Lawrence and Penny Higgins, personal interview, August 27, 2023.

2. "A History of Land Application as a Treatment Alternative," US Environmental Protection Agency, April 1979.

3. Annie Ropeik, "Sludge explained: What you need to know about 'forever chemical' contamination on some Maine farms," *Spectrum News*, March 8, 2022.

4. Nomawethu Moyo, Devki Rana, and Cassandra Smith, "The State of Municipal Solid Waste in Maine," Colby College / The State of Maine's Environment 2014, 2014.

5. "Maine DEP PFAS Investigation (Formerly the 'Septage and Sludge Map'),'" Maine Department of Environmental Protection, Arc Geographic Information System (ArcGIS) web application, https://maine.maps.arcgis.com/apps/webappviewer/index.html?id=468a9f7ddcd54309bc1ae8ba173965c7, accessed November 14, 2024.

6. "Status of Maine's PFAS Soil and Groundwater Investigation at Sludge and Septage Land Application Sites," Maine Department of Environmental Protection Bureau of Remediation and Waste Management, report to the Committee on the Environment

and Natural Resources, 131st Legislature, First Session, January 15, 2023; "H.P. 1189-L.D. 1600, An Act to Investigate Perfluoroalkyl and Polyfluoroalkyl Substance Contamination of Land and Groundwater," Chapter 478 Public Law, Maine Legislature, July 15, 2021.

7. Tom Perkins," Fury over 'forever chemicals' as US states spread toxic sewage sludge," *The Guardian*, 2022.

8. Jared Hayes, "EWG: 'Forever chemicals' may taint nearly 20 million cropland acres," Environmental Working Group, 2022.

9. Lawrence Higgins, Penelope Higgins, and Fairfield Water Concerned Citizens, "Supporting LD 1911 Bill," testimony to Maine State Legislature, January 24, 2022, https://legislature.maine.gov/testimony/resources/ENR20220124Higgins132869899448363750.pdf.

10. Higgins et al., "Supporting LD 1911 Bill"; "About the National Health and Nutrition Examination Survey (NHANES)," National Center for Health Statistics, Centers for Disease Control and Prevention, May 31, 2023, https://www.cdc.gov/nchs/nhanes/about_nhanes.htm.

11. Margaret Jackson, Perfluoroalkyl Substances (PFAS) Serum/Plasma tests for Lawrence Higgins, collected at MaineGeneral Health, Augusta, Maine / Nichols Institute on February 20, 2021; Report by Quest Diagnostics Nichols Institute, Chantilly, Virginia, on March 8, 2021.

12. Margaret Jackson, Perfluoroalkyl Substances (PFAS) Serum/Plasma tests for Penelope Higgins, collected at MaineGeneral Health, Augusta, Maine / Nichols Institute on February 20, 2021; Report by Quest Diagnostics Nichols Institute, Chantilly, Virginia, on March 13, 2021.

13. "Fairfield-Area PFAS Investigation," Maine Department of Environmental Protection, 2019, https://www.maine.gov/dep/spills/topics/pfas/fairfield/index.html.

14. David Madore, email correspondence, April 24, 2024.

15. Fred Stone, personal interview, August 26, 2023.

16. Normand R. Labbe, letter to Frederick Stone, Kennebunk, Kennebunkport and Wells Water District, November 3, 2016.

17. Kenneth C. Young, "Amendment to Department Order in the Matter of Kennebunk Sewer District Municipal Sewage Treatment Plant," State of Maine Department of Environmental Protection, October 22, 1986, W007034-61-A-N STONE; Kenneth C. Young, "Amendment to Utilization License," State of Maine Department of Environmental Protection, October 22, 1987, W007034-61-A-N STONE.

18. Labbe, letter to Frederick Stone.

19. "Title 38, §1310-N: Solid Waste Facility Licenses," Maine Legislature: Maine Revised Statute, November 1, 2024, https://legislature.maine.gov/statutes/38/title38sec1310-N.html.

20. Tess Richman et al., "Curation of a list of chemicals in biosolids from EPA National Sewage Sludge Surveys & Biennial Review Reports," *Nature* (April 19, 2022); "Standards for the Use or Disposal of Sewage Sludge," US Environmental Protection Agency; "Report: Biosolids Biennial Report No. 9," US Environmental Protection Agency, December 23, 2022.

21. *Farmer v. EPA*, D.C. District Court, 1:24-cv-01654, June 2024.

22. Kevin Miller, "MOFGA to sue federal government over forever chemicals in sludge used as fertilizer," Maine Public Radio, 2024.

23. E. Bizkarguenaga et al., "Uptake of 8:2 perfluoroalkyl phosphate diester and its degradation products by carrot and lettuce from compost-amended soil," *Chemosphere*, 2016.

24. "Analytical Results of Testing Food for PFAS from Environmental Contamination," U.S. FDA, June 26, 2024, https://www.fda.gov/food/environmental-contaminants-food/analytical-results-testing-food-pfas-environmental-contamination.

25. Marina Mastrantonio, et al., "Drinking Water Contamination from Perfluoroalkyl Substances (PFAS): An Ecological Mortality Study in the Veneto Region, Italy," *European Journal of Public Health* 28, no. 1 (May 23, 2017).

26. Josephine M. Brown-Leung and Jason R. Cannon, "Neurotransmission Targets of Per- and Polyfluoroalkyl Substance Neurotoxicity: Mechanisms and Potential Implications for Adverse Neurological Outcomes," *Chemical Research in Toxicology* 35, no. 8 (August 3, 2022).

27. "Rachel Criswell, MD, Skowhegan Family Medicine," Redington-Fairview General Hospital, November 1, 2024, https://www.rfgh.net/providers/pediatrics.xhtml.

28. "Guidance on PFAS Exposure, Testing, and Clinical Follow-Up," National Academies of Sciences, Engineering, and Medicine, 2022, https://nap.nationalacademies.org/catalog/26156/guidance-on-pfas-exposure-testing-and-clinical-follow-up.

29. Fred Stone, personal interview, April 24, 2024.

30. Fred Stone, personal interview, August 26, 2023.

31. Adam Nordell, personal interview, August 30, 2023.

32. Kristina Buckley, "Maine Farmland Trust Purchases Songbird Farm to Advance Research on PFAS in Agriculture," Maine Farmland Trust, October 6, 2023.

33. United Press International, "Permanent Ban Urged on Sludge in Farming," *New York Times*, September 20, 1981.

Chapter 9

1. Fred Stone, personal interview, August 26, 2023.

2. Henry Ingwersen, personal interview, August 26, 2023.

3. "An Act to Protect the Environment and Public Health by Further Reducing Toxic Chemicals in Packaging," Maine Legislature, March 18, 2019.

4. "Toxics in Food Packaging Program," Maine Department of Environmental Protection, 2019, https://www.maine.gov/dep/safechem/packaging/index.html.

5. "An Act Relating to the Statute of Limitations for Injuries or Harm Resulting from Perfluoroalkyl and Polyfluoroalkyl Substances," Maine Legislature, March 17, 2020.

6. "An Act Regarding the Statute of Limitations for Injuries or Harm Resulting from Perfluoroalkyl and Polyfluoroalkyl Substances," Maine Legislature, June 22, 2021.

7. "Resolve, To Protect Consumers of Public Drinking Water by Establishing Maximum Contaminant Levels for Certain Substances and Contaminants," Maine Legislature, June 21, 2021; "PFAS in Public Water Systems," Maine Division of Environmental

and Community Health, last updated September 6, 2024, https://www.maine.gov
/dhhs/mecdc/environmental-health/dwp/pws/pfas.shtml.

8. "An Act to Investigate Perfluoroalkyl and Polyfluoroalkyl Substance Contamination of
Land and Groundwater," Maine Legislature, July 15, 2021; "Groundbreaking PFAS
Bills in Maine," Defend Our Health, August 25, 2021.

9. "An Act to Stop Perfluoroalkyl and Polyfluoroalkyl Substances Pollution," Maine
Legislature, July 15, 2021.

10. "An Act to Support Manufacturers Whose Products Contain Perfluoroalkyl and Polyfluoroalkyl Substances," Maine Legislature, June 8, 2023.

11. "An Act to Restrict the Use of Perfluoroalkyl and Polyfluoroalkyl Substances in Firefighting Foam," Maine Legislature, July 9, 2021.

12. "PFAS Fund Advisory Committee," Maine Department of Agriculture; "An Act to
Make Supplemental Appropriations and Allocations for the Expenditures of State
Government . . . for the Fiscal Years Ending June 30, 2022 and June 30, 2023,"
Maine Legislature, April 20, 2022.

13. "PFAS Fund Advisory Committee."

14. "Maine Receives $5 Million Federal Grant to Bolster PFAS Response Efforts," Maine
Department of Agriculture, Conservation and Forestry, October 19, 2023.

15. David Madore, email correspondence, April 24, 2024.

16. Jim Britt, email correspondence, April 30, 2024.

17. Nikki Nelson, "Compare S Corporation vs. LLC: Differences & Benefits," Wolters
Kluwer, January 26, 2024.

18. Guides Legal Services Team, "LLC vs. S-Corp: What's the Difference?" Market Watch,
January 18, 2024; Abby Dorland, "What Is an S Corp, C Corp, & LLC?" Thomson
Reuters, March 1, 2024.

19. "An Act to Prevent the Further Contamination of the Soils and Waters of the State
with So-called Forever Chemicals," Maine Legislature, April 20, 2022.

20. "Analysis of State Legislation Addressing Toxic Chemicals and Materials," Safer States,
February 2024; "Safer States: Bill Tracker," selected filters: All States, All Statuses,
PFAS, Biosolids, https://www.saferstates.org/bill-tracker/?, accessed November 13,
2024.

21. "Michigan Biosolids PFAS-related Information and Links," Department of Environment, Great Lakes, and Energy, 2024, https://www.michigan.gov/egle/about/organi
zation/water-resources/biosolids/pfas-related.

22. Jacques Poitras, "Maine Has a Surplus of Human Waste. It's Being Shipped to New
Brunswick.," CBC, March 8, 2023.

23. "An Act to Prevent . . . Soils and Waters."

24. "An Act to Protect the Health and Welfare of Maine Communities and Reduce Harm-
ful Solid Waste," Maine Legislature, April 18, 2022; Popp, Evan, "Maine Legislature
Approves Bill to Close Juniper Ridge Out-of-state Waste Loophole," Maine Beacon,
September 24, 2022.

25. Dan Kusnierz, personal interview, August 28, 2023.

26. "Learn About Dioxin," US Environmental Protection Agency, December 7, 2023,
https://www.epa.gov/dioxin/learn-about-dioxin.

27. Federal Register, Volume 81 Issue 76, Government Publishing Office, April 20, 2016.

28. "Health Consultation: Review of Anadromous Fish: Penobscot River," Penobscot Indian Nation, US Department of Health and Human Services, ATSDR, and Office of Community Health and Hazard Assessment, May 19, 2021.

29. Ibid.

30. Nadia Barbo et al., "Locally Caught Freshwater Fish Across the United States Are Likely a Significant Source of Exposure to PFOS and Other Perfluorinated Compounds," *Environmental Research* 220, n. 9 (March 1, 2023), DOI:10.1016/j.envres .2022.115165.

31. Jeff Weld, email correspondence, May 3, 2024.

32. Paula M. Clark, "JRL Timeline: Timeline of Events Concerning the West Old Town Landfill," Maine Department of Environmental Protection, file posted by the Maine Department of Economic and Community Development, August 26, 2013; "Resolve, to Authorize the State to Purchase a Landfill in the City of Old Town," 121st Maine Legislature, June 23, 2003.

33. "Old Town Division," ND Paper, October 25, 2022.

34. "About Us: Sustainable Paper, Pulp, & Packaging," ND Paper, January 5, 2023.

35. Crawford Engineers, "Study to Assess Treatment Alternatives for Reducing PFAS in Leachate from State-Owned Landfills," Maine Department of Administrative and Financial Services, January 2023.

36. Crawford, "Study to Assess Treatment Alternatives."

37. "Effluent Guidelines Program Plan 15," US EPA, January 2023.

38. Brian Toth, email correspondence, August 22, 2024.

39. Ben Meyer, "It's 'raining PFAS,' even in remote areas of the Upper Peninsula," WXPR, September 9, 2021.

40. Bill Kearney, "Pollution taints even the most remote parts of Everglades, canoe journey reveals," *South Florida Sun Sentinel*, 2024.

41. Leah Santangelo et al., "Statewide survey of shallow soil concentrations of per- and polyfluoroalkyl substances (PFAS) and related chemical and physical data across New Hampshire, 2021," US Geological Survey, 2022.

42. Andrea Tokranov, personal interview, February 21, 2024.

43. Lawrence and Penny Higgins, personal interview, August 27, 2023.

44. Sharon Udasin, "Erin Brockovich and the people's agenda," *The Hill*, October 13, 2021; Rachel Frazin and Sharon Udasin, "State resistance foils law changes, hampering PFAS suits," *The Hill*, January 26, 2022.

45. Lawrence Higgins et al., "Original Complaint," Somerset County Court, Public Access to Court Electronic Records (PACER), September 7, 2021.

46. Frazin and Udasin, "State resistance."

47. Higgins, "Original Complaint."

48. "Waterville, ME," Huhtamaki, https://www.huhtamaki.com/en-us/north-america /about-us/locations/waterville-me/, accessed November 13, 2024.

49. *Lawrence Higgins et al. v. Huhtamaki, Inc., et al.*, Legal Complaint, United States District Court District of Maine, PACER, March 17, 2023.

50. "Defendant Huhtamaki, Inc.'s Answer to Plaintiffs' Third Amended Complaint," United States District Court District of Maine, PACER, April 17, 2023.

51. "Defendants Solenis International LLC, BASF Corp., and 3M Company's Joint Motion to Dismiss the Third Amended Complaint," US District Court District of Maine, PACER, April 17, 2023; *Lawrence Higgins et al. v. Huhtamaki, Inc., et al.*, "Order on Motion to Dismiss," US District Court District of Maine, PACER, October 5, 2023.

52. "Defendant Solenis, LLC's Answer and Defenses to Plaintiffs' Third Amended Complaint," US District Court District of Maine, PACER, November 20, 2023; "Defendant BASF's Answer and Affirmative Defenses to Plaintiffs' Third Amended Complaint," US District Court District of Maine, PACER, November 20, 2023.

53. "3M Company's Answer and Affirmative and Other Defenses to Plaintiffs' Third Amended Complaint," US District Court District of Maine, PACER, November 20, 2023.

54. BASF Media Relations, email correspondence, April 15, 2024.

55. Huhtamaki Media, email correspondence, April 22, 2024.

56. Russ Abney, email correspondence, May 3, 2024.

57. Nate Saunders, personal interview, August 27, 2023.

58. "Maine DEP PFAS Investigation (Formerly the 'Septage and Sludge Map')," Maine Department of Environmental Protection, Arc Geographic Information System (ArcGIS), web application, https://maine.maps.arcgis.com/apps/webappviewer/index.html?id=468a9f7ddcd54309bc1ae8ba173965c7, accessed November 14, 2024.

59. MaineGeneral Health Study, PFAS results for Nathan Saunders, 2021.

60. Nathan Saunders, PFAS levels: graph of personal health data, 2021–2023.

61. Saunders, graph.

62. Nathan Saunders, "Nathan Saunders Creatinine Over Eleven Years," graph of kidney function blood test, February 2, 2023.

63. "About the National Health and Nutrition Examination Survey (NHANES)," National Center for Health Statistics, Centers for Disease Control and Prevention, May 31, 2023, https://www.cdc.gov/nchs/nhanes/about_nhanes.htm.

64. "3M to Share Record on PFAS with House Oversight Subcommittee," 3M Statements, September 10, 2019, https://pfas.3m.com/3M-to-share-record-on-PFAS-with-House-Oversight-Subcommittee.

65. "Perfluoroalkyl and Polyfluoroalkyl Substances (PFAS) in the U.S. Population," Fourth Report on Human Exposure to Environmental Chemicals, CDC-ATSDR, January 2017.

66. "Business and Consumer Docket," State of Maine Judicial Branch, 2023, https://www.courts.maine.gov/courts/bcd/index.html.

Chapter 10

1. "3M TSCA [Toxic Substances Control Act] Section 8(e)—Perfluorooctane Sulfonate," substantial risk notification to EPA, Environmental Working Group, PFAS Timeline, May 14–15, 1998, https://static.ewg.org/reports/2020/pfas-epa-timeline/1998_3M-Alerts-EPA.pdf.

2. William Weppner (3M), letter to Frank Kover (EPA), December 21, 1998, AR226-0624.

3. David Barboza, "E.P.A. Says It Pressed 3M for Action on Scotchgard Chemical," *New York Times*, 2000.

4. Charles Auer, *Phaseout of PFOS*, archived email, May 16, 2000, AR226-0629.

5. EPA spokesperson, email correspondence, May 9, 2024.

6. "PFAS in the U.S. Population," ATSDR, CDC, January 18, 2024.

7. Charles Auer, personal interview, November 7, 2023.

8. *Complaint EPA v. DuPont*, Docket No. TSCA-HQ-2004-0016, RCRA-HQ-2004-0016, May 2016.

9. "President Bush to present DuPont with National Medal of Technology," DuPont, via EurekAlert, November 5, 2003.

10. Jennifer Orme-Zavaleta, personal interview, January 10, 2024.

11. Mark Strynar et al., "Identification of novel polyfluorinated compounds in natural waters using accurate mass TOFMS," Conference: SETAC 2012, Long Beach, CA; "Drinking Water Health Advisory: Hexafluoropropylene Oxide (HFPO) Dimer Acid. (CASRN 13252-13-6) and HFPO Dimer Acid Ammonium Salt (CASRN 62037-80-3), Also Known as 'GenX Chemicals,'" US EPA, June 2022.

12. Betsy Southerland, personal interview, September 26, 2023.

13. Charles Auer, personal interview, November 7, 2023.

14. Linda Birnbaum, personal interview, August 7, 2023.

15. Maria Doa, personal interview, March 4, 2024.

16. "In Case You Missed It: 'EPA Chief Vows That Clean Drinking Water Is National Priority,'" US EPA, May 22, 2018.

17. Tom Carper, "EPA Fails to Commit to Setting a Drinking Water Standard for PFAS," US Senate Committee on Environment and Public Works, February 14, 2019.

18. Radhika Fox, personal interview, May 7, 2024.

19. Steven Cook, personal interview, April 23, 2024.

20. "Peterson Air Force Base," Superfund Site Information, EPA ID: CO9571924191, US EPA, https://cumulis.epa.gov/supercpad/cursites/csitinfo.cfm?id=0800364; "Third Unregulated Contaminant Monitoring Rule," US Environmental Protection Agency, December 11, 2023.

21. Sean Houseworth, personal interview, May 5, 2023.

22. Jennifer Orme-Zavaleta, personal interview, personal interview, January 10, 2024.

23. Rachel Frazin, "EPA alleges political interference by Trump officials over toxic chemical," *The Hill*, February 9, 2021.

24. Betsy Behl, personal interview, January 16, 2024.

25. Betsy Southerland, personal interview, September 26, 2023.

26. Mark Garvey, personal interview, February 8, 2024.

27. "In Re: Swix Sport USA: Environmental Appeals Board United States Environmental Protection Agency Washington, D.C.," EPA, Docket No. TSCA-HQ-2020-5005, May 13, 2020.

28. Bill Donahue, "Nordic Skiing Has an Addiction to Toxic Wax," *Outside* magazine, January 24, 2020.

29. "PFAS Low Volume Exemption Stewardship Program," US Environmental Protection Agency, last updated September 4, 2024, https://www.epa.gov/reviewing-new-chemi cals-under-toxic-substances-control-act-tsca/pfas-low-volume-exemption.

30. "2021 TRI National Analysis," US EPA, March 2023; Sharon Udasin and Rachel Frazin, "Trump appointees barred EPA staff from warning Senate about 'forever chemical' loophole: Internal staff messages," *The Hill,* April 9, 2024.

31. Udasin and Frazin, "Trump appointees."

32. Ibid.

33. Ibid.

34. Nathan Saunders, personal interview, August 27, 2023.

35. "EPA Finalizes Rule to Require Enhanced PFAS Reporting to the Toxics Release Inventory," US EPA, October 20, 2023. https://www.epa.gov/newsreleases/epa -finalizes-rule-require-enhanced-pfas-reporting-toxics-release-inventory.

36. Michal Freedhoff, personal interview, April 25, 2024.

37. "PFAS Strategic Roadmap: EPA's Commitments to Action 2021–2024," US EPA, 2021.

38. Michal Freedhoff, "Changes to Reporting Requirements for Per- and Polyfluoroalkyl Substances and to Supplier Notifications for Chemicals of Special Concern; Commu nity Right-to-Know Toxic Chemical Release Reporting," US Environmental Pro tection Agency, October 18, 2023; "EPA Finalizes Rule to Require Enhanced PFAS Reporting to the Toxics Release Inventory," US EPA, October 20, 2023.

39. Radhika Fox, personal interview, May 7, 2024,

40. "3M to Exit PFAS Manufacturing by the End of 2025," 3M, December 20, 2022.

41. Dan Kildee, personal interview, March 5, 2024.

Chapter 11

1. Vaughn Hagerty, "Toxin taints CFPUA drinking water," *Wilmington Star-News*, June 7, 2017.

2. Quotations from Emily Donovan come from a series of phone and in-person inter views conducted between January 2023 and March 2024.

3. Vaughn Hagerty, personal interview, June 28, 2023.

4. Hagerty, "Toxin taints CFPUA drinking water"; M. Beekman et al., "Evaluation of substances used in the GenX technology by Chemours, Dordrecht," Netherlands National Institute for Public Health and the Environment, 2016.

5. Jessica Cannon, personal interview, June 28, 2023.

6. E. I. DU PONT DE NEMOURS AND COMPANY, Form 10-K 2012, Securities and Exchange Commission, 2012.

7. David Larcker, personal interview, April 2, 2024.

8. E. I. DU PONT DE NEMOURS AND COMPANY, Form 10-K 2015, Securities and Exchange Commission, 2015.

9. *The Chemours Company v. DowDuPont, NC Newsline*, Delaware Court of Chancery, July 2019.

10. "Motion for Leave to File Motion to Dismiss by Corteva, Inc. and Dupont De Nemours, Inc.," in re: Aqueous Film-Forming Foams Products Liability Litigation, in the United States District Court for the District of South Carolina, Charleston Division, November 16, 2020.

11. Dan Turner, email correspondence, May 2, 2024.

12. *The Chemours Company v. DowDuPont*, First Amended Complaint, Chemours, Delaware Court of Chancery, 2019.

13. Randall Chase "Judge dismisses Chemours lawsuit against DuPont," Associated Press, March 30, 2020.

14. "DuPont, Corteva, and Chemours announce resolution of legacy PFAS claims," January 22, 2021, *PR Newswire*, https://www.prnewswire.com/news-releases/dupont-corteva-and-chemours-announce-resolution-of-legacy-pfas-claims-301213118.html.

15. Mark Garvey, personal interview, February 15, 2024.

16. Michael Kane, "Live Blog: Outside the GenX Meeting in New Hanover County," *Port City Daily* (Wilmington, NC), June 15, 2017.

17. Adam Wagner, and Sherry Jones, "Notes from Chemours Meeting with Local, State Officials," *Wilmington Star-News*, New Hanover County Document Center, June 15, 2017.

18. "Human Health Toxicity Values for Hexafluoropropylene Oxide (HFPO) Dimer Acid and Its Ammonium Salt," US EPA, October 2021.

19. Shawn Taylor, email correspondence, May 6, 2024.

20. Chris Meek, personal interview, March 13, 2024.

21. Jonathan Shands, personal interview, January 30, 2024.

22. Cassie Olszewski, email correspondence, May 6, 2024.

23. "Summary of Selected Cancer Rates for Bladen, Brunswick, New Hanover and Pender Counties, 1996–2015, and Comparison to Statewide Rates," North Carolina Department of Health and Human Services, June 29, 2017.

24. "Human Health Toxicity Assessment for GenX Chemicals," Fact Sheet, US EPA, March 2023.

25. "What Are PFAS?" Cape Fear River Watch, https://capefearriverwatch.org/genx/, accessed November 13, 2024.

26. "State orders Chemours to stop chemical releases, begins legal action and steps to suspend permit," North Carolina DEQ, September 5, 2017.

27. "Chemours Consent Order," GenX Investigation, North Carolina Department of Environmental Quality, https://www.deq.nc.gov/news/key-issues/genx-investigation/chemours-consent-order, accessed November 13, 2024.

28. Fred Biddle, "DuPont confronted over chemical's safety," *Wilmington News Journal*, April 13, 2003.

29. "NPDES Permit Renewal Application: NPDES Permit No. NC0003573," DuPont, 2001.

30. Richard Abraham, personal interview, December 19, 2023.

31. Hope Taylor, personal interview, November 15, 2023.

32. Lisa Sorg, "Ex-DEQ Inspector Says He Shared DuPont Pollution Info with Federal Investigators," *NC Newsline*, February 26, 2019, https://ncnewsline.com/2019/02/25/ex-deq-inspector-says-he-shared-dupont-pollution-info-with-federal-investigators/.

33. Hope Taylor, personal interview, November 15, 2023.

Chapter 12

1. Zack Driver, "H2GO looks at reverse osmosis systems for schools," WECT, August 22, 2017.

2. WECT staff, "Brunswick Co. Schools: No discussions held with H2GO about reverse osmosis system," WECT News, August 23, 2017, https://www.wect.com/story/36199693/brunswick-co-schools-no-discussions-held-with-h2go-about-reverse-osmosis-systems/.

3. Meagan Kascsak, email correspondence, May 6, 2024.

4. Connor DelPrete, "Parent frustrated with school system's delayed response to reverse osmosis donation," WECT News, November 7, 2017.

5. "Brunswick Co. Schools pursues reverse osmosis filling stations following PFAS report," WECT, June 6, 2020; Sydney Evans et al., "PFAS Contamination of Drinking Water Far More Prevalent than Previously Reported," Environmental Working Group, January 23, 2020.

6. Kenneth Waldroup, personal interview, March 8, 2024.

7. "Granular Activated Carbon Treatment of Private Well Water," Private Well Program, Connecticut Department of Public Health Environmental Health Section, May 2018.

8. Vaughn Hagerty, interview during tour of CFPUA site, March 22, 2024.

9. John Nichols email correspondence, May 8, 2024.

10. Ann Truett, personal interview, March 4, 2024.

11. Betty Newkirk, personal interview, March 22, 2024.

12. Quotes from Janice Gaines come from interviews conducted between February and March 2024.

13. Donna Allen and Terrel Allen, personal interview, March 21, 2024.

14. Emerson Whitted, personal interview, March 21, 2024.

15. Alex Riley, email correspondence, May 8, 2024.

16. Quotations from Bernard Williams come from in-person and phone interviews conducted between February 2024 and May 2024.

17. "LaVerne Edwina Davis 'Scrappy' Whitted," obituary, *Wilmington (NC) Star-News*, Legacy.com, October 9, 2007, https://www.legacy.com/us/obituaries/starnewsonline/name/laverne-whitted-obituary?id=27565021.

18. Lena Williams, personal interview, March 22, 2024.

19. Kenneth Waldroup, personal interview, March 8, 2024.

20. "House Bill 259, An Act to Make Base Budget Appropriations for Current Operations of State Agencies, Departments, and Institutions," General Assembly of North Carolina, 2023.

21. Bernard Williams, personal interview, May 2024.

22. Quotations from Emily Donovan come from interviews conducted over the phone and in person between January 2023 and March 2024.

23. Rachel Frazin, "United Nations criticizes 'forever chemical' contamination in North Carolina," *The Hill*, February 22, 2024.

24. Cassie Olszewski, email correspondence, May 6, 2024.

25. Shawn Taylor, email correspondence, May 6, 2024.

26. "GenX Exposure Study: Our Findings, So Far," NC State University Center for Human Health and the Environment, 2024, https://genxstudy.ncsu.edu/our -findings/.

27. Jane Hoppin, personal interview, January 4, 2024.

28. Justin Conley et al., "Developmental toxicity of Nafion byproduct 2 (NBP2) in the Sprague-Dawley rat with comparisons to hexafluoropropylene oxide-dimer acid (HFPO-DA or GenX) and perfluorooctane sulfonate (PFOS)," *Environment International* 160 (February 2022).

29. Frannie Nilsen, "PFMOAA Summary," North Carolina Department of Environmental Quality, February 8, 2023.

30. Justin Conley et al., "Adverse Maternal and Neonatal Effects of Maternal Oral Exposure to Perfluoro-2-methoxyacetic Acid (PFMOAA) during Pregnancy and Early Lactation in the Sprague–Dawley Rat," *Environmental Science & Technology* 127, no. 3 (January 1, 2024).

31. Jason Lambert et. al., "ORD Human Health Toxicity Value for Perfluoropropanoic Acid," US EPA, June 2023.

32. Yishuang Duan et al., "Distribution of novel and legacy per-/polyfluoroalkyl substances in serum and its associations with two glycemic biomarkers among Chinese adult men and women with normal blood glucose levels," *Environment International* 134 (January 2020).

33. Lambert, "ORD Human Health."

34. Kenneth Waldroup, personal interview, March 8, 2024.

Chapter 13

1. John Adgate and Chris Higgins, personal interview, January 25, 2024.

2. Sara Ghorbani Gorji et al., "New PFASs Identified in AFFF Impacted Groundwater by Passive Sampling and Nontarget Analysis," *Environmental Science & Technology* 58, no. 3 (January 8, 2024): 1690–99, doi: 10.1021/acs.est.3c06591.

3. "Dr Jens Blotevogel," Commonwealth Scientific and Industrial Research Organisation, Australia, https://people.csiro.au/b/j/jens-blotevogel, accessed November 14, 2024.

4. National High Magnetic Field Laboratory, the National Science Foundation and the State of Florida, 2024, https://nationalmaglab.org/.

5. Robert B. Young et al., "PFAS Analysis with Ultrahigh Resolution 21T FT-ICR MS: Suspect and Nontargeted Screening with Unrivaled Mass Resolving Power and Accuracy," *Environmental Science & Technology* 56, no. 4 (January 31, 2022).

6. Jens Blotevogel, personal interview, March 21, 2024.

7. Guomao Zheng et al., "Elevated Levels of Ultrashort- and Short-Chain Perfluoroalkyl

Acids in US Homes and People," *Environmental Science & Technology* 57, no. 42 (October 11, 2023).

8. Linda Birnbaum, personal interview, February 25, 2022.

9. Jaeyun Sung et al., "Molecular Signatures from Omics Data: From Chaos to Consensus," *Biotechnology Journal* 7, no. 8 (April 23, 2012).

10. Lida Chatzi, personal interview, March 20, 2024.

11. E. Jane Costello et al., "Exposure to Per- and Polyfluoroalkyl Substances and Markers of Liver Injury: A Systematic Review and Meta-Analysis," *Environmental Health Perspectives* 130, no. 4 (April 1, 2022).

12. "Fountain Valley PFAS Study / PFAS Multi-Site Study Colorado: CO SCOPE," Agency for Toxic Substances and Disease Registry (ATSDR), Centers for Disease Control (CDC), June 14, 2022.

13. "The Norwegian Human Milk Study," Norwegian Institute of Public Health, June 26, 2017.

14. Rachel Criswell, personal interview, March 20, 2024.

15. "World-first Trial Finds Regular Blood and Plasma Donation Reduces Firefighters' PFAS Levels," *The Lighthouse*, March 16, 2023; Robin Gasiorowski et al., "Effect of Plasma and Blood Donations on Levels of Perfluoroalkyl and Polyfluoroalkyl Substances in Firefighters in Australia," *JAMA* Network Open 5, no. 4 (April 8, 2022).

16. "First Report of the Independent PFAS Scientific Advisory Panel for Jersey–the Potential for an Interim Therapeutic Phlebotomy Service," PFAS in Jersey, Information and public services for the Island of Jersey, November 2023, https://www.gov.je/Environment/Water/pages/pfas.aspx.

17. Sharon Udasin and Rachel Frazin, "'Forever chemicals' are known for lingering in the body. Menstruation helps expel them." *The Hill*, April 22, 2024.

18. Brittany P. Rickard et al., "Per- and Poly-fluoroalkyl Substances (PFAS) and Female Reproductive Outcomes: PFAS Elimination, Endocrine-mediated Effects, and Disease," *Toxicology* 465 (January 1, 2022); Fiona Wong et al., "Enhanced Elimination of Perfluorooctane Sulfonic Acid by Menstruating Women: Evidence from Population-Based Pharmacokinetic Modeling," *Environmental Science & Technology* 48, no. 15 (July 8, 2014).

19. Udasin and Frazin, "'Forever chemicals' are known for lingering."

20. "Point-of-Use Reverse Osmosis Systems," US Environmental Protection Agency, February 22, 2024.

21. "Reducing PFAS in Drinking Water with Treatment Technologies," US Environmental Protection Agency, 2018.

22. Fatemeh Asadi Zeidabadi et al., "Managing PFAS Exhausted Ion-exchange Resins Through Effective Regeneration/Electrochemical Process," *Water Research* 255 (May 1, 2024).

23. "Overview of Drinking Water Treatment Technologies," US Environmental Protection Agency, April 5, 2024.

24. "Granular Activated Carbon Treatment of Private Well Water," Connecticut Department of Public Health Environmental Health Section, Private Well Program, May 2018.

25. David Trueba, personal interview, March 28, 2024.

26. Sean Houseworth, personal interview, May 5, 2023.

27. "Incineration Moratorium," Department of Defense and Office of the Assistant Secretary of Defense for Energy, Installations, and Environment, February 2023.

28. Jay N. Meegoda et al., "A Review of PFAS Destruction Technologies," *International Journal of Environmental Research and Public Health* 19, no. 24 (December 7, 2022).

29. Jens Blotevogel, "An Electric Fix for Removing Long-lasting Chemicals in Groundwater," Colorado State University, October 9, 2019, https://source.colostate.edu/electric-fix-removing-long-lasting-chemicals-groundwater/.

30. Nasim E. Pica et al., "Electrochemical Oxidation of Hexafluoropropylene Oxide Dimer Acid (GenX): Mechanistic Insights and Efficient Treatment Train with Nanofiltration," *Environmental Science & Technology* 53, no. 21 (October 10, 2019).

31. "What Is Plasma?," Plasma Science and Fusion Center, Massachusetts Institute of Technology, 2024, https://www.psfc.mit.edu/vision/what_is_plasma.

32. Jens Blotevogel et al., "Scaling up Water Treatment Technologies for PFAS Destruction: Current Status and Potential for Fit-for-purpose Application," *Current Opinion in Chemical Engineering* 41 (September 1, 2023).

33. Blotevogel, "Scaling up."

34. "Battelle, Viking Global Investors Launch Revive Environmental," Battelle, January 7, 2023.

35. "Don't Move PFAS. Destroy It," PFAS Annihilator Destruction Technology White Paper, Battelle Memorial Institute, 2021, https://www.battelle.org/insights/white-papers/don't-move-pfas-destroy-it.

36. "Revive Environmental PFAS AnnihilatorTM Deployed in First-to-Market Commercial Destruction of 'Forever Chemicals,'" Revive Environmental, May 1, 2023.

37. "Statewide Study on Landfill Leachate PFOA and PFOS Impact Technical Report," Michigan Waste & Recycling Association and Ltd NTH Consultants, March 1, 2019.

38. Linda Birnbaum, personal interview, January 3, 2024.

39. Elizabeth Southerland, "Testimony of Dr. Elizabeth Southerland," House Committee on Science, Space, and Technology Subcommittee on Investigations and Oversight, March 17, 2021.

40. "Technical Fact Sheet: Drinking Water Health Advisories for Four PFAS (PFOA, PFOS, GenX chemicals, and PFBS)," US Environmental Protection Agency, June 2022.

41. Elizabeth (Betsy) Southerland, personal interview, September 26, 2023.

Epilogue

1. Brenda Hampton, personal interview, April 9, 2024.

2. Brenda Hampton, text messages, April 13–20, 2024.

Index

About the Authors

Sharon Udasin is an environment reporter, based in Boulder, Colorado, who has been delving into water contamination and conservation issues for fifteen years. She was first introduced to the PFAS problem by colleagues in 2019-2020 as a Ted Scripps Fellow in Environmental Journalism at the University of Colorado Boulder. After completing the fellowship, she covered US West climate issues for *The Hill*.

Sharon moved to Colorado after many years reporting on environment and energy for the *Jerusalem Post*—a role that followed her initial position at the *New York Jewish Week*. A graduate of both the University of Pennsylvania and Columbia Journalism School, Sharon also received a 2022 SEAL Environmental Journalism Award and was honored by the Heschel Center for Environmental Learning and Leadership in 2013.

Although born and raised in New Jersey, Sharon quickly adapted to the rugged beauty of the Rocky Mountain West, which she enjoys exploring with her husband and two children.

Rachel Frazin is a Washington, DC–based journalist who covers energy and environment politics and policy for *The Hill*. In this role, she writes about what people in power are doing about issues like climate change and toxic chemicals. It was through her in-depth coverage of these topics that she found out about— and became alarmed by—the prevalence of PFAS.

Rachel is originally from South Florida. Her work has appeared in the *Chicago Sun-Times*, *The Daily Beast*, the *Tampa Bay Times*, and the *Palm Beach Post*. She's a graduate of Northwestern University's Medill School of Journalism and was a recipient of a 2023 SEAL Environmental Journalism Award.

When she's not writing, Rachel can be found practicing her Spanish, singing show tunes, and trying new restaurants with family and friends.